Inside Relational Databases with Examples in Access

Mark Whitehorn and Bill Marklyn

 Springer

Mark Whitehorn
Applied Computing Division, University of Dundee, UK

Bill Marklyn
2332 E Aloha Street, Seattle WA 98112, USA

British Library Cataloguing in Publication Data
A catalogue record for this book is available from the British Library

Library of Congress Control Number: 2006931000

ISBN-10: 1-84628-394-9   Printed on acid-free paper
ISBN-13: 978-1-84628-394-9

Typeset by Fields Place Productions

9 8 7 6 5 4 3 2 1

Springer Science+Business Media
springer.com

Contents

Contents

Contents

Contents

Contents

Contents

Contents

Contents

Preface

Bill and I first wrote *Inside Relational Databases* to help people who were new to building databases. We could find lots of books that told people how to use their database engine of choice (Access, SQL Server, MySQL, whatever) but very few that described the underlying way in which relational databases work. So we wrote one. We guessed that many of the readers would be using Access, so we used Access to illustrate the relational model and called the book "Inside Relational Databases – with examples in Access". However, we did try very hard to make it clear that the book wasn't about how to drive Access; it was about the relational model that underpins all relational databases. We were simply using Access for illustrative purposes. To our enormous relief this was understood by those people kind enough to buy it and the book sold well.

For the second edition we expanded the book to include information about client-server databases and we illustrated that book with images from several database engines so we dropped 'with examples in Access' from the title.

That second edition was, happily, also well received, so eventually we turned our thoughts to another edition. It seemed to us very important that we continue to focus the book on the relational model and not turn it into a "Teach yourself about database X" book. On the other hand, we were nagged by the feeling that it is very convenient for the reader if we illustrate the relational model using their favorite product – such as Access. Eventually we realized that all we had to do was to produce several versions of the same book, each based on a different database engine.

Which is why you have in your hand a copy of "Inside Relational Databases – with examples in Access". If this isn't your database engine of choice, scan the internet and see if we have come up with one that matches your requirements. If not, email me Mark@Penguinsoft.co.uk. We're not proud. We'll do a version for any relational database engine if enough people want it.

Should we tell you the whole story?

Of course, there is an inevitable tension in trying to work like this. For example, in Chapter 16 we talk about referential integrity. There are essentially six different flavors of referential integrity but Access only supports four of them (they are the most important ones however, so you aren't missing out on too much). The problem is this. Should we tell you about the other two? If we do, as an Access user you have every right to be annoyed that we are telling you about a feature you can't use. On the other hand, the six different types that we describe are part of the relational world and this book is about that world – we are not trying to teach you how to use Access, we are simply using Access to illustrate the relational model. Ultimately we decided to risk your ire and to describe all of the features of the relational model as we see it, even if Access doesn't support all of them. One advantage of this approach is that if you need to use a different database engine you will almost certainly find the extra information useful.

Incidentally, this is not meant to imply that Access is somehow lacking as a relational database engine. The reason we chose it for the first book is that it is such a good example of a relational database tool. We are putting exactly the same warning in all the versions of the book that we write – there are no engines that support all aspects of the relational model.

Other changes

We have also taken this opportunity to restructure the book significantly. I (Mark) continue to teach database design and practice, both to undergraduates and in the commercial world. Without doubt the most popular topic in the commercial world is how to make databases run faster (no great surprise there) so we have added an entire section of brand new material – more than 10% of the entire book – on that topic. The section on designing databases has been reorganized and expanded and we also re-read the entire book (several times) and brought it all up to date.

Chapter 1

Introduction

Chapter 1 of Sir Henry Birkin's autobiography *"Full Throttle"*, published in 1932, ends with the following: "I can waste no more time on this matter; for the end is reached of what I now confess to have been 24 pages of deceit. I have disguised under the designation of Chapter One what was really nothing more than an introduction; but I know quite well, that had I been honest and called it an introduction, nobody would have read it."

If Henry Birkin wasn't my hero for racing two-ton motor cars on appalling road surfaces at speeds well in excess of 100 m.p.h., he would be my hero for sheer literary nerve.

I'll be less disingenuous. This chapter is an introduction. It defines the very basic terms that you may need like 'database', 'relational', 'DBMS' and 'RDBMS'. It tells you why the book was written, at whom it is aimed, and how it is organized.

If you know all of this already, or it sounds tedious and you really want to get down to the nitty gritty, please don't bother reading this chapter; dive straight into the book at Chapter 2 or wherever you fancy. As far as we're concerned, anyone who has paid us the considerable compliment of actually exchanging money for our words is entitled to read them as they please.

Who are we?

This book has two authors: Mark Whitehorn and Bill Marklyn.

Bill worked for Microsoft as the Development Manager for the first three versions of Access (1.0, 1.1 and 2.0). I (Mark) work as a database consultant, teach database theory and practice at two Universities and have written the UK Personal Computer World's database column for more than twelve years.

We met (at a database conference, not unreasonably, given our interests) in the summer before Access 1.0 was launched and found that we shared similar views on how databases should be designed and built. We wrote the original version of this book in 1997 and have worked together on book projects ever since.

I (Mark) penned most of the words and whenever the pronoun 'I' appears in the text, I accept full responsibility. So what is Bill doing there on the front cover? Well, writing down the words in a book is only one component. Books also need ideas and enthusiasm. I may have written the words, but Bill, more than anyone else, fired my interest in writing this book, provided his own inexhaustible enthusiasm and many of the ideas. I couldn't have written it without him, and he would probably not have found the time to write it himself, so it is truly a joint venture.

What is a database?

A database is simply a collection of data. Nowadays the term tends to be used about computerized systems, but the old cards which were used to classify and locate books in a library are a good example of a non-computerized database. The difference computers have made to databases is deceptively simple: computers make access to the data faster. That means, on a trivial level, that instead of hunting through 50,000 pieces of cardboard in a dusty room for three days, a computer will do the same job in under a second. However, there is more to this speed than meets the eye.

Suppose I asked you to find me the names and addresses of all male hospital patients in the country who are over 60 years old, have a history of diabetes in the family and have two children. Given a local paper-based system, the question is unanswerable in any meaningful way. By the time you have traveled around the country and searched all the available records, most of said patients would be dead. With centralized, computerized patient records, this question should be answerable in minutes or at worst a few hours. So computerizing databases hasn't simply speeded them up, it has opened up whole new ways of looking at data that simply weren't possible before.

And databases are becoming ever more pervasive. If you book a seat on a plane or train then someone, somewhere is using a database. A bank account is nothing more than a complex database; credit card purchases, your appointment with the doctor – all are likely to be entered into a database.

Databases vs. Database Management Systems

One important distinction which should be made early on in this book is the difference between a database and the software which is used to control and manipulate that database. A database is a collection of data – perhaps a list of your customers, their addresses, fax numbers and so on. In order to keep the data in your database under control, you need software known as a DBMS (Database Management System). The DBMS is to a database what a word processor is to a letter. The former is the controlling software, the latter the data that it manipulates. Examples of DBMSs include Access, SQL Server, MySQL, Oracle, DB2 – the list is not endless but certainly long. DBMSs are also referred to as database engines.

Relational Database Management Systems

There are several fundamentally different ways in which data can be handled or modeled – Hierarchical, Network and Relational are three such models. Without doubt the most widely used is the relational model, the brainchild of Dr Edgar Codd.

Codd is often described as 'the Father of the Relational Database' (with obligatory upper-case letters) and this is perfectly fair since he came up with the original idea which he announced to the world in 1970 with a paper entitled "A Relational Model of Data for Large Shared Data Banks". This is often quoted as Codd's first paper on the relational model but in fact he published one in 1969 called "Derivability, Redundancy, and Consistency of Relations Stored in Large Data Banks". However this paper was an IBM research report and carried a limited distribution notice, so it wasn't seen by many people at the time.

Codd wrote with enormous precision, for example:

Note that a view is theoretically updatable if there exists a time-independent algorithm for unambiguously determining a single series of changes to the base relations that will have as their effect precisely the requested changes in the view.

Since he is the original source, the very bedrock, from which this material comes, it was vital that he wrote in such a way as to leave no doubt whatsoever as to the meaning. Indeed, his ability to communicate with such precision to both mathematicians and database people undoubtedly helped to promote the relational model. However, a side effect is that his material can be a little difficult to follow on first reading.

Chris Date was at one time a co-worker of Codd's and has, in my opinion, done a wonderful job of explaining, popularizing and generally advancing the use and understanding of the relational model. These two guys rank alongside Henry Birkin in my hall of heroes.

So, why do you need to know anything about Codd and Date? Well, the world of databases is crowded with people who will try to impress you with their knowledge (which makes it exactly the same as every other branch of life). If you don't know these two names you can be seriously out-bluffed. For example, in 1985 Codd published a set of rules which defined the concept of a relational DBMS at that time. These rules have subsequently become enshrined in database lore and are constantly referred to in conversation – for example, "You can't do that, it contravenes Codd's 7th rule!" Experience suggests that very few people have actually gone back to the source material (*Computerworld*, 14-21 October 1985) and read them, so simply knowing who Ted Codd was and that he had a set of rules somewhere should be enough information to allow you to argue on even terms. However, if you want to know more about these rules, read Chapter 24 which lists and defines them all in (hopefully) understandable terms.

As an aside, there is nothing to stop you from playing the same game. If you find that you are being out-bluffed, you can try "Well, of course, when Chris contacted me about this last week he said that ... [fill in appropriate supporting statement]".

Very sadly, you can no longer substitute 'Ted' for 'Chris' because Edgar Codd died on the 18th. April 2003. Out of all the tributes paid to him, for me the most touching came from Sharon Weinberg, initially a colleague at IBM, later his second wife. "For a while, we had work stations side by side. I'd see him staring at his screen, thinking. I'd worry, and say, 'Breathe, Ted, breathe!' He'd work like a demon, you could not break his focus."

Any DBMSs you use are likely to be based on the relational model. Such DBMSs are, perfectly sensibly, known as RDBMSs (Relational Database Management Systems).

Why this book?

One of the main aims of this book is to demystify the relational database model. It is an excellent way of handling information and we want to make the relational model accessible to more people. This book attempts to introduce the concepts and ideas behind the relational model without the usual jargon.

A fair question at this point is "Why should anyone want to know about the relational model?". The answer to that lies in the distinction between knowing **how** to use a software package to perform a specific task and knowing **why** you would want to perform that task in the first place.

For example, if you browse through the Access help system, you will be able to find out how to, for example, declare a primary key for a table.

- Select the table.
- Open it in Design view.
- Select the field or fields you want to define as the primary key.
    - To select one field, click the row selector for the desired field.
    - To select multiple fields, hold down the CTRL key and then click the row selector for each field.
- Click Primary Key on the toolbar.

Great. Excellent, so now you know how to do it. But … what is a primary key? Are they really important? Should every table have one? What are they used for? The help system may give some pointers, but it is essentially focused on telling you how to achieve a desired end result. We have a totally different focus (although we may illustrate processes from time to time): we tell you why you would want to do it in the first place. This book is about the relational model because understanding the model is essential if you want to create excellent, stable and robust databases.

Who should read this book?

You should read this book if:

- You have created databases but they don't seem to work very well. Perhaps you:
    - can't retrieve the information that you want.
    - have to type in the same information over and over again.
    - type in data and it appears to go missing.
    - ask questions and get answers that you know are wrong.
    - can use Access but you don't know exactly what to do with it.
    - know that a relational database lets you create multiple tables in the database but you are uncertain why this is to your advantage.
    - find that there are lots of features in a database that sound interesting but you have no idea what you are supposed to do with them.

- Or perhaps you hear words in connection with databases like:
  - normalization
  - functional dependency
  - inner join
  - union
  - redundant data
  - data dictionary
  - meta-data
  - ER modeling
  - transaction
  - concurrency
  - locking

  and you haven't got the faintest idea what they mean and there is no one you can ask.

As we said above, you *shouldn't* read this book if you are looking for a 'How to use Access' book.

If you are looking for such a book we feel honor bound to recommend *"Accessible Access 2003"* published by Springer-Verlag, for the simple reason that we wrote it …

Organization of the book

Within a database itself, the data is stored in tables. A simple database will contain a single table; more complex ones can contain many tables. For example, if you want to keep your address book in a database (as I do on a hand-held computer) then a single table is perfect. However, if you want to store all of the business transactions of a company, you will find that it is more efficient to store the data in multiple tables – one for the customers, another for the goods you sell and so on.

This book is divided into five parts.

Part 1 concentrates on databases which contain only single tables because this should make some of the basic principles easier to understand. It describes the components which make up a typical database:

- tables
- queries/views
- user-interface components (forms)
- reports

Part 2 explains that when most people start building more complex databases they tend to try and put all of the data into one table. The section illustrates why this is a bad idea and then outlines how you can use multiple tables to overcome the problems inherent in single-table databases. Part 2 is a seriously chunky section since much of the relational model is explained in there.

Part 3 discusses, in broad terms, where the components of your database can be located. Databases (even when you are using a client-server database engine like SQL Server) can be created on single, stand-alone machines, in which case only one person can use the database at any one time. If you want the database to have multiple, concurrent users (clearly a major advantage if the database is used within a company), parts or all of it can be moved onto a networked machine. However, allowing multiple people to manipulate the same data at the same time introduces a whole host of new topics that you need to understand if you are to build and manage effective databases.

Part 4 is very different from the other parts. The first three are lovingly hand-crafted so that each chapter builds on the information in the previous one (or, at least, that was the idea). The chapters in Part 4 can be read in any order because the information in each one is essentially unconnected to that in the others. Much of the information in any given chapter in Part 4 assumes that you do understand the information in Parts 1-3 but there is essentially no cross-requirement between chapters in Part 4. Thus, if you understand the information in Parts 1-3 and want to know about SQL, go straight to Chapter 29 and read it. If someone is bugging you with terms like 'third normal form' or 'functional dependency' then read the chapter on normalization (Chapter 25).

Part 5 is about speeding up your database and a range of techniques is discussed there.

Some ground rules

This book assumes that the reader will be interested in relational databases. There are several other models for organizing data but the relational is the most common. Thus, in the text which follows, in order to avoid continually having to prefix the word 'database' with the word 'relational', you can assume that I mean relational unless it is explicitly stated otherwise.

I am all too aware of the fact (having been corrected many times) that 'datum' is the singular form of 'data', and so I should write 'every datum' rather than 'every piece of data'. The trouble is that using 'data' as both the singular and plural forms is now so widespread that to do otherwise smacks of pedantry and obscures rather than clarifies. I've been swayed by the common usage argument and have used just 'data'.

In fact, now is a good time to point out that this entire book fails to use exact terminology. I know that a table isn't a table, it is a 'relation'. Or to be precise, a table isn't *exactly* a relation, it's… and so on. I happily acknowledge that I shouldn't talk about the number of rows (or, slightly more accurately, the number of 'tuples'); what I really mean is the cardinality. Relational databases have their origins in the precise world of mathematics and that particular world has a very precise language. The trouble is that I also live and work in the real world and in it real people talk about tables, rows and columns. So, at the expense of a small degree of accuracy and the gain (I hope) of a great deal of clarity, I have elected to use less formal terminology whenever possible. Apologies are proffered in advance to those who are terminally offended.

Downloading files from the website

Where appropriate, the databases etc. which are used to illustrate this book are available for download from www.penguinsoft.co.uk.

The files are in Access 2000 format (which is compatible with Access 2000 and Access 2003): simply look in the folder with the appropriate name. Access 2003 was used for the screen shots.

Each Access file is tied to its chapter by name so, for example, the Access file associated with Chapter 2 is called CHAP2.MDB. Occasionally a chapter warranted more than one database file, so sometimes you will find names like CHAP25A.MDB and CHAP25B.MDB.

Acknowledgements

Very grateful thanks go to Mary Whitehorn, a talented writer in her own right and not unrelated to one of the authors. She put in so much work, both proof-reading and actually writing sections, that she easily qualified as another author. Only her innate modesty prevents her name appearing on the cover.

I (Mark) also acknowledge a huge debt to Professor John Parker. He was my PhD supervisor many years ago and is currently the Director of the Cambridge Botanic Garden. Whatever communication skills I have acquired came directly from sitting at the feet of a master of the art.

We don't have problems...

If you find a bug (sorry, bookware anomaly) anywhere in this book, I would be delighted if you would tell me by visiting www.penguinsoft.co.uk. where all known problems (and fixes) will also be posted.

Outroduction

So, that's the end of the introduction. I'd love to know how many people actually read it; perhaps Sir Henry is right. Either way, I hope that you get as much pleasure from the elegance of the relational model as I have done and I will be delighted if this book illuminates even a small section of it for you.

Part 1

A simple, single-table database

Chapter 2

Introduction to Part 1

The first database you ever build is likely to do something relatively simple, such as keeping a list of your customers or friends. Happily, even a simple database like this can be used to introduce the four most important components of a database, namely:

- Tables
- Queries/Views
- Forms
- Reports

It is difficult to over-stress the importance of these four components and we will start with a quick look at each.

Tables

Tables are the basic structures in which data is stored within a database. Think of a table as the container in which the data sits and the other three components as devices which manipulate the data contained in the table. A table that contains information about your employees might look like the one shown below. The name of the table (EMPLOYEES) is shown in upper-case.

EMPLOYEES				
EmployeeNo	FirstName	LastName	DateOfBirth	DateEmployed
1	Manny	Tomanny	12 Apr 1966	01 May 1999
2	Rosanne	Kolumn	21 Mar 1977	01 Jan 2000
3	Cas	Kade	01 May 1977	01 Apr 2002
4	Norma	Lyzation	03 Apr 1966	01 Apr 2002
5	Juan	Tomani	12 Apr 1966	01 Apr 2002

*If you do download the sample files (see **Chapter 1**) you'll find this EMPLOYEES table in CHAP2.MDB.*

Queries/Views

Queries are questions that you can ask of the data in a table. If you wanted to find all of your employees who were born after, say, 1970, you would use a query. Queries are used frequently within databases because typically the tables hold very large amounts of data and we often want to deal with, or look at, just a subset of that data.

Below is the result of a query to find the employees who were born after 1970.

EmployeesBornAfter1970				
EmployeeNo	**FirstName**	**LastName**	**DateOfBirth**	**DateEmployed**
2	Rosanne	Kolumn	21 Mar 1977	01 Jan 2000
3	Cas	Kade	01 May 1977	01 Apr 2002

The results of queries that we use to illustrate this book are usually shown with names; for example, in this case, it is EmployeesBornAfter1970, which is simply the name of the query. The query can be found in the appropriate .MDB file, in this case called CHAP2.MDB.

Views are very much like queries. Both are devices that are used to extract information from the database. Essentially the difference between a view and a query is simply its location. In a client-server database (such as SQL Server) any query that is stored on the workstation is a query. The same query, stored on the server (where it is accessible to lots of people) is typically called a view.

Since Access sits on your PC it becomes very difficult to say whether the query is on a server or a workstation, so Access simply uses the term Query and doesn't bother with the term View.

In large measure you can take every sentence written about queries, substitute the word "View" for the word "Query" and it still makes perfect sense.

Forms

Users need to gain access to the data in a database, so the database needs some kind of user interface. Generally a complete user interface will consist of a number of different components called forms. A form is a device which allows you to look at and edit the data in a table, like the one below showing information from a table of data about customers.

Some databases, such as Access, provide inbuilt tools for creating forms. Others, like Oracle, provide a separate tool (Oracle Forms which is a component of the Oracle Developer Suite) to build them. Forms can be produced as part of applications or as web pages (web forms). We'll drill into this later but for now you can think of forms as the user-friendly front end of the database.

This form allows you to look at and edit the data in the table. In fact, you can usually go directly to a table itself and perform both of these actions but typically they are accomplished via a form. A good question at this point is "Why use a form?" and a simple (but true) answer is that forms can be made more attractive and easier to use than tables. For more compelling reasons to use forms, see Chapter 5 – Forms.

Reports

Reports are used to produce printed output from the table. If you want a list of all of your customers' names and addresses, you would use a report to roll out just such a list from the printer.

EMPLOYEES

26-Jan-06

EmployeeNo	Name	DateOfBirth
3	Cas Kade	01 May 1977
2	Rosanne Kolumn	21 Mar 1977
4	Norma Lyzation	03 Apr 1966
5	Juan Tomani	12 Apr 1966
1	Manny Tomanny	12 Apr 1966

This report produces a printed list of information about employees, sorted by last name.

Simple, isn't it? And if you can get to grips with these four fundamental components – tables, queries, forms and reports – you will have acquired a very good handle on databases in general. Of course, there is more to them than just their definitions, so in the next four chapters we'll have at look at each in greater detail.

Chapter 3

Tables

Tables are containers for holding data which is similar in structure. If you collected information about your employees, the data about each would be similar and would therefore make the contents of a perfectly satisfactory table.

EMPLOYEES				
EmployeeNo	**FirstName**	**LastName**	**DateOfBirth**	**DateEmployed**
1	Manny	Tomanny	12 Apr 1966	01 May 2004
2	Rosanne	Kolumn	21 Mar 1977	01 Jan 2003
3	Cas	Kade	01 May 1977	01 Apr 2004
4	Norma	Lyzation	03 Apr 1966	01 Apr 2004
5	Juan	Tomani	12 Apr 1966	01 Apr 2004

This part is all about databases made up of a single table, so it may come as a bit of a shock to find that the CHAP3.MDB (the Access file which holds the sample files used for this chapter) has more than one table. However, this is simply because we use different tables to illustrate different points.

On the other hand, you cannot put one or more carefully spotted train numbers and a list of your favorite books into the same table.

NONSENSIBLE				
EmployeeNo	**FirstName**	**LastName**	**DateOfBirth**	**DateEmployed**
1	Manny	Tomanny	12 Apr 1966	01 May 1999
2	Rosanne	Kolumn	21 Mar 1977	01 Jan 2000
3	Cas	Kade	01 May 1977	01 Apr 2002
4	Norma	Lyzation	03 Apr 1966	01 Apr 2002
5	Juan	Tomani	12 Apr 1966	01 Apr 2002
6	2312234	Steam Train	Red and Black	3.45 to Bedford
7	The Egg-Shaped Thing	10c	Christopher Hodder-Williams	Hard Back
8	34223	Diesel	Black and Soot	2.17 to Seattle
9	The Mullenthorpe Thing	$2.50	Christopher Hood	Hard Back

To do so would entirely miss the point that tables should contain data with similar structure.

Rows & columns – records & fields

Tables consist of rows (horizontal) and columns (vertical). In the sensible sample table (shown again below) each row contains the data about one employee. The table has five columns, each of which has a name.

EMPLOYEES				
EmployeeNo	**FirstName**	**LastName**	**DateOfBirth**	**DateEmployed**
1	Manny	Tomanny	12 Apr 1966	01 May 1999
2	Rosanne	Kolumn	21 Mar 1977	01 Jan 2000
3	Cas	Kade	01 May 1977	01 Apr 2002
4	Norma	Lyzation	03 Apr 1966	01 Apr 2002
5	Juan	Tomani	12 Apr 1966	01 Apr 2002

Rows are also called records and columns are also called fields. In many cases the terms are used interchangeably. If I was being pedantic I'd say that the difference is that record and field are often used about the data:

> "Well, I'm looking at Fred's record on the screen now and he doesn't have an entry in the DOB field."

whereas row and column are often used about the table:

> "That table has 50,000,000 rows and 120 columns – it's a monster!"

However, it isn't quite as simple as that.

In some cases it isn't clear whether we are really talking about the table or the data. So a sentence like "If we run the query against that table we should get about 50 records." sounds just as appropriate as "If we run the query against that table we should get about 50 rows."

In addition the usage (in my experience) varies between communities of database engine users. For example, Access users tend to favor record and field whereas Oracle users favor row and column. In addition, row and column are usually favored by people from either camp when they are discussing the more formal aspects of databases (normalization, denormalization etc.).

And, just in case you still think this is simple, as discussed earlier there is a third set of terms that are used, for example, when Codd and Date write about the relational model.

Data terms	Table structure terms	Very formal terms
Table	Table	Relation
Record	Row	Tuple
Field	Column	Attribute
Number of records	Number of rows	Cardinality
Number of fields	Number of columns	Degree or Arity

In my opinion, people like Chris Date use the very formal terms for reasons of precision – a tuple isn't exactly the same as a row, neither is a relation exactly the same as a table, although they are very nearly the same. Other people seem to use them purely for reasons of obfuscation. (Bill added "Or elitism, a very common malady".)

You can see our problem. Which of these terms should we use in this book? Standardising on one set would provide a great deal of consistency. On the other hand, that doesn't help you gain a feel for the way the terms are used in practice. In the end we decided simply to use whichever term seemed appropriate to us for the context in which we were writing. We think this is ultimately better but it does, absolutely 100%, guarantee that we will have been inconsistent somewhere.

Numbers of rows and columns

In most databases, each table can be considered to be infinitely expandable in terms of the number of rows it can contain and so no limit is set on the number of (in this example) employees which can be accommodated in the table.

The same is not true for the number of columns which typically has some limit. In some database engines this limit may be absolute (like 255 columns) or it may be determined partially by the data types you choose (as it is in Access). In any event it is usually more than enough for most purposes.

Field Names

It is a characteristic of all tables that each field must have a name (called the 'field name' or 'column name') and that each column name, within a given table, must be unique. This is not unreasonable, since two fields in the EMPLOYEES table, both called FirstName, would be bound to cause confusion.

It should be clear that the EMPLOYEES table is designed to hold information about employees. For a start, the name of the table (EMPLOYEES) tends to give the game away but also the names on the tops of the columns (FirstName, LastName, DateOfBirth etc.) clearly indicate that this is a table for storing information about people rather than, say, items offered for sale.

Table structures

In a perfect world, the RDBMS would provide an infinite number of empty tables, each one designed to hold a different category of information – one for employees, one for customers, one for orders and so on. However, even if this were possible, it still wouldn't be much help, because different databases will require different information to be stored in the same category of table. Suppose that you and I are both setting up databases for our businesses and that we both need a Customer table. Clearly we would have some fields in common (PhoneNumber) but you might, for example, be interested in providing your customers with financial services and would need detailed information about credit rating and so on. I, on the other hand, might want to sell antique books for cash but provide a discount for members of the ABC (Antique Book Club) and therefore need to store information about each customer's membership status.

Access provides a set of 'Wizards' which let you choose the general class of table that you want (say, EMPLOYEES) and then step you through the process of making it. These are very helpful but it is impossible for the wizard to provide every possible variation of the EMPLOYEES table that everyone will need. So Access also provides a means by which we can build our own tables from scratch, like the one shown below, or modify the ones produced by the wizard.

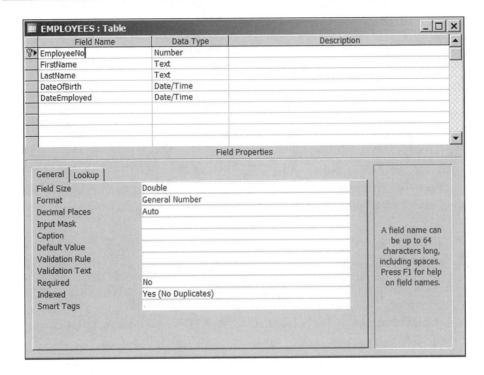

As a rule, once the structure of a table (in terms of the fields) is complete, it is rarely changed. This certainly isn't an absolute rule: I just make the point to highlight the difference between records and fields. The former will inevitably change as new information is added to, and subtracted from, the table; the latter are generally more fixed for any given table.

Your first task in setting up a database is to design a table to hold your data. In doing so you will have to specify the names of the fields that you think you will need.

All tables and all fields have names. Access allows the use of UPPER-CASE and lower-case characters in both table and field names. It also allows the use of spaces in these names. Thus it is possible to call a table Part time Employees and a field Rate Of Pay.

We have elected never to use spaces in field names for two reasons. The first is that it should make the text in the book clearer. Spaces in object names produce problems peculiar to writing about databases. For example, consider the text "... and obviously add the appropriate data to constraint and check carefully...". The field name in this case might be 'constraint', 'constraint and check' or, at a pinch, 'constraint and check carefully'. The meaning might become clear if we saw more of the context but it is intuitively clearer if both table and field names are always a single word.

Secondly, while Access allows spaces in field names, other RDBMSs do not. If you use spaces, you might be storing up problem for yourself in the future. Suppose, for example, that you build an Access application for your company that turns out to be wildly successful. Promotion quickly follows, with a place on the board and stock options: the world is your oyster. Then you are asked to upgrade the database to a client-server system (see Part 3). If the client-server RDBMS favored by your company doesn't support spaces in field names, you suddenly have a major headache. Take our advice and avoid spaces in field names.

We have also elected always to use UPPER-CASE for table names and the delightfully named CamelCaps for field names. Finally, if I need to refer to a specific field in a specific table, I will always do so by separating the two names with a dot or point(.). Thus:

> EMPLOYEES.EmployeeNo

refers to the *EmployeeNo* field of the table called *EMPLOYEES*.

Incidentally, one of the reviewers of the book commented "CamelCaps are more accurately known as BiCapitalization, but 'CamelCaps' is much more fun! Purely, for information, did you know that random CaPitaLizaTioN is known as StudlyCaps?"

That finishes with the aside. Now, back to the records. (As another aside, this expression "Now, back to the records" is a rare example of a database pun. We need to treasure it because there are so few of them.)

Building a table

So, tables have fields and fields have field names. However, if you elect to use the 'Design View' you will find that you are asked for more than just the field names. For each field you will be asked to choose the 'type' of data which the field will hold (known as the 'data type') and the size of the data which will be placed therein. We'll have a look at what each of these terms means and why it is usually to your advantage to choose wisely.

Types of data

The most commonly used data types are:

Text	Most characters found on the keyboard, including numbers; usually limited to 255 characters.
Memo	Large blocks of text.
Number (or numeric)	Numbers only, no text characters.
Date/Time	As the name suggests; dates, times or both.
Currency	Essentially numeric with four decimal places and a currency symbol.
AutoNumber	A number that is automatically incremented for each new record.
Yes/No	For discrete information that falls neatly into two categories; like True/False, Yes/No, Up/Down.
OLE Object	An object such as a Microsoft Excel spreadsheet, a Microsoft Word document or graphical information.
Hyperlink	For storing URLs (Uniform Resource Locators)

This is how data types are selected during the design of a table in Access.

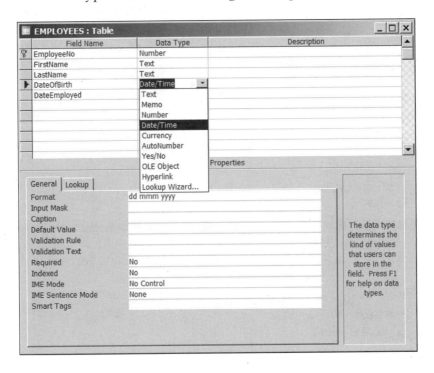

Choosing the correct data type for a given field is usually easy. If you create a field called FirstName, then Text is clearly likely to be the correct data type; Currency would be a good choice for a field called Salary and so on. But why do we have to tell the RDBMS what type of data is going into the table? Why can't it just store whatever we choose to put in as, indeed, some very simple DBMSs will do? The answer is that defining the data type has four advantages (in no particular order of importance). It can:

- allow more 'meaningful' operations to be performed upon the data
- exclude certain types of error
- make the storage of the data more efficient in terms of size
- make data recovery more rapid.

Meaningful operations

Suppose you want your EMPLOYEES table to store the date upon which each employee started to work for your company. You decide to declare a field called DateEmployed to store it. What data type would you choose? Date/Time seems like a good choice but it is common to find that people new to databases will choose the default data type which happens to be Text. Even more surprisingly, this appears to work (at least initially) because a text field will accept any alphanumeric character that you can find on the keyboard. The following are all acceptable in a text field:

> Penguin
>
> ROSS
>
> Sophie
>
> 45
>
> Salt & Pepper
>
> 12+45%
>
> 12/4/1966

Note that the last one looks like a date. Since text fields will accept data which looks like a date, why bother declaring the field type to be anything else? The answer is that dates, as you have probably noticed, are horrendously complex:

> *30 days hath September,*
> *April, June and November,*
> *All the rest hathn't*

(or words to that effect).

The good news is that if you declare this field to be of type Date/Time, the RDBMS will be able to perform what is known as 'date arithmetic'. For example, it should be able to tell you how long each employee has been with you simply by subtracting the date stored in DateEmployed from the current date. In addition, it should be able to give you the answer in days, months or years, whichever temporal currency you happen to prefer.

You can see this in action below, where Access is calculating the number of days for which an employee has been with the company, even allowing for leap years.

```
EMPLOYEES                                          _ □ ×
   EMPLOYEES
►
          Employee Number:  1
              First Name:  Manny
              Last Name:  Tomanny
            Date Of Birth:           12 Apr 1966
      Date First Employed:           01 May 1999
            Today's Date:           26 Jan 2006
      No. of Days Employed       2463

  Record: │◄│ ◄│        1 │ ► │►I│►*│ of 6
```

Incidentally, note that we are using a form here to look at the data in the table. It serves as an excellent illustration of exactly why forms are so useful. Tables cannot manipulate the data that they contain, they are simply storage vessels. Forms can do so and can also replace field names like DateOfBirth with text containing spaces

Clearly this is only possible because the RDBMS 'understands' that a date like '12 April 1966' is actually the twelfth day of the fourth month in 1966. It can only assume that this is so because we have effectively told it by declaring the field called DateOfBirth to be of type Date/Time.

As another example, consider telephone numbers. What sort of field type should be used to store them? (Be warned: this is a trick question.) The obvious answer is to store them in a number field but that happens to be the wrong answer. Number data types treat the data they contain as numbers, so they remove leading zeros, which catastrophically changes country codes like 001 to 1. In addition, they won't tolerate spaces or parentheses in numbers, which is also unfortunate. The net result is that you want to store, say:

> 001 234 123 4567

or

> (001) 234 123 4567

but all you can store is:

> 12341234567

which isn't the same thing at all.

The correct answer is to store telephone numbers in a text field where leading zeros, spaces and parentheses are happily tolerated. This use of text fields for telephone numbers isn't as counter-intuitive as it might appear. Numbers are values that we manipulate mathematically, and telephone numbers aren't numbers in that sense at all. When did you last calculate the average of your friends' phone numbers? Telephone numbers are actually identifiers which happen to be numeric; in practice they could equally well be a string of text characters.

Excluding certain errors

Given that the RDBMS will expect only dates to be entered into a Date/Time type field, it will reject dates like:

> 34th April 2005
> 29th February 2003

Incidentally, you don't have to type dates into the database as a mixture of text and numbers such as '21 Feb 2003'. You can type them in as numbers and you can set the expected format to be US or UK. Thus, if Windows is set for UK format dates, then typing in 7/4/96 means the seventh of April. If it is set for US format, then it is the fourth of July (and time for a party).

Making storage more efficient

Suppose you want a field to hold the number of offspring of each employee.

The obvious choice is to make the data type 'Number'. However, there are several different sub-types of 'Number'. You do not need to learn these off by heart but just to give you an idea of the range, the most commonly used are:

Sub type of Number	Storage capacity and size
Byte	Stores numbers from 0 to 255 (no decimals). Each occupies 1 byte.
Integer	Stores numbers from -32,768 to 32,767 (no decimals). Each occupies 2 bytes.
Long Integer	Stores numbers from -2,147,483,648 to 2,147,483,647 (no decimals). Each occupies 4 bytes.
Single	Big numbers. Numbers well into the billions and beyond. For the technically minded, numbers with six digits of precision, from approx. -3.4×10^{38} to $+3.4 \times 0^{38}$. Each occupies 4 bytes.
Double	Stores huge numbers, I mean really monstrous. In a double data type you can store a number which is far greater than the number of atoms in the entire observable universe. Since this number must, by definition, exceed the number of employees or customers you have, it should be big enough. For the technically minded, numbers are stored with 10 digits of precision and range from approx. -1.8×10^{308} to $+1.8 \times 10^{308}$ complete with decimals. Each occupies 8 bytes.

[A byte can be thought of as a single unit of storage in a computer. Disk space is usually measured in Megabytes (1 MByte = approximately 1 million Bytes) or Gigabytes (1 GByte = approximately 1,000 Megabytes).]

One of the reviewers wrote "Is this really true?" next to the bit about "you can store a number which is far greater than the number of atoms in the entire observable universe". "Yes" is the short answer. Last time I looked into this (which was a while ago) the estimate was 1×10^{73} atoms (1 with 73 zeros after it). Even if that estimate has risen ten million-fold, that would still only be 1×10^{80}, and a 'double' will store 1×10^{308}. Of course, these numbers are stored without much precision, but they are still mind-stretchingly vast.

Now, for a start, offspring are integers. Given a particularly obnoxious offspring you might attempt to claim responsibility for only a small part of it but we don't normally describe someone as having 0.1835 children. Secondly, how many people do you know with more than 255 children? How many people do you know with negative children? (This is not the same as asking, "How many people do you know who are negative about their children?") So the correct numeric sub-type in this case will be Byte which stores positive integers between zero and 255, or Integer if Byte is not available.

So, what major catastrophe occurs if you get it wrong and accept the default Number data type which isn't Byte or Integer? (Double was the default in Access 2.0 but it's Long Integer in the later versions.) The answer is 'Nothing too drastic really, unless you start to collects lots of data.' (see Field size below). However, since you are often unsure of exactly how much data you will collect, it is always a good idea to try to take the long-term view.

Making data recall more rapid

As a general rule, if you make a field a Long Integer and then fill it with positive integers between 1 and 20, you are wasting space. A digit between 1 and 20 would fit in a Byte field and therefore take up only one byte of disk space. However, the same number stored in a Long Integer field takes up four times as much disk space. This has the effect of making the table larger than it needs to be, which has the knock-on effect of slowing the database down when it is queried because there is more of it to be processed. However, it is important to keep a sense of proportion here.

Suppose you are building a table to hold a list of your friends. Popular as you are, you never expect the table to contain more than 300 rows. In this case, it really doesn't matter if you use a Byte or Double data type for storing how many children each friend has because neither size nor speed will ever be a noticeable problem. Having said that, of course, there is always the little matter of pride. There is a certain satisfaction in getting it right. In addition, many databases I have seen built for small companies have expanded beyond the designer's wildest dreams. So, on balance, even given a healthy sense of proportion, I would always try to get it right first time.

First time? Yes, because Access will allow you to change a data type, even after you have added data to the table. Exactly what happens to the data will depend upon the change you make and sometimes a loss of information is inevitable. For example, if you store data in a Double field, you can include numbers with decimal components. If you subsequently change it to an Integer type, Access will keep the whole numbers and will round them depending upon the decimal component. Thus 4.4 becomes 4 while 5.5 becomes 6.

Field size

If you declare a field called LastName to be of type Text, you will also need to tell Access how many characters that field can hold. This can be a bit of a guessing game; what's the longest last name you can think of? Marklyn? Whitehorn? Weatherbottom? Zimmer Van Kyllon? Most RDBMSs need to know this sort of information because the size of the field will affect storage space and retrieval speed. Suppose you decide to make the field 50 characters long; this means that for every record added to the table, 50 bytes are set aside to hold the person's last name. If the longest last name you ever store is 26 characters long (Zimmermann der Grossenamen), then you are wasting 24 bytes per record. Since tables are stored on disk, you are now wasting 24 bytes of disk space per record. Given that you want to store records for, say the population of Scotland (approximately 5 million souls), you will waste 120 MBytes of disk space by simply accepting a default value. If you make similar mistakes for 10 fields, that multiplies up to over a Gigabyte.

Surprisingly, this waste of disk space isn't too big a crime nowadays because disk space has become so cheap. But there is another problem: the bigger a table gets, the longer it takes to search. Choosing the wrong field size can contribute to a database which runs like congealed porridge. Such databases are generally unpopular with their users.

Excellent news for Access users is that ever since version 1.0, Access has been intelligent enough to store only the actual characters that you enter into each text field. Thus if you declare the text field to be 50 characters wide, but store 'Penguin' in the first record, this will only take up 7 bytes of disk space. In fact, Access only asks you to decide how many characters that field can hold so that you have control over the maximum number of characters which are entered. However, most RDBMSs are less forgiving with text fields and will waste space if you declare the size of the field unwisely.

General notes on table design

Think first

If you want a new table you shouldn't really sit down at the computer without doing some thinking first. Creating a table (and indeed a database) requires two fundamentally different stages which we can call 'Structure Definition' and 'Implementation'. (These are not formally recognized terms, they just happen to be useful here.)

Structure definition essentially means deciding which fields will be required, what information will go into them and how large each one should be. This is not a process which involves a computer; indeed it should be carried out as far away from a computer as possible.

Implementation means constructing a computerized representation of the design.

It could be imagined that because the first stage just takes pencil, paper and common sense, it is therefore a matter of little consequence. On the other hand, because the second step involves a computer and an RDBMS, it could be seen as more difficult.

In fact, the converse is true; design is difficult and implementation is easy. Having said that, design *is* mostly common sense (it just depends on how sensible you are). One golden rule of design is *not* to ask the question:

> "What information do I want to *put into* the table?"

Instead you should ask:

> "What information do I want to *get out* of the table?"

You are, after all, only building the database so that information can be extracted. Having decided what questions you are likely to ask of your table, you can then work backwards and decide what information needs to be put in and from that you can deduce the structure.

Again, an example helps make this clear. You need to be able to send mail to certain target groups of Influential People (IPs). (Make a note: you will need fields for names and others for addresses.) IPs are often fussy about their titles (note: separate field for title). You will need to target them based on their income group (field for income), number of children (integer field) and political party (text field). You want to include a direct reference to their spouse in the letter (text field for spouse's name) and so on.

If all this sounds far too obvious, believe me it isn't. I have seen several tables which have been stuffed with useless information, so well stuffed that the entire database was running like treacle, which was why I had been asked to take a look. The information wasn't there because anyone was going to use it but was there because it had been easy to collect. In two cases, the information had been available electronically so it didn't even have to be typed in. Ease of collection is not, on its own, a good reason for storing data.

Context

Another good rule is to think about the data that you will collect in the particular context in which it will be collected. The size of a field needed to hold people's last names will depend upon the ethnic group to which they belong.

PC or not PC? That is the question

Try to avoid field names like ChristianName; not everyone has one because not everyone is a Christian. I would hate this to sound like a sop to the great god 'Political Correctness' but why offend people when it is easy, with a little thought, to avoid doing so?

Hard-line political correctness makes table design a minefield in which even the wariest database designer can be caught. As one of the reviewers of an early draft of this book pointed out:

"Fine to abandon 'Christian' names because of cultural diversity, but not then to say 'First' or 'Last' name. 'Tsiao Ping' is not Mr. Deng's Christian name, but it is not his first name either; it is his given name (and 'Deng' is his *surname* or *family name*). Actually, you can't win: 'Magnusson' isn't Magnus's family name; it's his *patronymic*."

I suppose that we can take comfort in the fact that whatever we choose will be wrong, so at least we know where we are from the start.

Controlling data entry

Access allows you to set up filters which control the input of data into fields. It is worth mentioning here because you can use field types to help ensure that valid data ends up in the table.

Suppose you wish to collect information relating to a person's gender. You could set up a text field and expect the users of the database to type in 'Male' or 'Female' in response to the question 'Sex?'

Experience suggests that if male students are allowed to enter the data for themselves, about 5% will answer "Yes" and a further 10% will respond "Yes please!" While this data tells you that about two-thirds of the students with a sense of humor are also polite, it doesn't help you to collect the information you want.

There are several alternatives. You could set up the field to be of type Yes/No and entitle the field 'Female?' (or 'Male?' if you like). The system would then only allow the response 'Yes' or 'No'. By doing this you are making use of the data type to control data entry.

Another (and possibly better) way is to make use of a more specific control mechanism that Access allows during the construction of a table. You can choose a data type, such as text, set it to a specific size, say 6, and then specify that only the input "Male" or "Female" is acceptable for that field.

Of course, neither system will prevent any individual student from claiming to be the wrong sex (either from perversity or feeble-mindedness) but controlling such factors lies outside the remit of even the most advanced database.

Access allows the control of data input to the table to be set up in a very versatile manner. You can, for example, set up a numeric field which will accept values only between 1.34233 and 6.4453. As another example, you can set a field called Title to accept only the input 'Mr.', 'Mrs.', 'Miss', 'Ms', 'Dr.' or 'Prof.'.

One of the reviewers added "I wouldn't, though. I once tried to enumerate them all ('Sir', 'Lord', etc.) Ouch!"

True, there must be hundreds. However, have a look at the validation rule in the lower part of the screen below to see how it can be done.

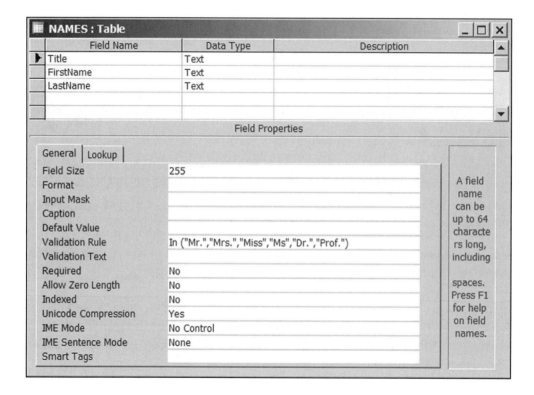

You can also use forms as a further level of control. This issue is discussed further in Chapter 5 – Forms and in considerably more detail in Chapter 16 – Integrity.

Field names

Most of the early RDBMSs put significant restrictions on the size of field names and the characters they could contain (such as eight letters or fewer, no lower-case letters and no spaces). In turn this has given rise to field names like FNAME, LNAME, CUST# and so on. I hate these because they are a barrier to understanding, and happily many of the modern RDBMSs remove these restrictions. Access allows field names with longer names like Customer Number. For reasons discussed above I would avoid spaces, but using more than eight characters can often make for more readable field names. Throughout this book I have carefully ignored my own advice, using as few letters as I can while still retaining some readability. In my defense I'll claim that when building databases for the 'real world' I do use longer field names. However, the databases used here are examples for a book. The printed page is an all too narrow medium for displaying tables, so I have tried to work as best I can within that rather odd restriction.

Splitting names, addresses etc.

It is tempting, but usually inadvisable, to store data in a single field if it can be logically subdivided. For example, if you store names like this:

Name
Prof. John Parker
Dr. Brian Featherstone
Miss Julie Arberlington
Mr. Mike Barham

all will be well until someone asks you to list all of the people in the table alphabetically by surname. In fact, with much effort and gnashing of teeth, it is possible to do this, but why make life difficult for yourself? If you store the same data in three fields like this:

Title	FirstName	LastName
Prof.	John	Parker
Dr.	Brian	Featherstone
Miss	Julie	Arberlington
Mr.	Mike	Barham

you can then simply sort on the contents of the third field:

Title	FirstName	LastName
Miss	Julie	Arberlington
Mr.	Mike	Barham
Dr.	Brian	Featherstone
Prof.	John	Parker

Subdividing data like this also makes it much easier to, say, extract all the Professors from the list.

The rule for subdividing data is quite simple. If you have data which can be logically split into sections, give serious consideration to doing so. If you can see any future need at all to manipulate the data via one of its possible subdivisions, it is almost essential to split it up into different fields.

Addresses are another good case in point. It is possible to argue that an address is usually used as a single unit. However, once the data is in a database, you are likely to be asked to perform operations such as finding all of the customers in Boston. This will be much easier if the address is split into separate fields, one of which is called something like City/Town. And, of course, postcodes and zip codes contain a plethora of information so long as you can get at it. Always store them in their own field.

Don't store redundant information

If, in an order table, you store CostOfItem and NumberOfItems, don't store the total cost since this is already inherently stored as the product of the other two fields. If we ever need the information we can calculate it as CostOfItem x NoOfItems (see Chapter 5 – Forms). Storing the product of these two in the table not only wastes space, it produces updating problems. Suppose you enter a record and complete the three fields – CostOfItem, NumberOfItems and TotalCost. Then your customer alters the order, doubling the number of items. You might update the number of items but forget to alter the value in the TotalCost field as has happened in the sample table shown below.

ORDERS					
OrderID	**Customer**	**Item**	**CostOfItem**	**NoOfItems**	**TotalCost**
1	Holly	Haddock	$3.45	23	$79.35
2	Bill	Herring	$2.56	45	$115.20
3	Jane	Haddock	$3.45	43	$148.35
4	Henry	Salmon	$5.67	34	$192.78
5	Mark	Shrimps	$3.23	100	$242.25
6	Mary	Prawns	$3.45	34	$117.30
7	Bill	Herring	$2.56	56	$143.36
8	Holly	Haddock	$3.75	45	$168.75

(To save you working it out, the record for Mark buying shrimps is incorrect. He originally ordered 75 which gives the price of $242.25 but later altered the order to 100. Since the TotalCost field wasn't updated to $323.00, he got a bargain, which means our company lost money.)

I have assumed that the price of fish varies with time, so it is perfectly reasonable for haddock to vary in price from one order to another.

In theory there are solutions to this problem which still allow you to store the redundant data. You could, for example, get the RDBMS to automatically recalculate the TotalCost whenever the values in either of the other two fields are altered. Actually ensuring that the recalculation takes place under all conditions takes time and effort. Experience has shown that in most cases it is far simpler and safer not to store redundant information.

Base tables – not defined here

Since this chapter is about tables, it feels instinctively like the right place to define a concept that you will probably need, that of a 'base' table. The problem is that base tables only really make sense when compared and contrasted with, well, tables which *aren't* base tables. All of the tables we have covered so far *are* base tables, so the definition is going to be cumbersome until we reach the other sort of table (which happens to appear in Chapter 4 – Queries/Views). So I'll salve my conscience by defining a base table as exactly the sort of table that you have met so far, namely those which you create and within which you store the data for your database. We can improve on that definition later.

Chapter 4

Queries/Views

Creating a database and then entering all the data takes time and effort. Simply creating a database is not an end in itself; unless you are one of those sad people (like me) who actually enjoys that sort of thing, there has to be some gain for the pain. That gain lies in the easy access to the data provided by an electronic database.

Queries usually find subsets of the data

By far the most common operation performed on the data in a table is to subset it.

EMPLOYEES

EmployeeNo	FirstName	LastName	DateOfBirth	DateEmployed
1	Manny	Tomanny	12 Apr 1966	01 May 1999
2	Rosanne	Kolumn	21 Mar 1977	01 Jan 2000
3	Cas	Kade	01 May 1977	01 Apr 2002
4	Norma	Lyzation	03 Apr 1966	01 Apr 2002
5	Juan	Tomani	12 Apr 1966	01 Apr 2002

This operation can be done by field,

JustNames

FirstName	LastName
Manny	Tomanny
Rosanne	Kolumn
Cas	Kade
Norma	Lyzation
Juan	Tomani

by record,

JustNorma				
EmployeeNo	**FirstName**	**LastName**	**DateOfBirth**	**DateEmployed**
4	Norma	Lyzation	03 Apr 1966	01 Apr 2002

or both.

JustNorma'sName	
FirstName	**LastName**
Norma	Lyzation

Operations which extract data from a table in this way are called queries. Given a table of five columns and five rows, there is no need to use a query; you can find the required information by eye. Given 50 columns and 100,000 rows your eye may need a little help. These subsetting operations rarely stem from a desire to play with the data *per se*; instead they arise because people ask questions. Subsetting by field, for example, answers a question which might be "What are the names of my employees?" Subsetting by record answers questions such as "What information is available about my employees called Norma?" Subsetting by both might have been produced to answer the question "What are the full names of all of my employees called Norma?"

Queries, answer tables and base tables finally defined properly and closure mentioned briefly

It is important not to become confused between a query and the answer that it produces.

A query is simply a question which can be asked of the data in a table. This query can be expressed in several ways (see the paragraphs on graphical querying tools and SQL at the end of this chapter) and it can even be expressed in human language. In this context, the method of expression is immaterial; a query is a question which you ask about the data in a table. Having asked that question, you expect an answer and the answer appears in a tabular layout called an answer table. An answer table will have columns and rows and it will look and feel like a table. Note that the last sentence sounds dictatorial "It *will* have columns and rows, it *will* look and feel like a table"; this is because one of the central tenets of relational database theory, known as *closure*, is that the result of a query will always be a table (see, for example, the subsetting examples shown above). This principle is very important but it is easier to explain why it is so important when we are dealing with multiple tables, so I'll leave more detailed discussions until Part 2.

Answer tables are such an important part of a database that it becomes essential to be able to distinguish them from the original tables. These original tables can be, and often are, referred to as *base tables*. The screen shots below illustrate the relationship, reading from bottom to top, between a base table, a query and an answer table.

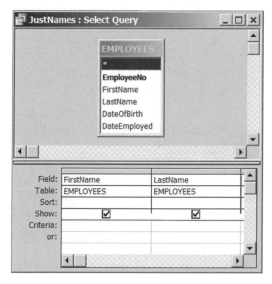

As we have seen above, base tables have certain characteristics, not the least of which is that the data they contain can be edited. The same should be true of the answer tables which arise from a query; the data you see in the answer table should be editable. This means you should be able to look at an answer table on screen and edit the data you see there. Those edits should 'pass through' the answer table and actually alter the data in the base table from which the data originally came.

I say 'should be' editable, because they often are. However, there are two main reasons why you may come across answer tables which are not editable.

The first is that not every DBMS implements this highly useful feature, a failure which, incidentally, excludes them from being true relational DBMSs (see Chapter 24). Access, you will be delighted to learn, supports this facility.

The second reason is that, under certain circumstances, allowing you to edit the data displayed in an answer table is, as we database professionals say, "incompatible with preserving the integrity of the data."

This situation can arise, for example, when certain types of query draw data from multiple tables or when a query summarizes data. Under these circumstances the RDBMS should not allow you to edit the data in an answer table. For example, we have already seen a table of information about employees. It stores the employees' dates of birth and the dates upon which they were employed. From these two pieces of information, it is clearly possible to work out how old each person was in years when employed and we can build a query to do this.

The answer table looks like this:

AgeWhenEmployed				
FirstName	**LastName**	**DateOfBirth**	**DateEmployed**	**AgeWhenEmployed**
Manny	Tomanny	12 Apr 1966	01 May 1999	33
Rosanne	Kolumn	21 Mar 1977	01 Jan 2000	22
Cas	Kade	01 May 1977	01 Apr 2002	24
Norma	Lyzation	03 Apr 1966	01 Apr 2002	35
Juan	Tomani	12 Apr 1966	01 Apr 2002	35

This answer table summarizes data and therefore parts should not be editable.

In this example, AgeWhenEmployed is being calculated as the integer value of the number of days between the dates divided by 365.25. I know this will very occasionally give the wrong answer, but then dates are notoriously tricky anyway...

The data in the first four fields comes directly from the base table EMPLOYEES and logically can be edited in the answer table above. The data in the fifth field, AgeWhenEmployed, is calculated and therefore cannot be edited. If this seems strange, ask yourself this question: "If we alter the value in the first record to read 35 instead of 33, which of the two date fields in the underlying base table should be altered to make the calculation yield 35?" The RDBMS cannot make this sort of decision, so the field is uneditable.

However, assuming that a given query is editable (both in theory and practice), I stress again that the actual changes you make to the data will be fed back to the underlying base tables. In other words, despite the fact that answer tables look like distinct entities on screen, in practice it is perhaps more accurate to think of them as windows onto the original base table. In fact, the name 'View', used for queries in a client-server database, gives a better flavor of how they behave.

There is another reason for stressing the fundamental difference between a query (which is, in essence, a question) and the answer table that a given query generates. Suppose you create a query, store it and use it on more than one occasion. Would you expect it to produce the same answer table every time it is run?

If the data in the base table is the same, the answer table will be identical. But if the data in the base table has changed, the data in the answer table may also have changed. A little thought shows that we can use this very much to our advantage.

Suppose you build a query which looks at the data in the table shown below

ORDERSFEW				
OrderID	**Customer**	**Item**	**CostOfItem**	**NoOfItems**
1	Holly	Haddock	$3.45	23
2	Bill	Herring	$2.56	45
3	Jane	Haddock	$3.45	43

and summarizes the total amount spent on each product.

TotalSalesForEachProduct-ORDERSFEW	
Item	**Total**
Haddock	$227.70
Herring	$115.20

Time passes and more orders arrive.

ORDERSMANY				
OrderID	**Customer**	**Item**	**CostOfItem**	**NoOfItems**
1	Holly	Haddock	$3.45	23
2	Bill	Herring	$2.56	45
3	Jane	Haddock	$3.45	43
4	Henry	Salmon	$5.67	34
5	Mark	Shrimps	$3.23	100
6	Mary	Prawns	$3.45	34
7	Bill	Herring	$2.56	56
8	Holly	Haddock	$3.75	45

When the same query is run again, it generates a different answer table which contains the up-to-date information.

TotalSalesForEachProduct-ORDERSMANY	
Item	**Total**
Haddock	$396.45
Herring	$258.56
Prawns	$117.30
Salmon	$192.78
Shrimps	$323.00

In the sample database these answer tables are actually produced by two queries. In fact, the two queries are effectively identical; they are just looking at two separate tables. This is to save you the effort of typing in the extra records. If you want to be sure I'm not fooling you, just type the extra records into the table called ORDERSFEW and re-run the appropriate query.

This separation of the query from the answer is wonderfully useful and many queries are used over and over again at different times. And if you ever need to take a snapshot of the data at a particular time, you can always get the query to generate a separate, new table which is written to disk under a different name, (making it, in effect, a base table) thus preserving the data for future reference.

One of the reviewers added "It might be worth saying that the table will no longer be an answer table in the sense that you can't update through it. However, you can still update the data it contains – including the fields that you couldn't update through before."

Summarizing data

At their most basic, queries extract a subset of the data in a table but they can do much more. It is perfectly possible to use a query not only to extract a subset of the data but also to perform some mathematical manipulation upon it. In the case of the table below the manipulation involves dates but given numerical data many other mathematical operations are possible (averages, standard deviations, variances, minimum and/or maximum values etc).

AgeWhenEmployed				
FirstName	**LastName**	**DateOfBirth**	**DateEmployed**	**AgeWhenEmployed**
Manny	Tomanny	12 Apr 1966	01 May 1999	33
Rosanne	Kolumn	21 Mar 1977	01 Jan 2000	22
Cas	Kade	01 May 1977	01 Apr 2002	24
Norma	Lyzation	03 Apr 1966	01 Apr 2002	35
Juan	Tomani	12 Apr 1966	01 Apr 2002	35

Other useful queries

And it just gets better and better. Apart from summarizing data and incorporating mathematical operations, they can be used to perform many other types of manipulation.

Update

Queries can be used to update the existing data in a table. For example, if you have a table of items for sale and you want to increase all of the prices by 10%, you can use an update query to do the job. You can be more selective and update the price by 10% only if the item costs more than $2.45.

Append

Queries can be created which will locate specific data in one table (find the names of the sales people who have exceeded this year's sales quotas) and add that data to another table (one which holds the names of everyone who is going on the company outing).

Delete

Queries can also be created which will locate specific records in one table (find the names of the sales people who have not exceeded this year's sales quotas) and delete those records from the table.

OK, perhaps this example is a bit brutal, but you get the idea.

Graphical querying tools

A query is a question you ask of a table and that question can be expressed in a variety of ways. It can be asked in a human language such as English: "Give me the phone numbers of all the customers who live in Dundee" or mangled French "Donnez-moi le phone number de tout les customers qui restent en Dundee." Work is proceeding on trying to get RDBMSs to understanding queries expressed in human languages. For example, SQL Server has a feature called English Query that can do a reasonable job of understanding some queries expressed in the English language.

However, we are still a long way from an RDBMS that can understand the full and rich ways that we humans choose to express questions. Until that day is reached, we need to use more formal ways of expressing questions to an RDBMS.

In order to make the process of querying a database more accessible to the majority of users, RDBMSs typically have graphical querying tools. The one supplied with Access looks like this:

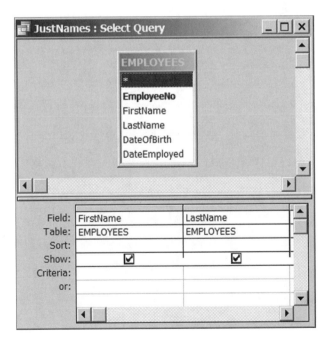

SQL and Views

Graphical querying tools are excellent, yet in the world of databases you will constantly hear people talking about SQL (Structured Query Language). SQL is a text-based querying system which takes slightly longer to learn and is less intuitive to use than a GUI-based querying system. Here is a sample:

```
SELECT EMPLOYEES.FirstName, EMPLOYEES.LastName
FROM EMPLOYEES;
```

So why would anyone bother with SQL? Well, SQL is a standard, meaning that many RDBMSs use it. In addition, it is more versatile than graphical querying tools: some complex queries which can be expressed in SQL cannot be expressed using a graphical tool.

If you are new to databases, I'd give SQL a miss for the moment. However, once you begin to get used to querying data, SQL is a subject which well repays some study. Those who feel the need are directed to Chapter 29.

Chapter 5

Forms

Data resides in the tables, but a database is more than simply data. It also includes components that are used as tools to look at, enter, delete and manipulate that data. Those components are called forms.

Below is, as you'll recognize, a table of data.

EMPLOYEES				
EmployeeNo	**FirstName**	**LastName**	**DateOfBirth**	**DateEmployed**
1	Manny	Tomanny	12 Apr 1966	01 May 1999
2	Rosanne	Kolumn	21 Mar 1977	01 Jan 2000
3	Cas	Kade	01 May 1977	01 Apr 2002
4	Norma	Lyzation	03 Apr 1966	01 Apr 2002
5	Juan	Tomani	12 Apr 1966	01 Apr 2002

Once you have defined a table, you can start putting data into it. Tables are usually represented on screen in a manner similar to that shown above, one row for each record and one column for each field. However, it is important not to lose sight of the fact that this 'table view' of the data is simply one way of representing the data. Your data is actually stored in a highly abstract way as a series of magnetic impressions on a disk and can be represented on screen in a whole variety of ways. In practice, data isn't usually entered directly into the kind of table representation shown above, although this is possible. Almost all data entry, editing and deleting operations are carried out via forms.

This is a form based on the table illustrated above.

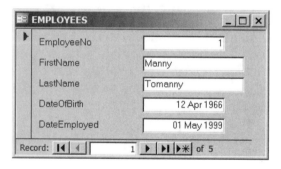

You can think of forms as being screens or filters which sit between the tables of data and the users of the database.

There is nothing intrinsically wicked about entering data directly into a table but forms are usually employed simply because human beings often prefer to be able to see each record in isolation rather than occupying a row on the screen alongside many other records. The type of presentation shown above is known as a form view of the data. Access has a Form designing section where you can build forms

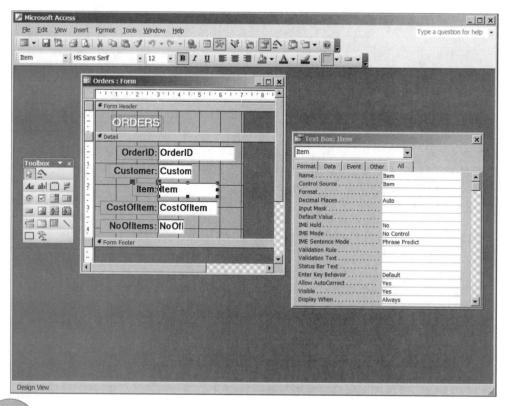

and it also has a Form Wizard that will design and build a form for you; all you have to give it is the table. In fact, the form shown above was constructed by the wizard.

As you can see, a basic form has one area for every field in the table. It is worth noting at this point that these areas on the form are not the fields themselves; rather, they are areas which allow you to view and (usually) edit the data in a field. In Access these areas on forms are known as 'text boxes'.

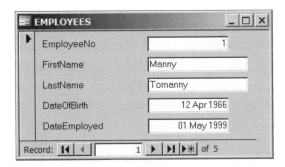

Typically a form shows one record on screen at a time and allows you to move between the text boxes by using the Tab key and to move between records with the PgUp and PgDn keys.

At their most basic, forms are simply devices for making it easier for people to interact with the table. After all, as discussed in the previous chapter, the restrictions of some RDBMSs can force field names to be rather cryptic. Care to guess what should be placed in a field called PatMass? A form allows you to place descriptive text beside a text box, so instead of having to enter data into field called PatMass, you can enter it into a text box labeled 'Patient's mass in kilograms'.

Even used in this very simple way, forms justify their existence by humanizing the database and the importance of this cannot be over emphasized: people still find computers intimidating, let alone databases. The easier the process of interacting with databases can be made the more effectively the database can be used. For example, it is often possible to use forms to make the interface to the database resemble the existing paper-based systems that the database is replacing.

Forms have many features which help towards this end. Perhaps the best way to understand how these help is to look at several in isolation and then see how they can be used together.

Multiple forms per table

The table is the repository of the actual data and the form is simply a 'window' onto that data. There is therefore nothing to stop you from creating more than one form based on a single table; each form can be used to give a different view of the same data.

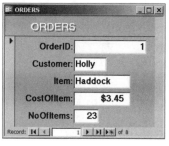

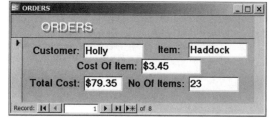

OrderID	Customer	Item	CostOfItem	NoOfItems
1	Holly	Haddock	$3.45	23
2	Bill	Herring	$2.56	45
3	Jane	Haddock	$3.45	43
4	Henry	Salmon	$5.67	34
5	Mark	Shrimps	$3.23	100
6	Mary	Prawns	$3.45	34
7	Bill	Herring	$2.56	56
8	Holly	Haddock	$3.75	45

Text boxes can be made read only

Remembering that text boxes are not the fields themselves, it is possible to alter the properties of a text box so that, for example, they become read-only; this means they will show the data in a given field but will not allow the user to change it. Combine this with the idea that you can have multiple forms per table and it becomes possible to have two very different forms. One could be for data entry, the other for simply viewing a subset of the information in the table.

Text boxes don't have to present data from just one field

As discussed in the previous chapter, it is excellent practice to ensure that you don't store several discrete pieces of data in the same field. For example, suppose you store names in two (or more) fields:

EMPLOYEES				
EmployeeNo	**FirstName**	**LastName**	**DateOfBirth**	**DateEmployed**
1	Manny	Tomanny	12 Apr 1966	01 May 1999
2	Rosanne	Kolumn	21 Mar 1977	01 Jan 2000
3	Cas	Kade	01 May 1977	01 Apr 2002
4	Norma	Lyzation	03 Apr 1966	01 Apr 2002
5	Juan	Tomani	12 Apr 1966	01 Apr 2002

Given this table and a form for data *entry*, you would have to present the user with two different text boxes, appropriately labeled so that the correct information was placed in the correct place. If you didn't, users might start entering the last name into the FirstName field.

However, suppose that you are using a form solely for *viewing* the data. There is then no need to treat these items of data as separate entities and they can be joined in one text box.

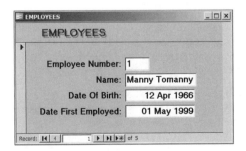

Note that this kind of manipulation doesn't affect the integrity of the data in any way and is worth doing because it makes life easier for the user of the database.

The example above is simply 'adding' (or concatenating) two text fields. It is equally easy to perform more complex mathematical manipulations on numerical fields. Again, as discussed in the previous chapter, it is not desirable to store information which can be calculated from data in existing fields. Clearly, since forms are the preferred way of looking at the data, they are also places for synthesizing the more complex form of the data.

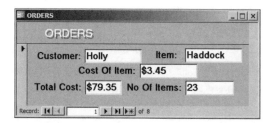

You can have a text box which is labeled 'Total Cost' and which displays the result of multiplying the values in CostOfItem and NumberOfItems. Unlike in the last chapter, there is no corresponding field called TotalCost in the ORDERS table.

ORDERS				
OrderID	Customer	Item	CostOfItem	NoOfItems
1	Holly	Haddock	$3.45	23
2	Bill	Herring	$2.56	45
3	Jane	Haddock	$3.45	43
4	Henry	Salmon	$5.67	34
5	Mark	Shrimps	$3.23	100
6	Mary	Prawns	$3.45	34
7	Bill	Herring	$2.56	56
8	Holly	Haddock	$3.75	45

The text box simply provides additional useful information for users of the form. If, as implied earlier, users of the database always interact with the table via a form, as far as they are concerned the Total Cost of the invoice is always visible. And if they alter either of the original values, the Total Cost text box will automatically update, precisely because it is solely dependent upon the other two.

It isn't necessary for each field in a table to appear on the form

Since a form is just a way of looking at the data in the table, it isn't necessary for every field in the table to appear on a given form. This is more significant than it first appears; see the summary at the end of this chapter.

Controlling data entry

As outlined in the previous chapter, choosing the correct data type for a field can help to ensure that the correct data is placed therein. In addition, it is possible to control data entry more closely at the table level, again described in the previous chapter. It is also possible to apply the same sort of control at the form level but as a *general* rule it should be applied at the table level. Why? Well, as has just been discussed, you can have multiple forms which are based on a single table. If you have a data entry rule that is crucial and you apply it at the form level, what will happen if you create a new form and forget to apply the rule there? Or what happens if you pass the database on to someone else and *they* don't know about the rule and create a new form? In both cases, there is now a strong possibility that corrupt/incorrect data will be allowed into your table, which has to be bad news. If you have a good reason for applying control at the form level, then clearly that is the best place. Otherwise, apply it at the table level. See Chapter 16 in Part 2 for more details.

Use of forms can be controlled

RDBMSs like Access allow you to control, via passwords if necessary, the access that any particular user has to the components of the database (tables, forms, queries, reports etc). In databases of any complexity it is common to forbid users direct access to the tables and to restrict their access to specific forms. Thus one group of users may be given access to one set of forms and another group may have access to a different set.

Forms can be web pages

Forms can also be created that are essentially web pages – or you can think of it the other way around: web pages can now act as forms. If your database is destined for use from the internet or a company-wide intranet, users can access the data and perform all the usual form-based functions from their browser. They can browse, search, add records and edit them, just as is possible from a form within a database application.

The means of generating web pages will differ between RDBMSs. Within Access, for instance, you can build data access pages, though these are designed primarily for use over an intranet. In these web-driven days, however, no matter what RDBMS you use, there will be some way of creating web pages to access your database. So wherever you see references in this book to a form, you can with equanimity substitute the words 'web page'.

Summary

- Forms are devices which allow users to see the data in a table, and it's possible to create one or more forms per table.

- Text boxes can be placed on a form which show the data from one field, or which combine and manipulate the data from more than one field.

- Not all fields have to be represented on a form and text boxes can be made read-only.

- Finally, the access that a user has to the set of forms can be controlled.

Given this level of flexibility, forms become quite remarkable tools. Imagine that you have a table which stores information about your employees. It contains some data that is generally available (name, address, phone number) and some which is confidential (salary, medical history, criminal record). Clearly it is unacceptable to give all of your employees direct access to this table. Nevertheless different people in different departments need access to different subsets of the data that it contains.

Three of the forms that you might consider building are:

- a read-only form designed to help employees locate and contact each other; this form is freely accessible. It shows only the individual's name (concatenated into a single text box), department, extension number and email address.

- one which is only available to the medical department and shows the name (again concatenated), department and medical history. Only the last field is editable and access to the form is controlled using a password known only to the medical department.

- one which shows the name (as two separate fields), address, home phone number, department and extension in editable text boxes . It is available to the personnel department for entering new records and editing existing ones.

The manner in which you set up these forms and the access that you allow different people to the data in the table is a matter for discussion within your company. The important point is that forms are the tools which can control access in this way.

Chapter 6

Reports

Reports are rather like queries in that they can be used to summarize the information in a database. One difference is that reports usually produce printed output, or produce web-based output that can be printed as required. Suppose that, at the end of every month, you need to produce a list of all invoices issued in that month, together with their individual values and a total. The best method is to use a report.

You need the invoices grouped by product with subtotals? Hey, no problem, use a report.

The sad truth is that the full power of reports cannot be demonstrated when they are used with single tables of data. Fear not: they will make more sense when we get on to using multiple tables. However, just to give you an idea of a simple one, here is a report which totals the numbers of items ordered by different customers.

Customer	NoOfItems	% of Total
Bill		
	45	
	56	
	101	27%
Henry		
	34	
	34	9%
Holly		
	23	
	45	
	68	18%
Jane		
	43	
	43	11%
Mark		
	100	
	100	26%
Mary		
	34	
	34	9%
Grand Total	380	

The report above is based on the data shown below.

ORDERSMANY				
OrderID	**Customer**	**Item**	**CostOfItem**	**NoOfItems**
1	Holly	Haddock	$3.45	23
2	Bill	Herring	$2.56	45
3	Jane	Haddock	$3.45	43
4	Henry	Salmon	$5.67	34
5	Mark	Shrimps	$3.23	100
6	Mary	Prawns	$3.45	34
7	Bill	Herring	$2.56	56
8	Holly	Haddock	$3.75	45

Chapter 7

Summary of Part 1

To summarize the basic components of a database:

- A base table is a repository for data.

- Queries/views are used to extract, subset and summarize data from the table and to update the table. Access doesn't distinguish between queries and views, so you only need to know about queries.

- Forms are devices for viewing and entering data into the table.

- Reports are used to print out some or all of the data in the table.

Tables, forms, reports and queries are the core components of a database. So far I have described each in isolation. However, when they are used together, they display a wonderful synergy. For example, as described above, a query is a storable question, the output from which is a table. Forms are based on tables, thus a form can be based on a query. Reports are based on tables, so they too can be based on a query. This is a really important point so it is worth repeating. Both forms and reports can be based upon queries.

Suppose you have a table that stores all of the orders that have come in from your customers. If you create a query that extracts only those orders which remain unpaid, you can then base a form on that query. Whenever you tell the software that you want to use the form, it will automatically run the query, extract the relevant information and display it in the form. A simple database constructed in this way is illustrated below.

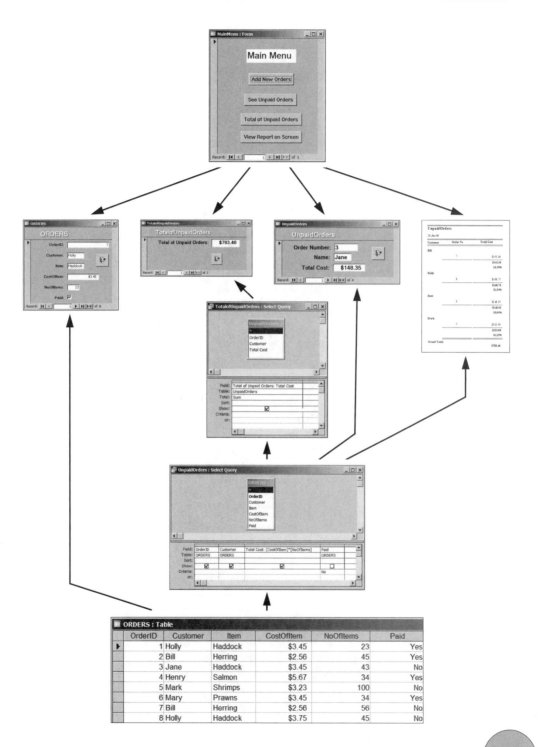

Part of the reason for building databases is to simplify the interface that the user encounters. Forms can be easy to use and understand, so they can be implemented as the sole way in which the user interacts with the data. To add a new order users choose the NewOrders form; to see how much money is currently outstanding, they select the form which displays this information and so on. Indeed, forms can be constructed whose sole function is to allow access to other forms. The one shown below simply provides a series of buttons which, when pressed, lead to other forms or cause reports to be generated.

This part of the book has looked at databases that are built around single tables of data. In practice, databases are often best built around multiple tables. The next part explains why multiple tables are such a good idea and describes the mechanisms that are used to make their use as painless as possible.

Part 2

A multi-table, single-user database

Chapter 8

Introduction to Part 2

So far we have confined ourselves to databases based upon a single table of data. These are great for learning about databases and occasionally the data you meet in the real world will actually fit neatly into just one table. For example, I once built a single-table database for SHARP (Scottish Heart and Arterial disease Risk Prevention).

Distressingly, Scotland remains one of the world leaders in the league table of premature deaths from cardiovascular disease. SHARP is a charity that aims to make people aware of both the problem and of possible remedies. From a base in a traveling bus, SHARP staff used to visit sites (factories, schools etc.) and assess individuals from the community for their risk of heart disease. The data collected consisted of 109 different pieces of information about each person. Since the data collected for each patient was unique, there was no advantage in using multiple tables. I built SHARP's database and it was a rare case, the only time I have ever used over 100 columns in a table and the only time I have built a single-table database (apart from simple address lists). So single-table databases do exist but experience suggests that almost all databases actually need multiple tables of data.

A perfectly reasonable question at this point is "Why?" After all, single tables are easy to manage and often feel intuitively right. We have lots of orders, we want to store information about each order, why can't we just use a single OR-DERS table? The Victorian clerks beloved of Dickens' novels put such orders into a ledger book which was essentially a single table of data.

What I have to do now is to convince you that single tables produce problems in computerized databases. Then I have to convince you that the extra effort involved in learning how to construct and maintain multiple-table databases is worthwhile. To put that more simply, I have to convince you that the gain is worth the pain. The next two chapters are designed to do just that.

After absorbing those two chapters, hopefully, you'll be convinced and will be prepared to read the rest of the part which tells you what you need to know in order to make multiple tables work together effectively.

Chapter 9

Serious problems with single tables

Suppose we decide, despite advice to the contrary, that we are going to use one and only one table in the database that we are building for our company. In that table we store the details of the orders that we process. These details include item sold, price, customer information, date of sale etc.. If we ran a bonus incentive scheme, we would also need to include the name of the employee who made the sale. We also need to store information about our employees – name, date of birth, date first employed, salary, address, home telephone number etc.. Since we only have one table, then that is the only place where we can put this additional information.

SINGLETABLE								
OrderNo	FirstName	LastName	DateOfBirth	DateEmployed	Customer	Supplier	Price	Item
1	Manny	Tomanny	12 Apr 1966	01 May 1999	Henderson	Harrison	$235.00	Desk
2	Norma	Lyzation	03 Apr 1966	01 Apr 2002	Thompson	Ford	$234.00	Chair
3	Manny	Tomanny	12 Apr 1966	01 May 1999	McColgan	Harrison	$415.00	Table
4	Rosanne	Kolumns	21 Mar 1977	01 Jan 2000	Wellington	Ford	$350.00	Lamp
5	Cas	Kade	01 May 1977	01 Apr 2002	Henderson	Ford	$234.00	Chair
6	Rosanne	Kolumns	21 Mar 1977	01 Jan 2000	Wellington	Ford	$350.00	Lamp
7	Rosanne	Kolumns	21 Mar 1977	01 Jan 2000	Henderson	Harrison	$235.00	Desk

We would also need to store the same sorts of details about the customers but I have left much of the detail out of the example so that the table doesn't spread right across the page and disappear off the edge.

However, even with its unrealistically small set of columns, this table can technically be described as a 'dog's breakfast' and for several reasons.

Redundant data

There is a considerable amount of repeated (or redundant) data in this table. Names, prices and dates are all stored multiple times, simultaneously wasting vast amounts of disk space and potentially slowing down any queries we run against the table. In addition, every time an employee makes another sale, we have to type in their name, date of birth, date first employed etc.. Would you want to type in all that data every time? And, since many of our customers (hopefully) will be giving us multiple orders, we will find that their details are also appearing over and over again. In addition, you will notice that we use Harrison as our supplier of desks. This fact is recorded twice already in the table and, if we sell a thousand desks, it will be immortalized 1,000 times; one can't help feeling that once would be enough. And the problems don't end with the amount of work required to input the data.

Typographical errors

Each row in this table represents a sale and we would hope that most customers come back for repeat purchases. If you had to type in words like 'Henderson' and 'Thompson' several hundred times (once for each sale to that customer), could you guarantee to do so perfectly every time? What about 'McCollgan' (one 'l' or two)? And even if you were sure you could do it correctly each time, what happens if several different people are entering data into the table? Will they all be consistent? It is all too easy to end up with a table like this:

VERYBADSINGLETABLE								
OrderNo	FirstName	LastName	DateOfBirth	DateEmployed	Customer	Supplier	Price	Item
1	Manny	Tomanny	12 Apr 1966	01 May 1999	Henderson	Harrison	$235.00	Desk
2	Norma	Lization	03 Apr 1966	01 Apr 2002	Tompson	Ford	$234.00	Chair
3	Manny	Tomanny	12 Apr 1966	01 May 1999	McCollgan	Harrison	$415.00	Table
4	Rosanne	Kolumns	21 Mar 1977	01 Jan 2000	Wellington	Ford	$350.00	Lamp
5	Cas	Kade	01 May 1977	01 Apr 2002	S. Henderson	Ford	$234.00	Chair
6	Rosanne	Fields	21 Mar 1977	01 Jan 2000	Ms Wellington	Ford	$350.00	Lamp
7	Rosa	Kolumn	21 Mar 1977	01 Jan 2000	Henderson	Harrison	$235.00	Desk

If we now search the table to find out how many sales a certain 'Rosanne Kolumns' has made for the company, we will get the answer 'one'. If she works on commission she will not be pleased.

Incidentally, just in case you don't believe that people really make typographical errors, the following is a list of variations of my name that I received in the post over a period of about five years. Many have been received multiple times and most appear to be in some kind of database or other. For the record, I do have two middle initials: they are A and F – and a PhD.

D Whitehorn
Dr A Whitehorns
Dr M A F Whiteh
Dr M A T Whitehorn
Dr M A Whitehord
Dr M F Whitehorn
Dr M Tehorn
Dr M Whiteham
Dr M Whitethorn
Dr M Whitewhorn

Dr M Whytehorn
Dr MAF Whitecorn
Dr Mark Whitehord
Dr Mark Whitekorn
Dr MHF Whitehorn, BSc, PhD
Dr N A F Whitehorn
Dr N Whitehorn
Dr Whipehorn

Dr Whitehall
Dr Whitehan
Dr Whitehorne

Dr Whitekor
Dr Whiteman

Dr Whytehorn
Dwhutehorn
Marie Whitehorn
Marj Whitehorn
Mark Whitburn
Mark Whitehall, Esq.,
Mark Whiteham
Mark Whitehaven
Mark Whitehern
Mark Whiteholn

Mark Witehorn
Mike Whitehorn
Mr D R Whitehorn
Mr D.A.M. Whitehorn
Mr M Horn
Mr M Whiteham
Mr Mack Horn
Mr Mark Whitehead

Mr Mark Whitehoarn
Mr Mark Whitehouse
Mr Mark Whithorn

Whitehorn Dark

I rather like 'Whitehorn Dark'; it's sophisticated and a little mysterious. Dwhutehorn is not bad either, but I'm not so sure about Whipehorn... nor about NAF Whitehorn.

Modifying data

Given that all of the data is placed in a single table, we have problems when we try to store or change certain types of information. These problems are generically called 'modification anomalies' and can be demonstrated with the table shown above and reproduced below.

OrderNo	FirstName	LastName	DateOfBirth	DateEmployed	Customer	Supplier	Price	Item
SINGLETABLE								
1	Manny	Tomanny	12 Apr 1966	01 May 1999	Henderson	Harrison	$235.00	Desk
2	Norma	Lyzation	03 Apr 1966	01 Apr 2002	Thompson	Ford	$234.00	Chair
3	Manny	Tomanny	12 Apr 1966	01 May 1999	McColgan	Harrison	$415.00	Table
4	Rosanne	Kolumns	21 Mar 1977	01 Jan 2000	Wellington	Ford	$350.00	Lamp
5	Cas	Kade	01 May 1977	01 Apr 2002	Henderson	Ford	$234.00	Chair
6	Rosanne	Kolumns	21 Mar 1977	01 Jan 2000	Wellington	Ford	$350.00	Lamp
7	Rosanne	Kolumns	21 Mar 1977	01 Jan 2000	Henderson	Harrison	$235.00	Desk

Suppose we delete the row for sale number 3 (the record with an OrderNo of 3). This happens to be the only record that contains the data which tells us that tables are supplied to our company by Harrison and that they cost $415.00. We can't afford to lose this information but, given a single table, we have nowhere else to store it.

And what happens if we want to store information about a new employee who has just started work but hasn't made any sales yet? If we insist on using this single-table structure, we have to wait until the new employee makes his or her first sale before we can record the fact that the new employee was born on 01 May 1967 or we have to use incomplete records to store such information.

Finally, if Rosanne gets married and decides to change her last name, we will have to find and change, not one piece of information, but several.

These three are known, respectively, as 'deletion', 'insertion' and 'update' anomalies. All three can be cured by using an additional pair of tables, one to store information about the items that we sell, the other for information about employees.

Summary

Single tables suffer from serious problems when they are used to store complex information. Those problems are:

- Redundant data which makes the table large, slow and unwieldy.

- Typographic errors caused by typing the same information multiple times.

- Difficulties in updating and modifying data.

I am aware that some of these problems can be overcome without the use of multiple tables. For example, consider the problem of Rosanne Kolumns' name change. We could use an update query to replace her old name with the new. In addition, we might even decide that we want to keep her old name on the old orders. The deletion and insertion anomalies are more difficult to deal with, although we could start storing records which are incomplete.

However, experience has shown that these solutions end up being more complicated than going over to a multi-table database. After all, multi-table databases don't have any virtue in themselves; the only reason that they have been widely adopted is that they solve the problems inherent in single-table databases in the most efficient way possible.

Chapter 10

Multiple tables
cure serious problems

So, let's have a look at the way in which multiple tables can remove these problems.

The two tables shown below hold the same information as the unwieldy one from the last chapter but together they take up less space on the hard disk. (In fact, the reduction in disk space is completely trivial in this example because the initial table was so small. However, as later examples will show, the saving becomes really significant with greater quantities of data.)

EMPLOYEES

EmployeeNo	FirstName	LastName	DateOfBirth	DateEmployed
1	Manny	Tomanny	12 Apr 1966	01 May 1999
2	Rosanne	Kolumns	21 Mar 1977	01 Jan 2000
3	Cas	Kade	01 May 1977	01 Apr 2002
4	Norma	Lyzation	03 Apr 1966	01 Apr 2002

ORDERS

OrderNo	EmployeeNo	Customer	Supplier	Price	Item
1	1	Henderson	Harrison	$235.00	Desk
2	4	Thompson	Ford	$234.00	Chair
3	1	McColgan	Harrison	$415.00	Table
4	2	Wellington	Ford	$350.00	Lamp
5	3	Henderson	Ford	$234.00	Chair
6	2	Wellington	Ford	$350.00	Lamp
7	2	Henderson	Harrison	$235.00	Desk

What I have done is to move the data relating to employees into a separate table and to use a 'pointer' to that data in the form of the EmployeeNo field in the ORDERS table. Thus from the ORDERS table we can see that sale number 2 was made by the employee with the EmployeeNo of 4. Referring to the EMPLOYEES table, we can then see that this is Norma Lyzation. (This use of 'pointers' is essentially part of the mechanism used to maintain a relational database and is covered in detail in Chapter 14 – How are relationships modeled?)

In fact, it is clear that we could continue this process and separate out the information about customers into a third table and the information about items into a fourth. However, with the very restricted number of columns shown in this cut-down table, that would be rather pointless. In addition, the process involved in creating each of those would be exactly the same as that required for the EMPLOYEES table, so we'll just use these two tables to illustrate the general principle for now.

It is true that to recover the original information, constant reference must be made to the employee number in both tables and the process feels horribly unwieldy. In practice the RDBMS will do this for you transparently (meaning that you don't even have to be aware that it is being done). As we will see later, once the database has been set up, you wouldn't normally look at these tables in their 'raw' state like this. Instead, you would interact with the data via forms which would show the data in whatever manner you desired, such as an order-centric view:

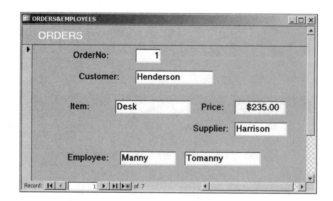

or an employee-centric view:

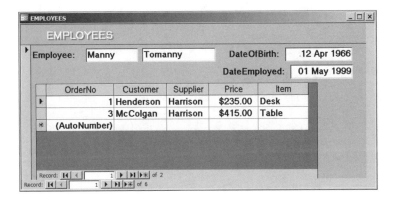

In the last chapter we looked at four areas that can be problematical if you use single tables, namely:

● Redundant data

● Typographical errors

● Updating data

● Modifying data

We'll cover the same four areas again, looking at how the use of multiple tables can reduce or eliminate those problems.

Redundant data

Given the small examples shown here, the savings in table size produced by splitting tables appear trivial but more realistic tables have significant savings. For example, suppose you have 1,000 employees and store 1 KByte of data about each. Your database also stores 2 KBytes of data about each of 100,000 sales. If you elect to use a single-table solution, each of the 100,000 rows will contain an extra 1 KByte of data about the sales person. Given a two-table solution, that information is held only once. Thus the sizes are:

	One Table	Two Tables
No. of rows	100,000	100,000 (from the ORDERS table) + 1,000 (EMPLOYEES table) = 101,000
Employee data	100,000 KBytes	1,000 KBytes
Sales data	200,000 KBytes	200,000 KBytes
Total data	300 MBytes	201 MBytes
Data saving		99 MBytes

The figures shown in the table have been rounded slightly as befits a rule of thumb estimate.

For information:

1,024 Bytes = 1 KByte

1,024 KBytes = 1,048,576 Bytes = 1 MByte.

The saving of one third is slightly exaggerated since adding the EmployeeNo fields to the two-table system produces a slight overhead but you probably get the general idea.

This looks good but it gets better. As the complexity of the data expands, the size problem inherent in using a single table increases catastrophically. Suppose we assume (quite reasonably) that each order can be for more than one item. Since each row in the single-table solution can only hold information about one item in the order, an order for three items will need three rows in the table.

MULTIPLEPARTORDERS									
Part	**OrderNo**	**FirstName**	**LastName**	**DateOfBirth**	**DateEmployed**	**Supplier**	**Item**	**Customer**	
1	1	Manny	Tomanny	12 Apr 1966	01 May 1999	Harrison	Table	Henderson	
2	1	Manny	Tomanny	12 Apr 1966	01 May 1999	Harrison	Desk	Henderson	
3	2	Norma	Lyzation	03 Apr 1966	01 Apr 2002	Ford	Chair	Thompson	
4	3	Manny	Tomanny	12 Apr 1966	01 May 1999	Harrison	Table	McColgan	
5	3	Manny	Tomanny	12 Apr 1966	01 May 1999	Ford	Chair	McColgan	
6	4	Rosanne	Kolumns	21 Mar 1977	01 Jan 2000	Ford	Chair	Wellington	
7	4	Rosanne	Kolumns	21 Mar 1977	01 Jan 2000	Ford	Lamp	Wellington	
8	4	Rosanne	Kolumns	21 Mar 1977	01 Jan 2000	Harrison	Desk	Wellington	
9	5	Cas	Kade	01 May 1977	01 Apr 2002	Ford	Chair	Henderson	
10	5	Cas	Kade	01 May 1977	01 Apr 2002	Ford	Lamp	Henderson	
11	6	Rosanne	Kolumns	21 Mar 1977	01 Jan 2000	Harrison	Table	Wellington	
12	6	Rosanne	Kolumns	21 Mar 1977	01 Jan 2000	Ford	Lamp	Wellington	
13	7	Rosanne	Kolumns	21 Mar 1977	01 Jan 1990	Harrison	Desk	Henderson	

We can make the same assumptions as before: 1,000 employees, 1 KByte of data about each one and 100,000 sales with 2 KBytes about each. We can add the assumption that we can sell any one of 2,000 different items (and hold 1 KByte on each one) and we will assume that an average order is for five items. The correct way of handling this data is to split it across four tables, one for the employees, one for the orders, one for the items and a fourth one which joins the items to the orders. The need for this fourth table hasn't been explained as yet (it will be in Chapter 14) but if you could take it on trust for the present, it will make my life a lot easier. (Trust me, I'm a database freak.) Each row in this joining table will be tiny, perhaps 8 bytes long, or 0.01 KBytes to be generous.

Again we can compare the efficiency of the single-table and multiple-table solutions in an approximate manner:

	One-table solution	Four-table solution
No. of rows	500,000	1,000(EMPLOYEES) + 100,000(SALES) + 2,000(ITEMS) + 500,000(JOIN) = 603,000
Employee data	500,000 x 1 KByte =	1,000 x 1 KByte = 1,000 KBytes
Sales data	500,000 x 2 KByte =	100,000 x 2 KByte = 200,000 KBytes
Items data	500,000 x 1 KByte =	2,000 x 1 KByte = 2,000 KBytes
Joining data	None	500,000 x 0.01 KByte = 5,000 KBytes
Total	500,000 KBytes + 1,000,000 KBytes + 500,000 KBytes = 2,000,000 KBytes = 2 Gbytes	1,000 KBytes + 200,000 KBytes + 2,000 KBytes + 5,000 KBytes = 207,000 KBytes = 207 MBytes
Saving		Approx. 1,800 MBytes = 1.8 GBytes

The four-table solution uses just a tenth of the space used by the one-table solution. While this waste of disk space is horribly inelegant, an even greater problem is that all of this repeated data will really slow the database down.

This example doesn't use a separate table for Customers. As an exercise, if you feel so inclined, you can calculate the additional savings if we assume that we have 2,000 customers and store 2 KBytes of data about each one.

Typographical errors

You are, of course, still at liberty to misspell poor Rosanne's last name. However, if you do, the error is likely to be much more obvious because every time her name appears it will be incorrect. In addition, since her name only has to be typed in once, we might hope that data entry boredom would be less of a factor.

Modifying data

The various modification anomalies described in the previous chapter disappear as soon as we move to a multi-table solution, assuming that the data is split up into an acceptable set of tables. For example, as you can see, we have been able to accommodate a couple of new employees without generating an incomplete record.

EMPLOYEES				
EmployeeNo	**FirstName**	**LastName**	**DateOfBirth**	**DateEmployed**
1	Manny	Tomanny	12 Apr 1966	01 May 1999
2	Rosanne	Kolumns	21 Mar 1977	01 Jan 2000
3	Cas	Kade	01 May 1977	01 Apr 2002
4	Norma	Lyzation	03 Apr 1966	01 Apr 2002
5	Juan	Tomani	12 Apr 1966	01 Apr 2002
6	Del	Eats	01 May 1967	01 May 2004

Chapter 11

Making multiple tables work together

You may wonder about the use of the word 'object' in this and subsequent chapters. You may have noticed heard about object-oriented programming and you might wonder if there is any connection. In fact, we are using the word 'object' here simply to mean 'thing' or 'entity'. The only reason we don't use the word 'thing' is that it looks thoroughly unprofessional to do so in a book about a serious subject like databases. There is, however, no hidden complex meaning in 'object' as the word is used here and if you want to mentally substitute the word 'thing', that's fine by me.

The only added complexity is that occasionally we will need to distinguish between an object itself and the class (or type) to which it belongs. For example, Norma Lyzation is an object and she happens to belong to the class of objects called Employees and information about her is therefore stored in the EMPLOYEES table. In practice, people often fail to distinguish between these in conversation. They will say, for example, "Employees and customers are clearly different objects"; in fact they mean "Employees and customers are clearly different classes of object".

Worrying about the distinction between an object and the class to which it belongs shouldn't keep you awake at night and we will follow common practice by not bothering to make the distinction unless we think it makes the text clearer to do so.

The last chapter should have convinced you that multiple tables are the only way in which to store complex data efficiently. Now we need to look at how they can be managed in a relational database. This in turn brings us to a consideration of what we want a database to do for us.

Databases are designed to model the real world

The real world is full of objects – employees, orders, customers, items for sale etc.

In the real world, these objects have relationships with each other – one employee will deal with multiple customers, one customer can buy multiple items and so on.

Databases, therefore, have to store information about these different objects and also about the relationships that exist between them.

What should you think about before you can build a database? There are five key areas which need to be considered:

1. How is information about the different objects to be stored in the database? In other words, how do we 'map' our real world objects onto our tables and ensure that we get the right data into the right tables?

2. What relationships can exist between real world objects?

3. How are these relationships modeled and maintained in a database?

4. How can we make the tables, forms, queries and reports work together in a database?

5. How do we maintain integrity within the data that we store in the database?

I suspect that it will come as no great surprise that these five topics make up the next five chapters.

Chapter 12

Getting the data into the correct tables

How do you ensure that you split up your data into an acceptable set of tables? For example, I might decide to store all of the information about employees in one table; but is that always the right decision? Is it always a good idea to have a separate table for the items that we sell? Again, if we sell mostly furniture and then start selling ice-cream, should the information relating to ice-cream sales go in the same table as that for furniture sales or a different one? How are you supposed to make these decisions?

Well, there's some good news and some bad news. The bad news is that this can develop into a complex question, with equally complex answers. The good news is that it usually doesn't. If, for example, you are trying to build a multi-table database for a small to medium-sized business, it is usually fairly obvious which tables you need and there is an excellent 'rule of thumb' to help you, which is as follows:

> Provide a separate table for each class of 'real world' object about which you are trying to store information in the database.

That's it. Thus an employee is one such class of object, a customer is another and an order is a third. (Chapter 14 discusses an 'extension' to this rule but I'd ignore it until you get there, unless, of course, I have inflamed your curiosity by mentioning it.) We then give each table only the fields that contain information which is unique to the object that the table represents. So the name of the customer goes into the CUSTOMERS table, the name of the employee into the EMPLOYEES table and so on.

Which bring us rather neatly to the problem that I posed above. If we sell mostly furniture and then start selling ice-cream, should the information relating to ice-cream sales go in the same table as that for furniture sales or a different one?

I can't give an immediate 'Yes/No' answer here because it will depend on the information that we need to store. So let's think about that information before deciding.

Suppose we sell furniture and want to store the following information about each piece that we stock:

> Stock no.
> Purchase date
> Purchase price
> Sale date
> Sale price
> Color

Then we start selling ice-cream and it so happens that we want to store the following information about ice-cream:

> Stock no.
> Purchase date
> Purchase price
> Sale date
> Sale price
> Color

Since we happen to be interested in exactly the same characteristics (or properties) for these two classes of object (furniture and ice-cream), then as far as the database is concerned, we actually have only one class of object here. In other words, we can happily store furniture and ice-cream in the same table.

If, on the other hand, the information we wanted to store about ice-cream was characterized like this:

> Stock no.
> Flavor
> Melting point
> Shelf life
> Viscosity

then it would clearly be foolish to try to store the information about ice-cream in the same table as the information about furniture.

Rather neatly, the act of considering this sort of problem gives us another mechanism for identifying classes of object in the database. This doesn't mean that we have to alter the rule of thumb given above, it simply means that we now have an additional way of identifying and classifying objects.

Objects can be distinguished by the properties (characteristics, attributes – call them what you will) that we want to store about them in the database. Suppose you are evaluating two apparently different object types, say full-time and part-time employees. Simply list the properties (fields) that you need to store about each one. If the list is the same, then they are actually one type of object and you only need one table. If the list is different, you have two classes of object and need two tables.

Not normalization (and not ER modeling either)

So, the rule of thumb is simple: give each 'real world' object class a table of its own.

However, I would be failing in my duty if I didn't tell you that there are times, particularly if you are working on large complex databases, where this rule of thumb (even in modified form discussed in Chapter 14) fails to ensure that you have chosen the correct tables and fields. This failing was noticed early in the history of relational databases and a process called normalization emerged and there is a large chapter dedicated to normalization in Part 4. The reason that it isn't covered here is simply that, under most circumstances with simple databases, the rule of thumb is sufficient.

Personally, if this was my first attempt to understand relational databases, I'd ignore normalization for now and concentrate on all the other concepts that have to be absorbed. Then, once I'd got a good grasp of those, I'd read the chapter on normalization. This isn't meant to imply that normalization is a particularly difficult concept, simply that you probably don't need it now.

While we are on the subject of 'nots', there is another process called Entity Relationship (ER) modeling which is worth mentioning (but not covering) here. ER modeling started as a way of representing the design of a database on paper. It is a formalized way of showing the overall design of the database without including so much detail that the complete picture is difficult or impossible to understand. Not surprisingly, computerized packages have subsequently been developed which allow you to lay out these designs on screen. ER modeling is wonderful and makes the process of database design much easier for a relatively complex database. So, don't bother with it for now, but when you feel the need, it's covered in Chapter 18.

Anyway, that's enough about what we are not going to cover here…

We are going to need an example to demonstrate how you can get the right data into the right tables, so let's rough out an example database now and try to identify the obvious objects that make up the data. I've tried to chose an example that is large enough to illustrate all of the principles we need but not so large that it becomes unwieldy.

Object identification

Imagine that you run a small business which exists to sell items to customers. Immediately we can see at least three object classes – Customers, Items and Orders (which records the transactions).

- You employ people who work for you (object class – Employee).
- Certain of your employees are allocated rooms in the head office in which to work (object class – Rooms).
- You also rent buildings such as warehouses (object class – Buildings).

We can go on for a while longer (an object class like 'Suppliers' springs instantly to mind) but these six objects are all we need to illustrate the principles.

So, we have six clearly defined object classes:

> Customers
>
> Items
>
> Orders
>
> Employees
>
> Rooms
>
> Buildings

Following the rule of thumb we need six tables:

> CUSTOMERS – information about customers.
>
> ITEMS – information about the items that we offer for sale.
>
> ORDERS – information about orders placed.
>
> EMPLOYEES – information about employees.
>
> ROOMS – information about the individual rooms in our head office.
>
> BUILDINGS – information concerning the rents that the company pays for its buildings.

What fields will go into each table? Only those which are unique to that table.

Consider into which table you would place the following potential pieces of information:

> Date of birth of employee
>
> Order number
>
> Customer name
>
> Employee name
>
> Item name
>
> Customer address
>
> Next of kin of employee
>
> Room numbers
>
> Rent

and the answers:

> Date of birth of employee – EMPLOYEES
>
> Order number – ORDERS
>
> Customer name – CUSTOMERS
>
> Employee name – EMPLOYEES
>
> Item name – ITEMS
>
> Customer address – CUSTOMER
>
> Next of kin of employee – EMPLOYEE
>
> Room numbers – ROOMS
>
> Rent – BUILDINGS

To stop this all sounding too abstract, here are a couple of the tables, each with a small quantity of data. Again I have tried to keep these as small as possible.

EMPLOYEES				
EmployeeNo	FirstName	LastName	DateOfBirth	DateEmployed
1	Manny	Tomanny	12 Apr 1966	01 May 1999
2	Rosanne	Kolumns	21 Mar 1977	01 Jan 2000
3	Cas	Kade	01 May 1977	01 Apr 2002
4	Norma	Lyzation	03 Apr 1966	01 Apr 2002
5	Juan	Tomani	12 Apr 1966	01 Apr 2002
6	Del	Eats	01 May 1967	01 May 2004

CUSTOMERS		
CustomerNo	**FirstName**	**LastName**
1	Brian	Thompson
2	Sally	Henderson
3	Harry	McColgan
4	Sandra	Wellington

That's it for now. As we've said, this process can become more complex but there are mechanisms to cope with that complexity (see Chapters 14 and 18). However, the basic principle really is as simple as this chapter suggests, so we'll move on to talk about the relationships that can exist between real world objects.

Chapter 13

Relationships in the real world

It is worth remembering that each table represents a type of object in the real world. If this were a real (rather than a demonstration) database, each record in the CUSTOMERS table would refer to a real customer and each entry in the EMPLOYEES table would represent a real employee. The first step in deciding what relationships we need to set up between the tables is to ask the question "What types of relationships can exist between these real world objects?"

The term 'relationship' as used here has nothing to do with the use of the word 'relational' in 'relational database' (see Chapter 21). It is used here simply to imply an association and/or interdependency.

It turns out that there are four possible kinds of relationship between any given pair of objects, as follows:

● One-to-many

● One-to-one

● Many-to-many

● None

One-to-many

The relationship between customers and the orders that they can place with our mythical company is a one-to-many relationship. This simply means that each customer can place none, one or more orders with the company. The relationship is asymmetrical in that any given order is placed by one and only one customer. Note that there is no implication that any one customer has to have placed an order before we can store that customer's details in the database.

Nor does the word 'many' imply that a customer must place lots of orders, only that we are allowing for that possibility.

One-to-many relationships happen to be very common; they appear over and over again in the business world.

One-to-one

Suppose that, for whatever reason, it is essential that each of our employees is allocated their own room in the company, perhaps because the company buys and sells bearer bonds and customers prefer to carry out these transactions in private. We therefore decide that it is a rule within the company that each employee must be allocated to one room but that owing to cost considerations, no employee is ever allocated more than one room.

The relationship that exists between rooms and employees is a one-to-one relationship. Note that, in this case, we might well have rooms that aren't allocated to employees, so again the relationship doesn't have to be symmetrical.

One-to-one relationships are uncommon.

Many-to-many

Consider the relationship between customers and employees. Over a period of time, would you expect a customer to be served by one or more than one employee and would you expect an employee to serve multiple customers? The answer to both of these questions is typically 'Yes', at least in most companies. Thus the relationship between customers and employees is a many-to-many relationship. In this case the relationship is symmetrical. Once again, there is no implication that a given customer *has* to be served by multiple employees, indeed after their *initial* contact with our company they will presumably have dealt with only one employee. However, the potential exists for each customer to interact with multiple employees and vice versa.

Many-to-many relationships are very common in business situations.

None

Some of the objects under consideration here do not have any relationship with each other. For example, the information about building rents has no relationship with the information about customers. We can ignore this class of relationship (or lack of it!); it is only included in this list for the sake of completeness.

Mapping real world relationships to tables

So, there are three possible kinds of relationship which we need to actively consider between the objects represented in a database:

- one-to-many
- one-to-one
- many-to-many

of which only the first and third are common.

I have taken the trouble to enumerate these because we can map the relationships between the objects in the real world (customers, employees etc.) onto the tables which hold information about those objects. For example, the one-to-many relationship between customers and orders maps directly onto the CUSTOMERS and ORDERS tables as we shall see in the next chapter.

As an exercise you might like to consider the six object classes in the database and decide upon the obvious relationships that exist. Unless you are a masochist, don't bother with the less obscure ones. I know it sounds unlikely but if we explicitly declare the obvious ones, the more obscure ones tend to take care of themselves. In addition, given six object classes there are 5+4+3+2+1=15 possible relationships so it will be a slightly tedious exercise if pursued to its conclusion.

Chapter 14

How are relationships modeled?

OK, so we've got our objects – employees, customers, orders etc. – nicely represented as tables in the database. We now understand the relationships that can exist between these objects. The next step is to see how we can model the relationships in the database.

The tools we use to perform this wizardry are:

* keys (both primary and foreign)
* joins

These two can be considered separately but in practice their use tends to be interwoven. For example, you need to create one or more primary keys before you can create a join but it is the act of creating a join which essentially completes the creation of a foreign key. In case this makes these tools sound horribly complicated, they aren't at all. In fact, once you understand them, they have a wonderful elegance and simplicity which makes you wonder how you ever lived without them. Me, I lie in bed at night just dreaming about them.

The easiest way to discuss these two is to see them in action. A very common form of relationship is the one-to-many relationship already discussed in the previous chapter. This is exemplified by the relationship which exists between customers and the orders that they place with a company, so we'll use that as the first example.

Remember the naming convention discussed in Chapter 3? I have elected always to use UPPER-CASE for table names and CamelCaps for field names. If I need to refer to a specific field in a specific table, I will always do so by separating the two names with a dot or point (.). Thus:

CUSTOMERS.CustomerNo

refers to the CustomerNo field of the table called CUSTOMERS.

I have extended the simplified version of the ORDERS table we used earlier; it now has pointers to the CUSTOMERS table as well as the EMPLOYEES table.

CUSTOMERS

CustomerNo	FirstName	LastName
1	Brian	Thompson
2	Sally	Henderson
3	Harry	McColgan
4	Sandra	Wellington

ORDERS

OrderNo	EmployeeNo	CustomerNo	Supplier	Price	Item
1	1	2	Harrison	$235.00	Desk
2	4	1	Ford	$234.00	Chair
3	1	3	Harrison	$415.00	Table
4	2	4	Ford	$350.00	Lamp
5	3	2	Ford	$234.00	Chair
6	2	4	Ford	$350.00	Lamp
7	2	2	Harrison	$235.00	Desk

EMPLOYEES

EmployeeNo	FirstName	LastName	DateOfBirth	DateEmployed
1	Manny	Tomanny	12 Apr 1966	01 May 1999
2	Rosanne	Kolumns	21 Mar 1977	01 Jan 2000
3	Cas	Kade	01 May 1977	01 Apr 2002
4	Norma	Lyzation	03 Apr 1966	01 Apr 2002
5	Juan	Tomani	12 Apr 1966	01 Apr 2002
6	Del	Eats	01 May 1967	01 May 2004

These three tables come from the sample database (CHAP14A.MDB): their primary keys are emboldened and the foreign keys italicized.

This version of the ORDERS table is not perfect since it still stores redundant information about the items which should really be in the ITEMS table. However, this is as complex a structure as we need for now and the ORDERS table will be improved later on in the chapter.

If you have a look at the CUSTOMERS and ORDERS tables above you can see that the data which ties them together is contained in two fields (one in each table), both of which are called CustomerNo. It should be reasonably clear that the number 2 in the first record of ORDERS.CustomerNo means that Sally Henderson bought a desk. We are using the value 2 here as a pointer to the record in CUSTOMERS which refers to Sally. You can use the same logical process to deduce that Manny Tomanny was the employee who clinched the deal.

We could use either the relationship between CUSTOMERS and ORDERS or the relationship between EMPLOYEES and ORDERS to illustrate the use of keys because both are built and managed in exactly the same way. In an entirely arbitrary manner, I'll elect to use CUSTOMERS and ORDERS, so you can forget about the EMPLOYEES table for a while (but it will return in due course).

In order for the two CustomerNo fields to be able to tie the tables together in a sane and meaningful way, each field must display certain characteristics. These characteristics can be summed up by saying that CUSTOMERS.CustomerNo must be a *primary* key and that ORDERS.CustomerNo must be a *foreign* key.

So, to create a one-to-many relationship between two tables, you need a primary key in one table and a foreign key in the other. The primary key models the 'one' end of the relationship and the foreign key models the 'many' end. We are using these fields and numbers to represent the relationship that exists in real life between customers and the orders they place, namely that one individual customer can place multiple orders with the company.

Clearly, primary and foreign keys are important, so we'll have a look at their characteristics in more detail now.

Primary keys

The exact requirements for a primary key are simple. I could list them for you now but it is considerably more fun (and hopefully more memorable) to derive them. So much of relational theory is actually common sense that you can derive many of the rules for yourself.

Remember that the CustomerNo field in CUSTOMERS is the primary key of that particular table. So consider this field: CUSTOMERS.CustomerNo. It contains a number which identifies each customer: 1 is Brian Thompson, 2 is Sally Henderson and so on. What would happen if both of these customers were given the same number, say, 1? The tables would look like this:

CUSTOMERS		
CustomerNo	**FirstName**	**LastName**
1	Brian	Thompson
1	Sally	Henderson
3	Harry	McColgan
4	Sandra	Wellington

ORDERS					
OrderNo	**EmployeeNo**	**CustomerNo**	**Supplier**	**Price**	**Item**
1	1	2	Harrison	$235.00	Desk
2	4	1	Ford	$234.00	Chair
3	1	3	Harrison	$415.00	Table
4	2	4	Ford	$350.00	Lamp
5	3	2	Ford	$234.00	Chair
6	2	4	Ford	$350.00	Lamp
7	2	2	Harrison	$235.00	Desk

and it is now impossible to determine who should be sent the bill for order number 2; it could have been either Brian or Sally who bought the chair. (In addition, order numbers 1, 5 and 7 are also problematical but we'll deal with that class of problem in the section on foreign keys.) So, the first rule we can derive about primary keys is that the values placed in primary key fields must be unique for each record: no duplicates can be tolerated.

Next, what happens if a value in a primary key field isn't entered?

CUSTOMERS		
CustomerNo	**FirstName**	**LastName**
1	Brian	Thompson
2	Sally	Henderson
	Harry	McColgan
4	Sandra	Wellington

ORDERS					
OrderNo	*EmployeeNo*	*CustomerNo*	**Supplier**	**Price**	**Item**
1	*1*	*2*	Harrison	$235.00	Desk
2	*4*	*1*	Ford	$234.00	Chair
3	*1*	*3*	Harrison	$415.00	Table
4	*2*	*4*	Ford	$350.00	Lamp
5	*3*	*2*	Ford	$234.00	Chair
6	*2*	*4*	Ford	$350.00	Lamp
7	*2*	*2*	Harrison	$235.00	Desk

Harry hasn't got a value for CUSTOMERS.CustomerNo. Does he have to pay for that third order or not? Even if the tables looked like this:

CUSTOMERS		
CustomerNo	**FirstName**	**LastName**
1	Brian	Thompson
2	Sally	Henderson
	Harry	McColgan
4	Sandra	Wellington

ORDERS					
OrderNo	*EmployeeNo*	*CustomerNo*	**Supplier**	**Price**	**Item**
1	*1*	*2*	Harrison	$235.00	Desk
2	*4*	*1*	Ford	$234.00	Chair
3	*1*		Harrison	$415.00	Table
4	*2*	*4*	Ford	$350.00	Lamp
5	*3*	*2*	Ford	$234.00	Chair
6	*2*	*4*	Ford	$350.00	Lamp
7	*2*	*2*	Harrison	$235.00	Desk

the answer is still not clear. The easiest way to avoid this kind of ambiguity is to insist that all primary keys have a value. A missing value in a database is called a *null* value and the problems (sorry, challenges) associated with nulls make them worthy of their own small chapter (Chapter 31) in Part 4. See that for more details.

Finally, it seems worth stating explicitly that there is no need for primary key values to be sequential. The following are perfectly fine as primary key values.

CUSTOMERS		
CustomerNo	**FirstName**	**LastName**
1	Brian	Thompson
42	Sally	Henderson
68	Harry	McColgan
112	Sandra	Wellington

ORDERS					
OrderNo	*EmployeeNo*	*CustomerNo*	**Supplier**	**Price**	**Item**
1	1	42	Harrison	$235.00	Desk
2	4	1	Ford	$234.00	Chair
3	1	68	Harrison	$415.00	Table
4	2	112	Ford	$350.00	Lamp
5	3	42	Ford	$234.00	Chair
6	2	112	Ford	$350.00	Lamp
7	2	42	Harrison	$235.00	Desk

That's it. We have just derived the important characteristics of a primary key – namely that the information it contains for each record must be unique and must not be a null value. RDBMSs like Access, of course, 'understand' these rules. All we have to do is to tell Access which fields are primary keys and it will ensure that we are never allowed to create a record which breaks either of these rules. "Hmm," you're probably thinking. "Does he really mean that if a table contains 100,000 customers, Access will check each and every new one that I add against all of the other to ensure that the rule about 'no duplicates' is obeyed and none of the values in CustomerNo is duplicated?" Yes, that's what I mean. In fact, Access (and any good RDBMS) can do this so quickly and with so little effort that you won't even notice it happening.

It isn't obligatory that primary keys are numeric values, but they probably will be in most cases.

Using multiple fields as primary keys

Although it may not immediately be apparent, these two requirements (unique values and no nulls) don't limit a primary key to a single field.

There is nothing to stop you from declaring two fields, say FirstName and Last-Name, to be the primary key. If you do that, then the contents of both fields in both records have to be identical before the uniqueness of the data is compromised. So you would be able to have 'John Smith' and 'John Smyth' in your table but not two people called 'John Smith'. Despite the fact that it is possible to create a primary key from more than one field, as a general rule it is usually a bad idea, unless there is a clear reason to do so. However, there are some cases where it is *essential*. We'll have a look at an example later in this chapter, in the section on many-to-many joins.

What makes a good primary key?

So, having told you that it is possible to use one or more fields as a primary key, how do you decide which fields (and how many) to choose?

Well, as outlined above, there are times when it is advisable or essential to use multiple fields. However, if you cannot see an immediate reason to use two or more fields, then use one. This isn't an absolute rule, it is simply advice. However, primary keys made up of single fields are generally easier to maintain and faster in operation. This means that if you query the database, you will usually get the answer back faster if the tables have single field primary keys.

Next question – which field should you pick? Well, the value in the chosen field must uniquely identify the record in which it appears. In a table of employees, clearly any field like FirstName is a poor choice since you would only be able to have one employee called 'Bill'.

There is a story which I have heard several times. It says that in the early days of the company, Bill Gates wouldn't employ anyone else at Microsoft called Bill. The usual figure quoted (see Accidental Empires by Robert X. Cringely) is that the company had to get to well over 500 employees before another Bill was hired. It's a great story; it just happens to be untrue. Bill Marklyn, the co-author of this book, was hired long before that. Clearly Microsoft doesn't use FirstName as the primary key in its EMPLOYEE table.

The easiest way to choose a field as a primary key (and a method that is reasonably commonly employed) is to get the database itself to automatically allocate a unique number to each record. Access has a field type called AutoNumber which will do this for you. It is excellent for objects like orders, employees and so on. However, you might find that you are already storing a unique identifier in the table. In the UK, for example, you might well want to record an employee's National Insurance number, and in the USA there is the Social Security number. These are guaranteed to be unique, so you might well use the appropriate one as a primary key.

Finding truly unique identifiers is not as easy as it first appears. See Chapter 32 for more details.

How do I create a primary key?

Creating primary keys is an important process and although this isn't a book about 'how to use Access', illustrating how it is done at each step helps clarify the differences that exist between primary and foreign keys. For example, creating a primary key is done during table design, whereas creating a foreign key is not done explicitly; rather, it is done as part of the process of creating a join.

So to answer the question about how you create a primary key: during table design, you simply click on the field you want to be the primary key and then click on the 'Set Primary Key' button in the toolbar. By convention, the primary key field is placed first in the table, although it doesn't have to be. If you want to set two fields to be the primary key, simply select both at the same time before clicking the 'Set Primary Key' button. That's it.

Foreign keys

Since we've been using CUSTOMERS and ORDERS as an example, we'll stay with them and demonstrate the characteristics of a foreign key in a one-to-many relationship. A foreign key is simply one which references a primary key; in this case the foreign key is the field ORDERS.CustomerNo.

Once again we can derive the most important 'rules' about foreign keys intuitively. Consider the values in these tables:

CUSTOMERS		
CustomerNo	**FirstName**	**LastName**
1	Brian	Thompson
2	Sally	Henderson
3	Harry	McColgan
4	Sandra	Wellington

ORDERS					
OrderNo	*EmployeeNo*	*CustomerNo*	**Supplier**	**Price**	**Item**
1	*1*	*2*	Harrison	$235.00	Desk
2	*4*	*1*	Ford	$234.00	Chair
3	*1*	*3*	Harrison	$415.00	Table
4	*2*	*4*	Ford	$350.00	Lamp
5	*3*	*2*	Ford	$234.00	Chair
6	*2*	*4*	Ford	$350.00	Lamp
7	*2*	*5*	Harrison	$235.00	Desk

(Hint: the last row in ORDERS is worth examining.)

The last row in ORDERS contains the value 5 in CustomerNo, which is a little odd because we don't have a customer with the number 5. So, given this particular set of data, we have no idea who should be sent the bill for order number 7. You will be way ahead of me by this point and will have worked out that we cannot tolerate this sort of inexact information in the database, so a foreign key must only contain values which are represented in the primary key.

How do I create a foreign key?

Foreign keys are created/defined during the process of creating a join, so we'll cover it when that process is described.

Summary so far

A couple of quick, slightly more formal definitions before we move on to joins. The tables below are for reference should you need them.

CUSTOMERS		
CustomerNo	**FirstName**	**LastName**
1	Brian	Thompson
2	Sally	Henderson
3	Harry	McColgan
4	Sandra	Wellington

ORDERS					
OrderNo	EmployeeNo	CustomerNo	Supplier	Price	Item
1	1	2	Harrison	$235.00	Desk
2	4	1	Ford	$234.00	Chair
3	1	3	Harrison	$415.00	Table
4	2	4	Ford	$350.00	Lamp
5	3	2	Ford	$234.00	Chair
6	2	4	Ford	$350.00	Lamp
7	2	2	Harrison	$235.00	Desk

Primary key

Every table in a relational database must have a primary key. A primary key consists of one or more fields. No value in a primary key can be a null value (that is to say, no entry in a primary key may be left blank). Each row in a table must be uniquely identified by the value contained within its primary key, which is simply another way of saying that each value that appears in the primary key must be unique. Primary keys are defined as part of the table structure.

Foreign key

Foreign keys are not essential requirements for each table. In other words, although each table must have a primary key, each one doesn't have to have a foreign key. However, if a relationship exists between two tables, one of those tables will have a foreign key in which the values are drawn from the primary key of the other table. In practice, most tables do have foreign keys and it is perfectly possible for a table to have more than one. If it has more than one, the table must be involved in more than one relationship. Foreign keys are defined when a join is made, a process that has so far been glossed over but will now be described.

Joins

In this chapter we are looking at how we model relationships in a database. I said at the start that the tools we use are:

- keys (both primary and foreign)
- joins

We've covered keys, so let's turn our attention to joins. In the previous chapter we said that there are three possible types of relationship that can be modeled in a database:

- one-to-many
- many-to-many
- one-to-one

We'll start with the most common, which is one-to-many.

One-to-many

Suppose that we have two tables like these:

CUSTOMERS		
CustomerNo	**FirstName**	**LastName**
1	Brian	Thompson
2	Sally	Henderson
3	Harry	McColgan
4	Sandra	Wellington

ORDERS						
OrderNo	**EmployeeNo**	**CustomerNo**	**Supplier**	**Price**	**Item**	
1	1	2	Harrison	$235.00	Desk	
2	4	1	Ford	$234.00	Chair	
3	1	3	Harrison	$415.00	Table	
4	2	4	Ford	$350.00	Lamp	
5	3	2	Ford	$234.00	Chair	
6	2	4	Ford	$350.00	Lamp	
7	2	2	Harrison	$235.00	Desk	

Can we, *just by looking at these tables*, deduce what relationships exist between them? The answer (like all good answers) is "Well, yes and no." We can't be absolutely sure about any relationships that exist but we could have a good guess.

We could guess that the ORDERS.OrderNo is a primary key; the field name sounds promising and the values in the field uniquely identify the records. We could also guess that CUSTOMERS.CustomerNo is also a primary key for the same reasons.

We could notice that the values in ORDERS.CustomerNo are all drawn from the values in CUSTOMERS.CustomerNo which would lead us to suspect that ORDERS.CustomerNo is a foreign key.

Why am I telling you this? Do I expect you to go around looking at tables and guessing what relationships exist? No. What this exercise does is to highlight the important bits which go into creating and maintaining a relationship between two tables.

With those firmly recalled, we can look at the entire process of modeling a one-to-many join, which tends to go like this:

- We decide that the database needs to contain information about two objects – customers and orders.

- The relationship between these objects is a one-to-many relationship. That is, one customer can have many orders.

- We will create one table for each class of object – CUSTOMERS and ORDERS.

- Each table will have a primary key for the simple reason that all tables must have primary keys. These primary keys will be called CUSTOMERS.CustomerNo and ORDERS.OrderNo.

- Since we want the database to mimic real life, we want a one-to-many relationship to exist between the two tables.

- In order to make this relationship possible, we will need a foreign key in the table which is at the 'many' end of the relationship – in this case, the table ORDERS.

- This foreign key field can have any name but it is often given the same name as the primary key it references. It must, however, be of the same field *type* as the primary key it references.

- So, we add a field called CustomerNo to the table ORDERS.

- Finally (the moment you have all been waiting for) we tell Access that a one-to-many join exists between these tables.

In practical terms, this simply means that you open up the relationship editor, add the two tables to the editor, drag CUSTOMERS.CustomerNo onto ORDERS.CustomerNo and let go. When the dialog box appears, you select 'Enforce Referential Integrity', accept the default one-to-many option and click on OK. (In case you are wondering what 'Referential Integrity' does, see Chapter 16 – Integrity).

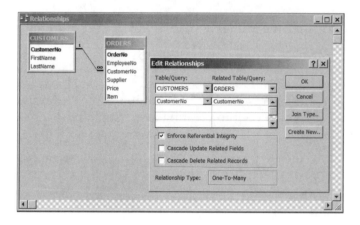

This process tells Access that a join now exists. In addition, creating the join has made ORDERS.CustomerNo a foreign key. You can play around, trying to put a number into ORDERS.CustomerNo that doesn't exist in CUSTOM-ERS.CustomerNo. Every time you do, Access will refuse to accept it.

You can probably see now why joins and keys are so intimately tied together. In order to put a join like this in place you need a primary key and you need a field which is set up to be a foreign key. However, it is the act of creating the join which actually confirms the field as a foreign key.

There are a few points that are worth noting here in passing. The join (with referential integrity) will fail to be established if:

● the field used at the 'one' end of the relationship isn't a primary key.

● the data types of the two fields used in the join are not identical.

● data already exists in the table at the 'many' end which is not found in the 'one' end.

On the subject of similar data types, I have said that it is common to use an AutoNumber field as a primary key. You cannot use this as the data type at the many end of a join. The data type to choose in this case is Number – Long Integer. This isn't as weird as it sounds. AutoNumbers are simply Long Integer fields that are automatically incremented.

One-to-one

One-to-one joins are uncommon. However, they are easy to understand and create because they are very similar, in terms of construction, to one-to-many joins. As in those, the join goes from a primary key in one table to a foreign key in the other. The only difference is that the foreign key in the second table is not allowed to contain duplicate values. There are two ways of ensuring that the foreign key doesn't contain duplicate values.

One is to ensure that the foreign key of the second table is also its primary key. In other words the join can be between two primary keys, one of which also acts as a foreign key.

The other way is to give the foreign key a unique index, which again ensures that it doesn't contain duplicate values. Indexes are discussed in detail in Chapter 34. This is the one I will demonstrate below.

In the sample database outlined above, some employees don't have rooms (traveling sales staff) and some do. The rooms are small, so only ever one employee is allocated to a room.

EMPLOYEES				
EmployeeNo	**FirstName**	**LastName**	**DateOfBirth**	**DateEmployed**
1	Manny	Tomanny	12 Apr 1966	01 May 1999
2	Rosanne	Kolumns	21 Mar 1977	01 Jan 2000
3	Cas	Kade	01 May 1977	01 Apr 2002
4	Norma	Lyzation	03 Apr 1966	01 Apr 2002
5	Juan	Tomani	12 Apr 1966	01 Apr 2002
6	Del	Eats	01 May 1967	01 May 2004

ROOMS	
RoomNo	*EmployeeNo*
1	2
12	4
23	1
24	6

EMPLOYEES.EmployeeNo is a primary key, so no duplicates are allowed. ROOMS.EmployeeNo has been given a unique index (during table design), so no duplicates are allowed. In addition, it is also a foreign key and can only contain values which already exist in EMPLOYEES.EmployeeNo.

Thus:

ROOMS	
RoomNo	***EmployeeNo***
1	*2*
12	*4*
23	*1*
24	*9*

is not allowed since the value 9 is not found in the primary key EMPLOY-EES.EmployeeNo. In addition, the following:

ROOMS	
RoomNo	***EmployeeNo***
1	*2*
12	*4*
23	*1*
24	*2*

is not allowed because the value 2 is repeated in ROOMS.EmployeeNo.

Creating a one-to-one join simply involves opening up the relationship editor, adding the two tables to the editor, dragging EMPLOYEES.EmployeeNo onto ROOMS.EmployeeNo and letting go. When the dialog box appears, you select 'Enforce Referential Integrity', accept the default one-to-one option and click on OK.

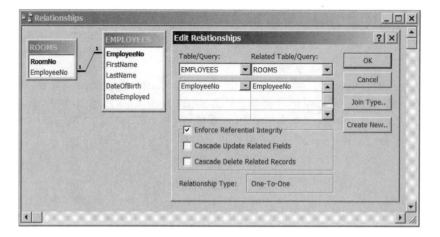

Note that ROOMS.EmployeeNo must have a unique index set before this join can be created.

Further note that although the relationship exists between two primary keys, it is not symmetrical. A value can exist in EMPLOYEES.EmployeeNo which doesn't exist in ROOMS.EmployeeNo but not vice versa.

Many-to-many

Many-to-many joins are common and, once mastered, are incredibly easy to create.

Consider the relationship between customers and employees. Over the course of time, one customer can be seen by many different employees; in addition, one employee will typically deal with many customers. Thus the relationship between customers and employees is a many-to-many relationship. The next question to ask is "What defines an interaction between a customer and an employee?" Well, while it is true that a customer might interact with an employee without actually buying anything, such interactions are unlikely to be of interest, at least in terms of the database. The only time we are interested in a customer/employee interaction is when an item is bought. Whenever an item is bought, an order is generated, so it is the orders that define the interaction between customers and employees.

Now consider what relationship exists between customers and orders. Answer – one-to-many. The same kind of relationship exists between employees and orders.

CUSTOMERS		
CustomerNo	**FirstName**	**LastName**
1	Brian	Thompson
2	Sally	Henderson
3	Harry	McColgan
4	Sandra	Wellington

ORDERS

OrderNo	EmployeeNo	CustomerNo	Supplier	Price	Item
1	1	2	Harrison	$235.00	Desk
2	4	1	Ford	$234.00	Chair
3	1	3	Harrison	$415.00	Table
4	2	4	Ford	$350.00	Lamp
5	3	2	Ford	$234.00	Chair
6	2	4	Ford	$350.00	Lamp
7	2	2	Harrison	$235.00	Desk

EMPLOYEES

EmployeeNo	FirstName	LastName	DateOfBirth	DateEmployed
1	Manny	Tomanny	12 Apr 1966	01 May 1999
2	Rosanne	Kolumns	21 Mar 1977	01 Jan 2000
3	Cas	Kade	01 May 1977	01 Apr 2002
4	Norma	Lyzation	03 Apr 1966	01 Apr 2002
5	Juan	Tomani	12 Apr 1966	01 Apr 2002
6	Del	Eats	01 May 1967	01 May 2004

Unlikely as it sounds, creating a pair of one-to-many joins like this is all that is required to create a many-to-many relationship between CUSTOMERS and EMPLOYEES. In fact, there is no special mechanism for making a many-to-many join – you always build them from two one-to-many joins. However, they have to be constructed in the particular orientation shown here.

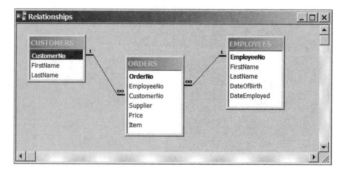

For example, the two one-to-many joins shown below do not create a many-to-many join between the two outer tables.

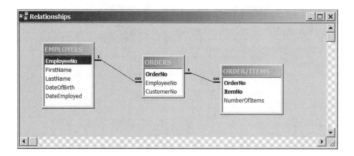

Often, in my experience, when you identify a many-to-many relationship, there is a handy table, like ORDERS in this case, which can act as the required link in the middle. On other occasions this is not so and it is worth looking at such a case because it will make our sample database slightly more realistic. It also illustrates a case where a two-field primary key is essential (more or less).

When multiple-field primary keys are essential

Consider our sample database from Chapter 12. In it, we identified six object classes:

- Customers
- Items
- Orders
- Employees
- Buildings
- Rooms

We have been concentrating on three of these:

- CUSTOMERS
- ORDERS
- EMPLOYEES

and initially we kept the structure of ORDERS relatively simple because we were using it for demonstration purposes. Now we can look at ORDERS with the structure that it needs in order to fit our initial model properly. I've also included another three tables for easy reference. These tables are from the sample database called CHAP14B, which will be used briefly, before we move onto CHAP14C.

ORDERS

OrderNo	EmployeeNo	CustomerNo	ItemNo
1	1	2	1
2	4	1	3
3	1	3	4
4	2	4	2
5	3	2	3
6	2	4	2
7	2	2	1

EMPLOYEES

EmployeeNo	FirstName	LastName	DateOfBirth	DateEmployed
1	Manny	Tomanny	12 Apr 1966	01 May 1999
2	Rosanne	Kolumns	21 Mar 1977	01 Jan 2000
3	Cas	Kade	01 May 1977	01 Apr 2002
4	Norma	Lyzation	03 Apr 1966	01 Apr 2002
5	Juan	Tomani	12 Apr 1966	01 Apr 2002
6	Del	Eats	01 May 1967	01 May 2004

CUSTOMERS

CustomerNo	FirstName	LastName
1	Brian	Thompson
2	Sally	Henderson
3	Harry	McColgan
4	Sandra	Wellington

ITEMS

ItemNo	Supplier	Price	Item
1	Harrison	$235.00	Desk
2	Ford	$350.00	Lamp
3	Ford	$234.00	Chair
4	Harrison	$415.00	Table

As you can see, the ORDERS table is made up of a primary key ORDERS.OrderNo and three foreign keys which reference the other tables.

It should be clear (hopefully) that this collection of tables, set up as they are, only allows one item to appear on each order. For example, order number 3 is from Harry McColgan and he ordered item number 4, a table. But what if he wanted a chair (or even four chairs) to go with it? As the tables are currently constructed, there is nowhere to store information about multiple items per order so each item requires a separate order.

There are several solutions to this problem, two of which can appear to be both logical and easy to build; however, both can result in serious damage to your database. It seems best to show them to you, if only to poke fun at them and to ensure that you never try to use them.

Here is the first common (and bad) solution.

OrderNo	EmployeeNo	CustomerNo	ItemNo1	ItemNo2	ItemNo3	ItemNo4	ItemNo5
1	1	2	1	4			
2	4	1	3				
3	1	3	4	3	3	3	3
4	2	4	2	1	3		
5	3	2	3	2			
6	2	4	2	4			
7	2	2	1	2			

BAD-ORDERS-TABLE

It looks good, doesn't it? Instead of a single field for storing a reference to an item, we have five. Harry now has his four chairs and the others can have additional items on their orders if they so desire.

It may look good but it's terrible in practice. For a start, adding four extra fields may be enough for the present but what happens if a customer orders two tables, a dozen chairs and a lamp? We can, of course, continue to add fields. Suppose that we do this and it turns out that the greatest number of items ever ordered on a single order is 28: we end up with 28 fields for items. The problem is that the average number of items may be 3 so, on average, 25 of the fields will be wasted per record. This wastes disk space and slows the database down.

In addition, look at the way the data is dispersed in the table. Suppose that we want to find out how many chairs we have sold. It is impossible to be sure which of the fields contain information about chairs, so we have to indulge in complex searches of all the fields. This is a bad solution.

A better (but not great) solution is this:

BAD-ORDERS-TABLE-2						
OrderNo	EmployeeNo	CustomerNo	Desk	Lamp	Chair	Table
1	1	2	1			1
2	4	1			1	
3	1	3			4	1
4	2	4	1	1	1	
5	3	2		1	1	
6	2	4		1		1
7	2	2	1			

Now the field names provide the information about the nature of the item ordered and the value tells us how many of each item was ordered. Harry can now have his chairs, we know where to find the information about chairs and we no longer have to worry about the number of different items on an order; there's always a field for each item in our range. Great. Sadly, this is still a poor solution. What happens if we add an item to the range that we sell? We have to add another field to the ORDERS table. If we add another, we again have to alter the structure of the table ORDERS. What happens if we run out of fields (many RDBMSs are limited to around 255 per table)? We also have exactly the same wasted space problem as before. No, this one looks better but it is still too bad to consider using.

So now we come to the right solution (you knew we'd get there in the end). The rest of the tables shown in this chapter are taken from CHAP14C.MDB.

The best way to solve this problem is simple, once your brain is geared to using multiple tables. We have a many-to-many relationship between ORDERS and ITEMS. We construct a many-to-many relationship from two one-to-many joins used back to back. Clearly what we need is a table to put in between ORDERS and ITEMS which allows us to model the relationship. A reasonable name for this table might be ORDER/ITEMS and the three relevant tables would look like this:

ORDERS		
OrderNo	EmployeeNo	CustomerNo
1	1	2
2	4	1
3	1	3
4	2	4
5	3	2
6	2	4
7	2	2

ORDER/ITEMS

OrderNo	ItemNo	NumberOfItems
1	1	1
1	4	1
2	3	1
3	3	4
3	4	1
4	1	1
4	2	1
4	3	1
5	2	1
5	3	1
6	2	1
6	4	1
7	1	1

ITEMS

ItemNo	Supplier	Price	Item
1	Harrison	$235.00	Desk
2	Ford	$350.00	Lamp
3	Ford	$234.00	Chair
4	Harrison	$415.00	Table

These three tables contain all of the information that is included in the two poor solutions quoted above, so Harry gets his four chairs to go with his table. In addition, this solution solves the problems inherent in the other solutions (or rather, it doesn't introduce the problems in the first place).

There is no wasted space in the tables: all of the fields in all of the records are complete.

There is no artificial restriction on the number of different items that can appear in a single order. Adding a lamp to an order which held only chairs simply means adding a single row to the ORDER/ITEMS table.

Finally, if we add another item to our product range, we simply add a row to the ITEMS table. We don't have to alter the structure of the ORDERS table or any other table.

So, we have improved the flexibility of our ordering system but what has all of this got to do with multiple fields in primary keys?

Well, ORDERS.OrderNo has to be a primary key, ensuring that each order has a unique number. Similarly, ITEMS.ItemNo must be a primary key. However, neither OrderNo nor ItemNo on its own can be the primary key in the table ORDER/ITEMS; instead, the primary key must be composed of these two fields used together. If both are used then the table can have identical values in the OrderNo field, as it can in the ItemNo field like this:

ORDER/ITEMS		
OrderNo	*ItemNo*	**NumberOfItems**
1	*1*	1
1	*4*	1
2	*3*	1
3	*3*	4
etc.	*etc.*	etc.

but the following is forbidden because of the identical values in the second and third rows of the primary key column:

ORDER/ITEMS		
OrderNo	*ItemNo*	**NumberOfItems**
1	*1*	1
1	*4*	1
1	*4*	2
2	*3*	1
3	*3*	4
etc.	*etc.*	etc.

This actually matches reality very well, since the order should not have the same item appearing more than once. Instead the NumberOfItems field should be used to record multiple instances of an item in an order.

General lessons about joins

The discussion about many-to-many joins has covered a lot of ground, so it is probably worth pausing to highlight some general points.

Add flexibility by adding records, not fields

The solution discussed above for allowing multiple items per order provides a high level of flexibility. You can add items to orders, change the number of a particular item on a given order or add to the range of items without altering the structure of a single table.

I said above that modern RDBMSs like Access allow you to alter the structure of a table reasonably easily. This ability is essential during database development but once the database is operational, changes of this kind should only be undertaken in extremis. Remember that you will have based forms, queries and reports on those tables. Every time you alter the structure of a table, you will have to check all of these to see if they need to be changed as well. So, as a general principle, any solution to a problem which will require you to constantly change the structure of a table should be regarded with suspicion. Not only is it likely to be troublesome, such a restriction almost certainly means that you have overlooked a more elegant solution somewhere.

GUIs, not numbers

These joins constantly deal with numbers in primary keys and foreign keys. We tend to use numbers because they are convenient (although you can use text if you so desire). It is worth stressing that you aren't expected to go to the ORDER/ITEMS table and write these numbers into the table manually.

We use an attractive GUI interface which allows us to pick the customer's name from one combo box, the employee's from another, the item from a third,

and then to type in the number of items required. The system will look after the tedious job of writing the abstract numbers into the tables for us.

How such forms or, indeed, web pages that behave like forms, are constructed falls outside the remit of this book because the book is essentially about the relational model, not about how to build interfaces in Access. However, just to show that it really isn't difficult, look at the form called Orders in the sample database CHAP14C which demonstrates just such a GUI.

There is more on this general subject of using a GUI to 'protect' the user of the database from the rather abstract nature of the tables in the next chapter.

Less obvious objects

I told you that you can decide on the tables required in a database just by identifying the real world object classes and giving each a table. Yet I have just added one (ORDER/ITEMS) which isn't an obvious object class. In my defense, what I proposed earlier was simply a rule of thumb. This is about the only major exception to it and it's pretty easy to remember. If you can identify a many-to-many relationship between two real world objects and there isn't an obvious object that sits in between those two objects, then you are probably going to need to create a table like ORDER/ITEMS.

A little obfuscation

So, joins and keys are easy to use and incredibly useful. However, it is vital to remember that you are slowly but surely entering the world of the database specialist. In that world, it is essential that you are able to describe what you are doing in the obfuscative terms commonly employed by such people, otherwise you won't be treated with the respect that you deserve. Important words here are Parent, Child, Own, Owned, Superior, Subordinate, Dependency and Foreign key.

For example, the ORDERS table is **owned** by the EMPLOYEES table and is therefore its **child**. ORDERS is **subordinate** to EMPLOYEES and also **subordinate** to its other **parent**, CUSTOMERS, which also **owns** ORDERS and is therefore **superior** to it. All **child** tables have at least one **foreign key** and because ORDERS has two **parent** tables, it has two **foreign keys** – EmployeeNo and CustomerNo. These **foreign keys** establish a **dependency** between the **parent** and **child**; in this case there are two **foreign keys**, so there are two **dependencies**.

There, I think that I managed to get in all of the important words. Note that the foreign keys in ORDERS form relationships with primary key fields in each of the parents. A little reflection should convince you that this is an essential prerequisite, since the parent table is always at the 'one' end of a one-to-many relationship.

The relationships between the tables are shown below

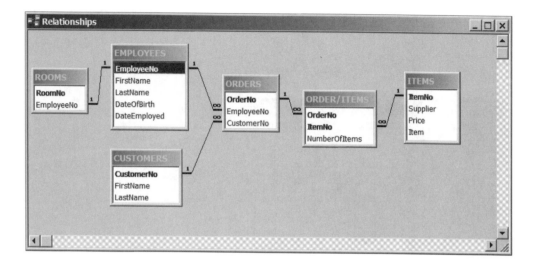

and these are the six tables in the database.

EMPLOYEES				
EmployeeNo	**FirstName**	**LastName**	**DateOfBirth**	**DateEmployed**
1	Manny	Tomanny	12 Apr 1966	01 May 1999
2	Rosanne	Kolumns	21 Mar 1977	01 Jan 2000
3	Cas	Kade	01 May 1977	01 Apr 2002
4	Norma	Lyzation	03 Apr 1966	01 Apr 2002
5	Juan	Tomani	12 Apr 1966	01 Apr 2002
6	Del	Eats	01 May 1967	01 May 2004

CUSTOMERS		
CustomerNo	**FirstName**	**LastName**
1	Brian	Thompson
2	Sally	Henderson
3	Harry	McColgan
4	Sandra	Wellington

ORDERS

OrderNo	EmployeeNo	CustomerNo
1	1	2
2	4	1
3	1	3
4	2	4
5	3	2
6	2	4
7	2	2

ORDER/ITEMS

OrderNo	ItemNo	NumberOfItems
1	1	1
1	4	1
2	3	1
3	3	4
3	4	1
4	1	1
4	2	1
4	3	1
5	2	1
5	3	1
6	2	1
6	4	1
7	1	1

ITEMS

ItemNo	Supplier	Price	Item
1	Harrison	$235.00	Desk
2	Ford	$350.00	Lamp
3	Ford	$234.00	Chair
4	Harrison	$415.00	Table

ROOMS

RoomNo	EmployeeNo
1	2
12	4
23	1
24	6

I shouldn't make *too* much fun of the words used in database construction since all specialist subjects acquire a verbal shorthand which is useful for rapid communication. However, this shorthand should be used to speed up communication, not to play a smoke-and-mirrors game of confusing non-initiates and obscuring principles which are essentially simple. The important point is to understand the principles; after that the words make sense and follow naturally.

These tables are still not perfect, since, for example, the ITEMS table still contains repeated data (such as the name of the supplier). I'm leaving them in this slightly imperfect state since these imperfections will be used in Chapter 15 to illustrate why you should remove redundant data from tables.

Chapter 15

Revisiting the big four – the synergy begins

In this part we have been looking at why single tables are bad, why multiple tables are good and latterly at how you actually arrange the data into separate tables. Now seems like a good time to look at the gains you get from splitting up data in this way. At the same time we can revisit the four basic components of a database that were covered in Part 1, namely:

- Tables (briefly)
- Queries (extensively)
- Forms
- Reports

and see how they work with multiple tables of data.

However, just before we do that, there is one more topic that we need to cover – closure.

Closure

Closure is an important part of the relational database model, so much so that it forms one of Ted Codd's rules. You can, of course, go and read Chapter 24 but it's more fun to derive the need for closure logically than just to accept it as a rule. After all, closure isn't important simply because it is a rule, it is important because it fixes an otherwise insoluble problem. So we'll start with the problem and show how closure fixes it. Hopefully by the end you will be one of closure's biggest fans.

For this chapter, I will be using tables from the database in CHAP15.MDB; however, the tables it contains are essentially identical to those in CHAP14C.MDB.

The data has been split up into several tables and I have spent some considerable time and effort convincing you that this is a good thing to do because it reduces repeated data and has other major benefits. I have also told you that tables are the containers in which data is stored and that queries, forms and reports can all be based on tables.

However, one major disadvantage arises when we combine this idea of splitting data between several tables with the idea of basing forms (for example) on base tables. This disadvantage is neatly summed up in the form shown below (called BadOrdersForm in CHAP15.MDB).

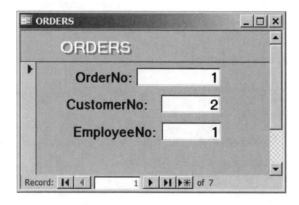

This is the table upon which the form above is based.

ORDERS		
OrderNo	*EmployeeNo*	*CustomerNo*
1	1	2
2	4	1
3	1	3
4	2	4
5	3	2
6	2	4
7	2	2

The very act of splitting up the data has left it in a highly human-unfriendly state.

The solution is remarkably easy. Queries are perfectly capable of pulling together the information that we need from different tables (see below). Here is the result of a query which pulls data from the three tables – ORDERS,

EMPLOYEES and CUSTOMERS:

OrdersInformation		
OrderNo	**Customer**	**Employee**
1	Sally Henderson	Manny Tomanny
2	Brian Thompson	Norma Lyzation
3	Harry McColgan	Manny Tomanny
4	Sandra Wellington	Rosanne Kolumns
5	Sally Henderson	Cas Kade
6	Sandra Wellington	Rosanne Kolumns
7	Sally Henderson	Rosanne Kolumns

and here is a form based upon it.

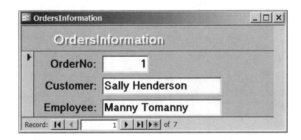

Suddenly the data is readable again and the problem goes away. But (and it is a big but) notice that the form above is based not upon a base table but upon the answer table from a query. This is what closure is all about. In a relational database, it is imperative that the answer tables generated by queries must not only *look like* base tables, they must have the same behavior as base tables. That is, they have to allow forms and reports to be based upon them without complaining.

This relational property (that the answer to a query is a full and proper table in its own right) is known as closure and it is much more important than it first appears because it can be used in several ways.

Suppose that you have a table containing the details of 40,000 customers world-wide. You might build a query which lists only those who live in the USA and you might call that query USCustomers. Now suppose that you want a list of all of the customers based in the USA who have spent more than $10,000 with your company. Instead of querying the main CUSTOMER table, you can query the answer table called USCustomers and look for those who have spent more than $10,000, safe in the knowledge that this will only return

US-based customers.

In theory there is no limit to the number of answer tables that you can use in a stack like this. However, in practice I have rarely seen more than about four or five queries stacked on top of each other.

Another example which makes use of closure is this form called Orders.

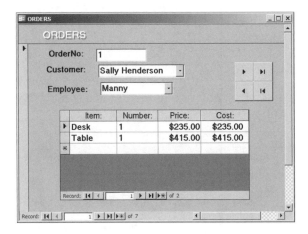

This form lets you see the information pertinent to each order. However, this form is actually drawing information from several sources. One is the table called ORDERS and another is the query called SubForm which is providing the details about Item, Price etc. in the lower half of the form. This Orders form is only possible because the query SubForm is producing an answer table which is behaving just like a normal table.

Indeed, closure is such an important part of the relational model that we take it for granted. Often you will hear people talking about a form which is based on a given query, rather than saying that the form is based on the answer table from a query. Closure will appear in the discussions which follow, particularly with regard to queries, forms and reports.

Tables

Base tables are the repositories of the data that you collect and store in the database. The data you want to store should be split up into suitable sets of tables (either formally or by rule of thumb) to reduce/eliminate redundant data and to enhance data integrity. Moving to a multi-table database has (reasonably obviously) increased the number of tables in the database but apart from that there is not much to say about them that hasn't been covered earlier in this part.

Queries (and a bit on forms)

The use of queries, on the other hand, changes substantially in a multi-table database.

In a single-table database, queries are essentially used to subset the data. In addition, they can be used to perform calculations on the data. These can be very simple calculations – for example, the query shown below is 'adding together' the data from first and last name fields to make the names appear in a more readable way:

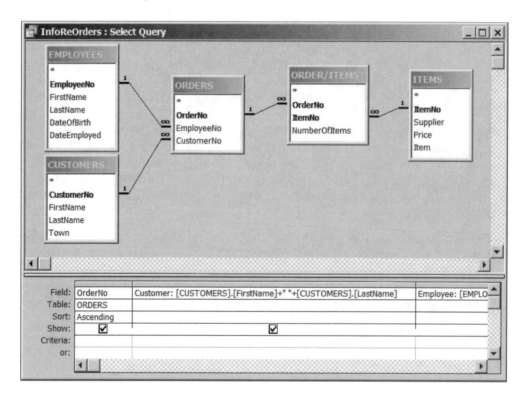

Calculations can also be much more complex mathematical manipulations (summing, multiplying, performing standard deviation calculations etc.) as discussed in Chapter 4 – Queries/Views.

In a multi-table database queries can, of course, still be used to do all of this but they are also used extensively to pull data together from the different tables.

For example, in the sample database in CHAP15.MDB, customer information is stored in one table, employee information in another and order information in a third. While splitting the data up into several tables ensures that this data is stored efficiently, the data is not readily accessible in this state to the average user of the database. Queries can be used to pull the data together with consummate ease; for example, the query above called InfoReOrders produces this data which is much more accessible to the average user:

InfoReOrders						
OrderNo	**Customer**	**Employee**	**Item**	**NumberOfItems**	**Supplier**	**Price**
1	Sally Henderson	Manny Tomanny	Table	1	Harrison	$415.00
1	Sally Henderson	Manny Tomanny	Desk	1	Harrison	$235.00
2	Brian Thompson	Norma Lyzation	Chair	1	Ford	$234.00
3	Harry McColgan	Manny Tomanny	Table	1	Harrison	$415.00
3	Harry McColgan	Manny Tomanny	Chair	4	Ford	$234.00
4	Sandra Wellington	Rosanne Kolumns	Chair	1	Ford	$234.00
4	Sandra Wellington	Rosanne Kolumns	Lamp	1	Ford	$350.00
4	Sandra Wellington	Rosanne Kolumns	Desk	1	Harrison	$235.00
5	Sally Henderson	Cas Kade	Chair	1	Ford	$234.00
5	Sally Henderson	Cas Kade	Lamp	1	Ford	$350.00
6	Sandra Wellington	Rosanne Kolumns	Table	1	Harrison	$415.00
6	Sandra Wellington	Rosanne Kolumns	Lamp	1	Ford	$350.00
7	Sally Henderson	Rosanne Kolumns	Desk	1	Harrison	$235.00

Note that this query is automatically making use of the information in the primary and foreign keys to produce the data that we see in the answer table. This is one of the major strengths of the relational database model. Once you have set up the joins between the tables, queries can automatically make use of them to provide the correct data.

As mentioned above, the answer tables that queries produce can also have forms and reports based upon them.

So, queries can subset the data in tables, they can perform manipulations on the data, they can draw together data from many tables and they can also have forms and reports based upon the answer tables that they produce, all of which makes them pretty talented. However, the multi-faceted nature of their abilities raises a question. Suppose that you build a database along these lines. The data is stored in the base tables, you use queries to pull the data together and then base the users' forms on the queries. The burning question is "Can the users edit the data that they see on the form?" The answer is that, with certain restrictions, yes, it's perfectly possible.

This is an important point because most well designed databases make extensive use of this facility so we'll have a look at a series of examples which will gradually increase in complexity.

The customer table in this example has been extended to contain the town in which the customer lives. (We could get into an argument about whether this information represents repeated data in this table but it is only for an example.)

CUSTOMERS			
CustomerNo	**FirstName**	**LastName**	**Town**
1	Brian	Thompson	Boston
2	Sally	Henderson	Dundee
3	Harry	McColgan	Seattle
...	...	...	...
103	William	Johnston	London
104	Agnes	Keith	Dundee
105	Robert	Edgar	Boston

If we build a query which extracts only the Bostonians, we can then base a form on that query:

Should we be able to edit the data shown here? Logically there is no reason why not. True, we are only seeing a subset of the data but those records that the form does show us would look no different if we based the form directly upon the CUSTOMERS base table.

Any RDBMS worthy of the name will allow you to edit the data shown in this form. The edits that you make will be written 'through' the query and will end up in the base table. Thus if we change a customer's name, that change will appear in the CUSTOMERS base table. Access certainly permits this type of edit.

Now, let's make it a little more complicated. Suppose that you sell wood. It comes in all different shapes and sizes, so you sell it by the cubic unit. You don't care if it is in a plank or a block, you simply multiply height by width by depth and sell it by volume.

You store these dimensions in a table:

WOOD			
Item	Length	Breadth	Height
1	6	4	4
2	1	1	4
3	6	6	1
4	3	3	3
5	2	3	4
6	1	2	1
7	5	5	1

but you are smart enough not to store the volume in the table (Chapter 3 tells you why you never store derivable data). Instead you get a query to work it out for you and base a form upon the query:

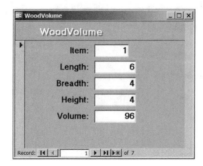

Some of the data in this form should be editable but not the text box which shows the volume. A good RDBMS will allow you to edit any of the dimensions since those edits can be written back to the underlying table. Indeed, when you do so, it will update the volume information to reflect those changes. However, imagine if you were allowed to edit the data in the volume text box. Which of the dimensions should alter to accommodate that change? One of them or all of them? How is the RDBMS supposed to make decisions like that? The answer is that it can't, so this text box will be uneditable.

Now have a look at the query and answer table you met earlier:

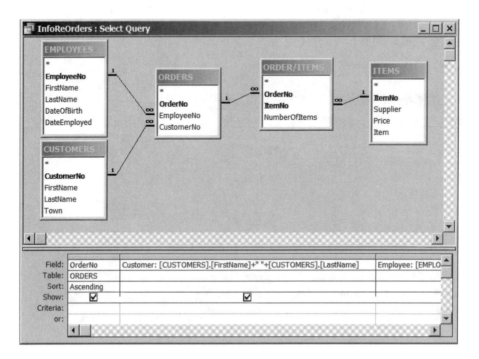

InfoReOrders

OrderNo	Customer	Employee	Item	NumberOfItems	Supplier	Price
1	Sally Henderson	Manny Tomanny	Table	1	Harrison	$415.00
1	Sally Henderson	Manny Tomanny	Desk	1	Harrison	$235.00
2	Brian Thompson	Norma Lyzation	Chair	1	Ford	$234.00
3	Harry McColgan	Manny Tomanny	Table	1	Harrison	$415.00
3	Harry McColgan	Manny Tomanny	Chair	4	Ford	$234.00
4	Sandra Wellington	Rosanne Kolumns	Chair	1	Ford	$234.00
4	Sandra Wellington	Rosanne Kolumns	Lamp	1	Ford	$350.00
4	Sandra Wellington	Rosanne Kolumns	Desk	1	Harrison	$235.00
5	Sally Henderson	Cas Kade	Chair	1	Ford	$234.00
5	Sally Henderson	Cas Kade	Lamp	1	Ford	$350.00
6	Sandra Wellington	Rosanne Kolumns	Table	1	Harrison	$415.00
6	Sandra Wellington	Rosanne Kolumns	Lamp	1	Ford	$350.00
7	Sally Henderson	Rosanne Kolumns	Desk	1	Harrison	$235.00

This query is drawing data from several tables and is manipulating some of the data by 'adding together' the first and last name fields. (Combining text fields in this way is known as 'concatenation').

Here is a form based on that query:

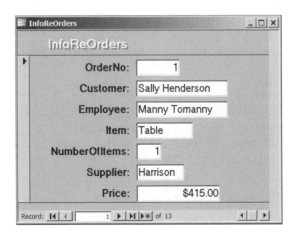

Should the data shown in this form be editable? The answer, now familiar, is 'yes and no'. The name fields from the original base tables have been manipulated (by concatenation) so they can't be edited. Most of the data in the other boxes can be edited, sometimes with interesting results. For example, the word 'Desk' appears in several of these orders but it is stored only once in the database (in the ITEMS table). Changing any entry from 'Desk' to 'Lectern' will alter the entry in the ITEMS table. Thus all of the other records in the answer table which refer to this entry in ITEMS will show 'Lectern' instead of 'Desk'. You can try this for yourself in the sample database CHAP15.MDB. It can be done from the form but the effect is more impressive if you make changes to the underlying answer table itself, where multiple records can be seen at the same time. As soon as you change one of the records, a ripple of change runs across the table as the other records update to reflect that change.

Intriguingly, if you edit the name of a supplier (e.g. change 'Harrison' to 'Harisson'), some, but not all, of the records will update. If you follow the connections back to the original table, you'll find that the name of the supplier is stored several times in the ITEMS table.

ITEMS			
ItemNo	**Supplier**	**Price**	**Item**
1	Harrison	$235.00	Desk
2	Ford	$350.00	Lamp
3	Ford	$234.00	Chair
4	Harrison	$415.00	Table

Earlier in the book, I pointed out that there was duplicated data in this sample table but allowed it to remain. Here it serves as (yet another) excellent illustration of why redundant information in tables is to be avoided.

Finally, the OrderNo isn't editable in this form but this is simply because it happens to be an AutoNumber field in the underlying base table. Auto-Number fields are inherently uneditable, even in the base table, so we wouldn't expect it to suddenly become editable here.

We could go on looking at examples but the underlying rule should be becoming clear. Queries can be used to pull data together and forms can be based on those queries. Whether the data that appears on such forms is editable or not depends upon the nature of the query (or queries) which have been used. Most RDBMSs provide lists of the different types of queries that you can run and whether or not the resulting answer table can be edited.

Some interesting research has been carried out into which classes of answer table are inherently safe to edit and which aren't. It turns out that there are some queries for which a satisfactory 'Yes' or 'No' can never be given; (see Chapter 24.) We don't have to worry about them; RDBMSs generally take a cautious view and if there is any doubt will default to rendering the answer table uneditable.

Once again, just like in Chapter 4, we feel the need to mention Views at this point, if only for completeness. These are essentially queries that happen to be stored on a database server. If you have an interest in client-server databases take a look at Chapter 20. If not, ignore Views for now.

Forms

Forms also become more versatile in multi-table databases and some of this increased functionality has been covered during the discussion on queries (see above). However, the main benefits can be seen in this Orders form:

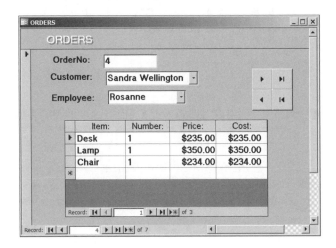

This form is drawing information from three tables. Several queries are being used to feed data to the sub-form (which shows the items in the order) and to the combo boxes (used for the fields labeled 'Customer' and 'Employee'). New orders can be constructed by moving to a blank record, selecting a customer's name, employee's name, choosing the items for the order and entering the number purchased. Now, you and I know that underneath all of this, the data is being stored as entries like:

OrderNo	EmployeeNo	CustomerNo
4	2	4

OrderNo	ItemNo	NumberOfItems
4	1	1
4	2	1
4	3	1

but the users simply see a form from which they can make choices.

This form sums up much about, not just how the relational model works, but why it has become so omnipresent. The model requires that we split the data up into separate tables and use all sorts of unhelpful numbers in primary and foreign keys. We do all of this because it ensures that the data is more difficult to corrupt. In other words, it is a pain but the pain is eminently worth the gain, which is that the data is kept clean. We cannot expect the average user of a database to cope with all of this complexity, but that's OK because we can use other aspects of the relational model (closure, queries etc.), together with forms to shield the user from that complexity.

Reports

Not only do reports allow us to print out data, we can use them to summarize and group the information in the database. In a multi-table database, we can base the reports on multiple tables.

For example, given the information in the sample database, we might be interested in which customers bought which items. We can generate a report which draws information from CUSTOMERS and ITEMS. Such a report might look like this:

Item Buyers

Item	Customer
Chair	
	Sally Henderson
	Harry McColgan
	Brian Thompson
	Sandra Wellington
Desk	
	Sally Henderson
	Sally Henderson
	Sandra Wellington
Lamp	
	Sally Henderson
	Sandra Wellington
	Sandra Wellington
Table	
	Sally Henderson
	Harry McColgan
	Sandra Wellington

This very simple report lists each item alphabetically and alongside each is a list of the customers who have bought the item. The customers are sorted alphabetically on surname.

A somewhat more informative report might show the amount each customer has spent and on which items, part of which might look like this:

Customer Totals

Customer	Item	Price	No.	Total Cost
Sally Henderson				
	Chair	$234.00	1	$234.00
	Desk	$235.00	1	$235.00
	Desk	$235.00	1	$235.00
	Lamp	$350.00	1	$350.00
	Table	$415.00	1	$415.00
				$1,469.00
Harry McColgan				
	Chair	$234.00	4	$936.00
	Table	$415.00	1	$415.00
				$1,351.00
Brian Thompson				
	Chair	$234.00	1	$234.00
				$234.00
Sandra Wellington				
	Chair	$234.00	1	$234.00
	Desk	$235.00	1	$235.00
	Lamp	$350.00	1	$350.00
	Lamp	$350.00	1	$350.00
	Table	$415.00	1	$415.00
				$1,584.00

The name of each customer, sorted alphabetically by surname, is shown on the left-hand side, with a list of the items purchased, the price of each item and the number of items purchased. Then the total spent on each type of item is generated, with a total of each customer's purchases at the bottom of the list. A grand total of all customers' purchases (not shown above) appears at the end of the report.

Reports can be much more complex than these examples, using data drawn from many tables. Subtotals, totals, averages and other summary statistics can be generated from entries in the relevant tables to generate informative reports on the data in your database.

Chapter 16

Integrity

Data integrity – is it worth the effort?

How accurate should the data in a database be? 100% would be good, of course, but what is realistically acceptable in a database of reasonable size? 90%? 95%? The answer is that we need to go much higher than 95% for one very simple reason.

Imagine we have a database of, say 10,000 patients in a hospital and that 95% of the data held about each patient is accurate. Further imagine that the average question we ask of the data is one which spans a number of records – "How many of the patients are male?"; "How many are over 40?"; "How many are on insulin?" The number of records from which these queries draw data will vary considerably but let's imagine that the average number is a conservative 200.

What is the probability that any one query will return the correct answer?

Since each record that is used in the query has a 95% chance of being correct, then, very simplistically, the chance that 200 be queried and that none contains false data is 0.95 to the power of 200, which equals:

0.000035

which means 0.0035% of answers will be correct. To put that another way, well over 99.99% of the answers will be wrong, very probably only slightly wrong, but incorrect nevertheless.

Before anyone objects, this calculation is badly flawed for a variety of reasons. Not the least is that although the average number of records might be 200, if the distribution of records is very skewed with the majority of queries actually only drawing data from 5 records, (and the odd one from 10,000), then the accuracy of the answers improves dramatically. We can also argue that many inaccuracies don't matter. If the actual number of diabetic patients is 545 and we get an answer of 547, this probably won't alter our plans for ordering insulin.

I agree with these arguments and I would hate anyone to take these figures as definitive or even particularly accurate. What they are intended to show is that, contrary to what many people appear to believe, 95% accurate data does not give you 95% accurate answers: the actual figure will be much lower than this. This makes it imperative that you strive to ensure that the data in the database is as accurate as you can possibly make it. In practice, the effort is worth it because if you can improve the accuracy of the data to 99%, then using the same very simplistic measure, the probability of a correct answer rockets up to 0.13, meaning 13 % of your queries will return correct answers. Increase the accuracy up to 99.9% and you get 0.82, so 82% of the answers will be correct.

Striving for data integrity is well worth the effort. Now we'll have a look at the main types of data integrity errors that can arise.

Types of data integrity error (and some cures)

Data integrity is a general term which refers to several processes that keep the data in your database error-free (or as close to error-free as we can get). Very broadly there are four types of integrity error that can occur in a database.

1. *Errors in unique data within a single field.* You can mis-enter unique data, such as a customer's name, into a single field. For example, you could type 'Smath' instead of 'Smith' into a LastName field. The database cannot realistically be expected to detect or prevent this kind of error.

2. *Errors in standard data within a single field.* You can mis-enter standard data, such as a customer's title into a Title field. Suppose that you normally enter 'Prof' as the title for a Professor but for a few of them you happen to use the title 'Prof.' (which has a period after the 'f'). When you search the database for all customers who have the title 'Prof', you will certainly find them all but you will not be finding all of those customers who are Professors. This differs from the example given above for a last name only because the number of possible titles is small and readily definable. The difference is significant because the database can easily be designed to eliminate this second type of error.

3. *Errors between data in different fields.* Suppose that you record both the date of birth of your employees and their date of employment. Clearly

if the date of birth for a given employee is greater (that is, later) than their date of employment, an error has been made during data entry (or else you have very odd employment rules!). We can use a type of data checking to detect this sort of error at the time of entry and ensure that it never gets into the database. In addition, there is nothing to stop us from making the checking more useful.

For example, if we assume that you don't employ under-age workers, then any entry which has a date of birth less than 16 years before the date of employment must be an error. If we understand the rules of the business for which the database is designed, we can set up data integrity rules which look for data which contravenes those rules. Such rules are known, perfectly reasonably, as 'business rules'.

Note that the fields concerned in this type of data integrity check are often in the same table but don't have to be. For example, you might want to ensure that the value of an order (stored in an ORDERS table) never exceeded a customer's credit rating (stored in a CUSTOMERS table).

4. *Errors between keys in different tables affecting referential integrity.* Finally there is a class of error that occurs between different tables, more specifically between the values that are stored in primary and foreign keys. The system which controls (and prevents) this type of error is known as referential integrity. If a value appears in a foreign key it must also appear in the primary key. This sounds straightforward and it is, but there are several cases where the designer of the database (that's you!) has several choices, each of which has a different consequence.

Now we'll have a look at the four types of error in more detail.

Errors in unique data within a single field

There's not much advice I can give you here except, of course, be very careful; sadly the database can't help when you enter erroneous data of this type. The good news is that it can help with the other three which are generally more serious anyway.

Errors in standard data within a single field

Given data that is essentially drawn from a small pool of possible values (for example, Ms., Mrs., Miss, Mr., Dr., Prof.) it is perfectly possible and highly desirable to ensure that no 'rogue' values (such as Professor or Missus) are entered. Most RDBMSs provide mechanisms to ensure this. Such control can also be applied to numerical data. For example, you can specify that a value, such as a height, must be between 1.5 and 2.5 meters.

As an example of numerical control, we could specify that the NumberOfItems field in the ORDER/ITEMS table must contain a value between 1 and 100:

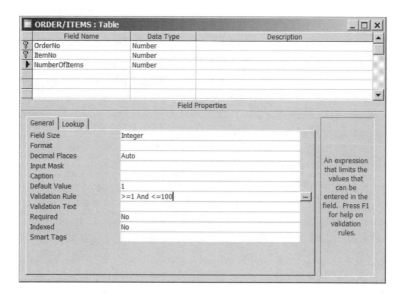

We can also specify a set of values for the Title field in CUSTOMERS in much the same way:

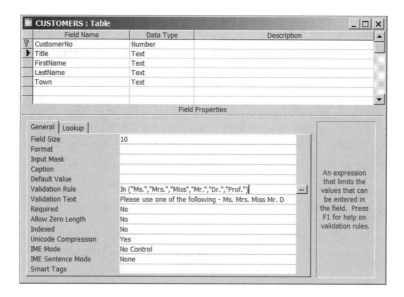

The actual validation rule in this case is:

In ("Ms.", "Mrs.", "Miss", "Mr.", "Dr.", "Prof.")

These screen shots show the integrity control being applied at the table level. It can also be applied on the form used to enter the data; the application designer can provide a combo box which only allows the 'acceptable' values to be selected:

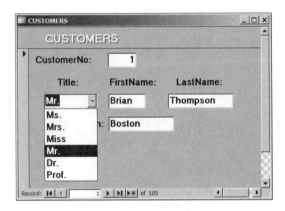

This combo box can be made to work in conjunction with, or independently of, the control applied at the table level.

The pros and cons of these two approaches (that is, whether control should be applied at the form level or the table level) are discussed towards the end of this chapter.

We need a general term for the set of values that are acceptable in a given field. That term is 'domain' and we go into more detail about domains in Chapter 30.

Errors between data in different fields

In Access errors between fields can most easily be controlled at the form level. Within a form it is relatively easy to set up quite complex checks which control data entry. As an example, this form, shown in the design stage, checks to see if the employment date is approximately 16 years after the person's date of birth:

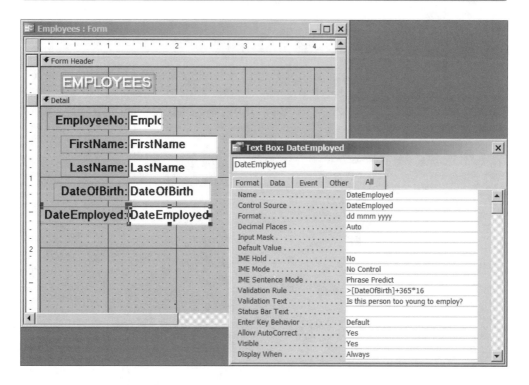

In practice, you need to be careful setting up checks like this one. For a start, 365.25 x 16 doesn't always check for exactly 16 years difference between two dates. However, an exact check is more complex to set up and this one is going to be good enough in most cases. More importantly, this check operates only on the employment date, which means that it assumes that the date of birth has been entered and will not be changed after the employment date is entered. In other words, a user of the database can circumvent this check by filling in a date of birth such as 1 Apr 1960, filling in an employment date of 1 Apr 2000 (which is more than 16 years after the date of birth) and finally changing the date of birth to 1 Apr 1990. As the database designer, you are expected to foresee this sort of devious behavior on the part of the user and trap it. Depending upon the complexity of the checking that needs to be done, you may have to use a snippet of code (see Appendix 1).

In other database engines, particularly client-server ones, you can also use Triggers to manage (and hopefully limit) this kind of error. Triggers don't appear in Access, but it is still useful to know about them because you may use other database engines in the future. There's more information about them in Chapter 22.

Errors between keys in different tables – referential integrity

This subject has been discussed in some detail in Chapter 14 but just in case you aren't reading this book sequentially (which I rarely do with books) we'll look at it again briefly.

This is the type of data integrity control which looks after integrity between tables. Why do you need to check integrity between tables?

EMPLOYEES				
EmployeeNo	**FirstName**	**LastName**	**DateOfBirth**	**DateEmployed**
1	Manny	Tomanny	12 Apr 1966	01 May 1999
2	Rosanne	Kolumns	21 Mar 1977	01 Jan 2000
3	Cas	Kade	01 May 1977	01 Apr 2002
4	Norma	Lyzation	03 Apr 1966	01 Apr 2002
5	Juan	Tomani	12 Apr 1966	01 Apr 2002
6	Del	Eats	01 May 1967	01 May 2004

ORDERS		
OrderNo	*EmployeeNo*	*CustomerNo*
1	1	2
2	4	1
3	1	3
4	2	4
5	3	2
6	2	4
7	2	2

The field EmployeeNo in parent table EMPLOYEES is a primary key so it only contains unique data. By contrast, the field EmployeeNo in child table ORDERS is a foreign key and it can contain duplicate values. In fact, the more successful your employees, the more frequently their EmployeeNo appears in the ORDERS table. We want a so-called 'one-to-many' relationship to exist between these fields: one number for each employee but many entries for that employee in the ORDERS table.

In terms of data integrity, it may not matter if an employee appears in the EMPLOYEES table but not in the ORDERS table; perhaps they are new to the company and are still undergoing training. However, data integrity is violated if the opposite condition is allowed to arise, whereby a value (such as 9) appears in ORDERS.EmployeeNo which does not appear in EMPLOY-EES.EmployeeNo.

ORDERS		
OrderNo	*EmployeeNo*	*CustomerNo*
1	*1*	*2*
2	*4*	*1*
3	*1*	*3*
4	*2*	*4*
5	*3*	*2*
6	*2*	*4*
7	*9*	*2*

So we need to actively manage the numbers that appear in the key fields, always ensuring that any number which appears in a foreign key already exists in the corresponding primary key. In theory we could ask the people using the database to be *very careful* when they enter data but that's somewhat unrealistic. So that, in a nutshell, is referential integrity; in practice there are two broad ways in which we can enforce it.

Declarative and procedural referential integrity

For once the names seem reasonably appropriate: 'declarative' means that you declare to the database engine that you want it to enforce referential integrity and henceforth it will go ahead and do it. Once you've opted for the declarative method, the engine takes responsibility for referential integrity and handles everything.

The alternative, procedural, means that you have to write specific procedures yourself in order to enforce referential integrity. These procedures are typically implemented using triggers (again, see Chapter 22 for more on triggers). You retain responsibility for handling all referential integrity issues.

The procedural approach involves you in a lot more work so an inevitable (and sensible) question at this point is "Why would anyone ever choose anything other than the declarative method?" The answer is that declarative referential integrity is easy for database designers (you and me) to use but it is difficult for the database engine designers (the guys at Microsoft who write Access) to build into the engine. So the early versions of some database engines only supported the procedural method; declarative was added later. Access, being a more modern database engine, has always supported declarative referential integrity (but it doesn't support all the different flavors, see below).

Procedural enforcement used to be very important because it was the only way of ensuring referential integrity. Now it's a dying art form. You may hear about it and even see it on odd occasions, but generally speaking you would need a very good reason not to use the declarative method, and good enough reasons are very rare.

Flavors of declarative referential integrity

So, referential integrity keeps the values in foreign and primary keys in synchronization but it turns out that most database engines will offer you several different flavors of referential integrity.

Why do we need different flavors? Well, it all comes down to the fact that we want to build databases that accurately model what happens in the real world.

On Delete Cascade

Consider the tables shown here:

ORDERS

OrderNo	EmployeeNo	CustomerNo
1	1	2
2	4	1
3	1	3
4	2	4

ORDER/ITEMS

OrderNo	ItemNo	NumberOfItems
1	1	1
1	4	1
2	3	1
3	3	4
3	4	1
4	1	1
4	2	1
4	3	1

Suppose that we record all orders as soon as they are placed. Inevitably some are later cancelled. If the orders in the Order table have no sub-orders (that is, corresponding records in the ORDER/ITEMS table), then normal referential integrity will happily allow the order to be deleted. But if we try to deleted order number 3 (which has child records) the standard flavor of referential integrity will simply refuse to allow us to do it because doing so would leave two orphan records in the ORDER/ITEMS table (they would be child records without parents). So in practice, every time an order is deleted, the user must first delete all of the associated sub-orders. This is fine as an occasional job but very tedious if orders are frequently deleted.

It is for precisely this kind of reason that we have different types of referential integrity and the one we would use in this case is called 'On Delete Cascade'.

We have just described this type of referential integrity in terms of the business rule it would be supporting but we can also describe it in terms of how it actually works; in other words in terms of the key values. On Delete Cascade says that if we delete a record in the parent table then all of the records in the child table that reference it are also automatically deleted. The delete cascades down from the parent to the child.

How do you apply this kind of referential integrity? If you double click on a join between two tables in the Relationship editor and select Edit Relationship…, a dialog opens up:

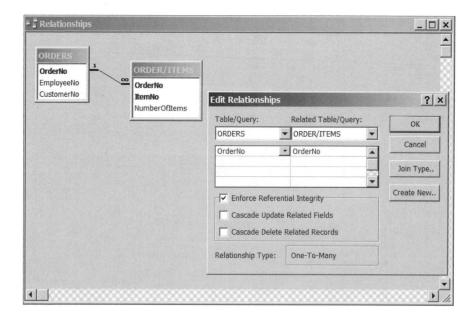

136

You can select Enforce Referential Integrity in the dialog box. If you do select that, one of the other options you can then choose is Cascade Delete Related Records.

Access uses the term 'Cascade Delete' rather than 'On Delete Cascade' but the functionality is identical.

How do you know when to select this type of referential integrity? Simple: it depends on the requirements of the users. If they have a business rule that says "Orders must not be deleted if sub-orders have already been entered", then On Delete Cascade is inappropriate. If not, then it may well be the referential integrity flavor you need for this join.

The important point here is that we are matching the type of referential integrity to the business requirements. For other business requirements we have other flavors of referential integrity.

On Delete Set Null (or Set Default)

Suppose that your ordering system is an internet-based one. People frequently start to create an order, put items in the shopping basket but never actually complete the order. You want to delete the order but for analytical reasons you want to keep track of the items that are selected for incomplete orders.

In database terms this means you want to be able to delete the parent record but keep the children. You can use a type of referential integrity called On Delete Set Null which sets the foreign key values of the children to null when the parent is deleted. (This will clearly only work if the foreign key field has been set to accept null values. See below for more about nulls in foreign key fields.)

Many database designers avoid nulls where possible (see Chapter 31) and so alternatively you can set the foreign key to some chosen default value. The value chosen would have to be one that existed in the parent table. It would be common in a case like this to set up a dummy order with an unusual order number (e.g. 10,000,000) and use this as the default value.

On Delete No Action

This is the official description of what we have been referring to as standard referential integrity. In other words, if you try to delete an order and it has child records, that the deletion of the parent will not be permitted. You can, of course, delete the child records manually first, in which case the deletion of the parent will be permitted.

Summary of On Delete

So that covers the possible actions we can have if the user tries to delete a parent record – we can cascade the deletion, we can set the child to a null (or a default value) or we can stop the deletion of the parent. All of these are reasonable courses of action and all maintain referential integrity.

But the user can also try to update an existing primary key value in a parent table. Under that circumstance we can, again, cascade the change, set a null or default or refuse the update. For the sake of completeness we feel we ought to spell these out but you may already have got the message so feel free to fast-forward briefly at this point.

On Update Cascade

Suppose that for EmployeeNo you use a government-generated unique identifier – some kind of Social Security number. A new employee arrives who has forgotten this crucial piece of information. This isn't a crime (depending upon the country in which you live) so you insert a temporary number. Finally, after several months, the person's paperwork arrives and you can enter their 'proper' unique identifier. But wait. Referential integrity will refuse to allow you to change the temporary number in the EMPLOYEES table if there are entries in the ORDERS table which use that number. Enter (stage left) On Update Cascade, which will permit you to make this change. It manages to do this without upsetting referential integrity because it will obligingly locate and change all the records in ORDERS from the temporary to the new number.

If you set On Update Cascade for a join then updates to the primary key are allowed and the child values in the foreign key are automatically updated so that they remain in step with the new parent value. In other words, the change to the parent value is cascaded down to the children.

On Update Set Null (Default)

When the user updates a parent value then the foreign key values in the child records are set to null or to a chosen default value.

On Update No Action

This is the vanilla flavor of referential integrity. Updates to primary key values in the parent table are refused if there are child records.

Are there options we can set for changes to foreign key values?

We've talked about six flavors:

- On Delete
    - Cascade
    - Set Null (Default)
    - No Action
- On Update
    - Cascade
    - Set Null (Default)
    - No Action

These all refer to the changes that users can make to the primary key values, not the foreign key values. The reason for this is simple – referential integrity doesn't allow for much choice when it comes to foreign keys. If we delete a foreign key value (i.e. a record in the ORDERS table) we can't possibly be offending referential integrity. If we insert a new record (with a new foreign key value) or update an existing one, the new value that appears in the foreign key must be one that already exists in the primary key field. If it isn't, the change is refused. There is really no discussion.

Nulls in foreign keys

Foreign key values are, according to referential integrity, supposed to point to existing primary key values. Nevertheless, many database engines will allow you to enter null values into a foreign key. In fact, Access allows this by default.

Now, on the face of it, this is a little weird. True, we couldn't say it is pointing to the wrong parent record, it is just that it isn't pointing at any parent record. No problem. First of all we'll show you how to fix the problem and then we'll try to convince you that it wasn't really a problem at all, just an opportunity.

To fix it, you simple edit the child table and set the Required property of the foreign key field to be true.

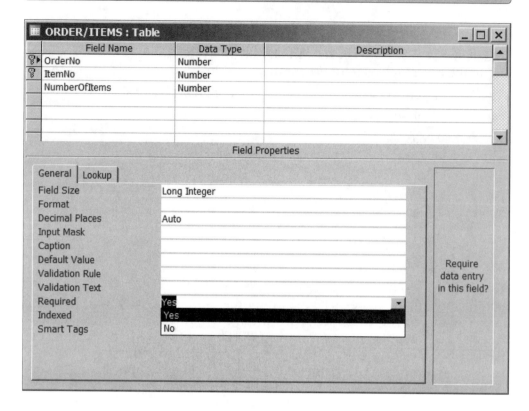

'Required' means that a value is required in the field, so nulls are excluded.

As to why this isn't really a bug, we need to remember that referential integrity isn't some theoretical abstract, it is there to ensure that the databases we build store data that accurately reflects what happens in the real world. In other words, our databases have to be able to cope with the rules that appertain to our business processes.

Imagine a business where Orders are always credited to Employees. In this case we would set the properties of the foreign key field so that it did not allow nulls to be entered. Now imagine a company where most orders are credited to an employee, but some aren't. In this case we can allow nulls in the foreign key field.

So, null values in foreign key fields are perfectly acceptable because they enable us to model a particular type of business rule.

Null values, as discussed in Chapter 31, can cause problems in practice. Suppose that you want some orders not to be credited to specific employees and you also want to avoid using nulls. In this case you could set up a record in the Employee table where the employee name was "No Employee" and give it a primary key value (say, 1). You could then have orders that are not credited to a particular employee by inserting the value 1 in the foreign key field of those orders.

ORDERS		
OrderNo	*EmployeeNo*	*CustomerNo*
1	1	2
2	4	1
3	1	3
4	2	4
5	3	2
6	2	4
7	2	93

EMPLOYEES		
EmployeeNo	**FirstName**	**LastName**
1	No Employee	No Employee
2	Rosanne	Kolumns
3	Cas	Kade
4	Norma	Lyzation
5	Juan	Tomani
6	Del	Eats

However, this is certainly not obligatory and it may bring associated problems, such as what you enter for the date of birth of Employee number 1. The main point here is that by allowing null values in foreign keys, the database engine is allowing you to choose the solution that is best suited to your business requirements.

Access Support

Access supports all of the flavors described here apart from:

- On Delete
  - Set Null (Default)
- On Update
  - Set Null (Default)

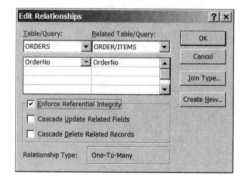

If you tick the box for Enforce Referential Integrity then you get:

● On Delete
    − No Action
● On Update
    − No Action

You can then select either or both of the Cascade options which give you:

● On Delete
    − Cascade
● On Update
    − Cascade

These options in context

If this has made sense so far, try this question. Is there any logical reason why you shouldn't be allowed to set, say, both cascade delete and cascade update on the same join?

You have, of course, thought about it carefully and come to the conclusion that the answer is 'No'. That is, no, there is no reason why you can't have both. And your answer is correct. Perhaps you have an ordering system that uses order numbers generated by a complex interaction of customer name, date etc. You want to be able to delete orders which are cancelled and you might also need, occasionally, to be able to give an order a temporary number if some of the other information is unavailable. I'm not suggesting that this is a good or bad idea, just that if you come across a situation where both forms of cascade are desirable, there is no data integrity reason why you shouldn't be allowed to set both.

Other integrity issues

It is worth remembering that in applying data integrity mechanisms, we are usually trying to protect the data from the users of the database. This is not meant to imply that database users are normally malicious or mischievous, it is simply that they will often enter data which seems to them to be reasonable but isn't in terms of the database (the 'Prof.' vs. 'Prof' problem as discussed earlier). Before we discuss where the integrity rules, checks and controls can and should be placed in the database, it is worth pointing out that RDBMSs often provide other security mechanisms which can be used in conjunction with data integrity mechanisms. For example, it is possible and often desirable to limit the access that a user has to a database. We often limit this access to just the forms that have been designed for the users; we deny them access to the base tables and also deny them the ability to create new forms. As discussed below, if we do this, it can have a profound effect on the way in which we then use other types of data integrity enforcement.

Integrity – where should you set it?

We can consider a database to be composed of layers. At the bottom layer are the base tables, above those are the queries (or views, depending on your RDBMS) which extract and manipulate the data in the base tables, and then there are the forms which are based on the queries and occasionally directly on the base tables:

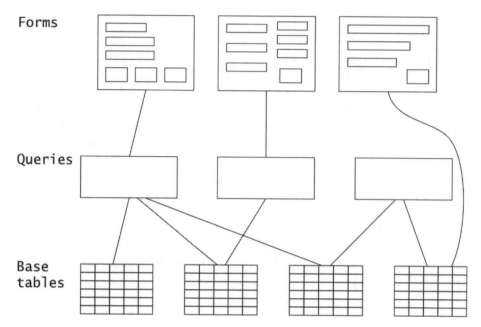

Forms

Queries

Base
tables

Where, within this model, should integrity checking be applied?

It's a pretty fundamental question. If integrity checks are applied at the base table level then they propagate upwards. That is to say, if you apply a data integrity control at the base table level, then all of the forms which are based on that table (or on queries that are based on that table) will inherit that integrity control. To put that another way, if you apply data integrity at the table level, then that integrity cannot be subverted by, for example, creating a new form. The only way to enter data into that table which disobeys the integrity rule is first to remove the rule from the table.

If, on the other hand, you apply data integrity at the form level, then any new form that is created will not apply the same integrity rules automatically.

In general it is best to apply data integrity rules in such a way as to ensure that:

1.   they cannot be subverted

2.   the workload required to maintain the database is kept at a minimum.

In turn, this leads to a more general rule which says that data integrity rules are best applied at the table level whenever possible because that makes them more difficult to subvert. However, it is only a general rule and there are times when it should be ignored.

Consider a particular company that sells, say, computers. The company gives discounts and sales people are allowed to give up to 5% at their discretion. Supervisors can give up to 10% while managers can give up to 50% (in times of dire need to pacify customers already dissatisfied with a previous product). Clearly the upper limit is 50%, but if we simply set that at the table level, a sales person might accidentally give a discount greater than 5%. The answer is to give each type of employee a different form, each with a different integrity rule.

The bad news is, of course, that this integrity could be subverted if the users of the database were able to access the base tables directly. However, if you know from the start of the design process that users will not be allowed to access the base tables directly (see above), then this is no longer a consideration. You are free to apply data integrity at the form level if it is (as in this case) to your advantage.

As a final general rule, use your common sense. If you can't imagine any reason to allow a rule ever to be subverted, then place it at the base table level if that isn't going to impose a maintenance problem (which it usually doesn't). However, there are times when it is a positive advantage to place a data integrity rule at a higher level and if you can see such an advantage, go for it.

Chapter 17

Summary of Part 2

This is an exceedingly short chapter which simply summarizes what Part 2 is all about and points the way to the next part.

I sincerely hope that Part 2 has convinced you that single tables are fine for very simple data but catastrophic for more complex data, which is the sort of data that most people actually want to store and manipulate.

The relational model gives us the mechanisms we need to store and manipulate complex data in a way that ensures we will be able to query it later and get out the answers that we need. Part 2 outlines most of what you need to know about the relational model to get started building databases.

If you have read and understood Part 2, I reckon that you are more qualified than most people to construct multi-table databases for single users. Ah – you noticed the qualification that slipped in there; that 'for single users' bit. So far we have only considered databases which run on a stand-alone PC and can therefore be used by only one person at a time. Part 3 outlines the ways in which a single-user database can be expanded to allow multiple users to access it at the same time.

Part 3

Database Design
& Architecture

Chapter 18

Database design

Designing databases – user, logical and physical models

The process of database design is typically separated out into three different layers:

- User
- Logical
- Physical

The idea of splitting it like this arose very early in the development of databases. These three layers were first described in an interim paper published by the ANSI/SPARC Study Group on Data Base Management Systems in 1975.

It is certainly not essential to remember that ANSI stands for American National Standards Institute and SPARC for Standards Planning and Requirements Committee.

It is easier to introduce these layers not in terms of what they do, but in terms of the problem they were introduced to address. The broad problem turns out to be very easy to state – database design wasn't working.

At that time, only very large, important and wealthy organizations could afford to develop databases (governments and very serious corporations). What they discovered was that most database projects were failing or, at best, going way over budget and timescale. We are talking millions of dollars and many years here. So, the ANSI/SPARC committee was set up to try to find:

- why the projects were failing
- a solution that could be applied generically to all database projects

Two conflicting views of the same database – user and physical

The committee realized that the fundamental problem with database design at the time was a lack of communication.

Users who want a database often have a model in their brains of what they want.

Incidentally, we are aware that the term 'user' is sometimes used in a mildly pejorative sense. We decided to continue to use the term because it is now very firmly embedded in the literature of database design (as in 'user view' etc.) but it certainly carries only positive connotations here. In a database design context, users are the people who employ us. Without them, we would be out of work.

Users tend not to think about databases in a formal sense; rather they tend to think in terms of the information that they want to appear on screen in order to allow them to complete their work.

"I want to be able to enter details about all the products I have to sell." They also think in terms of the functionality that they want. "I also want to be able to manage the orders that customers place with me."

Then there are the database designers (DBDs) who essentially think in terms of database structures. Relational database designers tend to think in terms of tables, columns, rows, primary keys, referential integrity, clustered and non-clustered indexes (see Chapter 34), etc.

The problem comes when these two talk about the database. There is exactly and precisely zero common ground between them. The following (admittedly imaginary) conversation sums up the problem.

Client: "Hi, we need a database to store information about our real estate business."

DBD: "Great, what sort of tables did you have in mind?"

Client: "Uh, no, not the content of the houses, just the property itself."

DBD: "Do you want fields with that?"

Client: "No, not all houses come with land. But the new system does need to tell us which houses are on the property index."

DBD: "Clustered or non-clustered?"

Both groups have a perfectly valid model in their heads of the proposed database. The user's model is expressed in terms of the business functionality that they want; the DBD's model is expressed in terms of the way in which the database should be physically constructed. The former is very business oriented and relatively un-formalized, the latter is very structural and extremely formal.

So, we may have a communication problem but at least we now understand the problem and defining these two models, the User model and the Physical model, is a large step on the way to solving it.

In practice these models can also be known as views or layers. You will hear people using the terms more or less interchangeably – talking about the 'user view/layer' as well as 'the user model'. This isn't a problem; indeed it can be useful. Sometimes it seems more natural to talk about the different layers, at others the user's view of the database or the model that they have formed seems better.

Now also seems like a good time to break it to you, just for the sake of completeness, that the ANSI/SPARC committee actually used the terms External (in place of User) and Internal (in place of Physical). It also used the term 'Schema' in place of 'View'… but you really don't have to remember this either because the modern terms are much more memorable.

It would be difficult to imagine two groups with more different views of the same database, and yet it is these two very groups that have to work together to produce a database. This was essentially the problem that the ANSI committee identified. The solution it proposed was inspired. Rather than attempt to make either group modify its view, which would have been disastrous since both views are perfectly valid, it proposed the introduction of a third model that sits between the two and acts as an interpretation layer. This is called the logical model (or 'conceptual schema' in ANSI/SPARC-speak).

The Logical model – overview

The logical model concentrates on formalizing the user's view of the database, turning it from a relatively unstructured state into a definitive description of the user's requirements. Once this has been done, it is relatively easy to map this onto the physical model that the DBD is so keen to produce. Logical models can be constructed in a variety of ways, but one of the most commonly used is called ER (Entity Relationship) Modeling. The ER model gets its name from the fact that it records the entities that are identifiable in the user's requirements and the relationships that exist between them.

During a process called Business Requirement Analysis, business analysts (BAs) talk to the users and examine the user model that exists in the users' heads. With the co-operation of the users, this is formalized into an ER model which essentially forms the logical model.

It is important to realize that this logical model is based entirely upon the users' requirements. There is no input from the DBDs. Indeed, at this stage, not only has it not been necessary to decide which database engine the database will run upon (DB2, SQL Server etc.), it hasn't even been necessary to chose a database model (relational, hierarchical etc.).

Once the logical model is complete, it is handed over to the DBDs. At this point a decision is made about the database model and (most commonly) the database engine that will be used. In the logical model the DBDs receive a well understood, formalized description of the business requirements (entities, relationships etc.) that can be mapped relatively easily onto the world that they understand (tables, joins etc). DBDs also add a huge amount of detail that is of no interest to the users (data types, primary keys, indexes etc.). The logical model gradually turns into the physical model that the DBDs wanted in the first place.

Let's take a very simple example. The user model is:

"I want to be able to enter details about all the products I have to sell and I also want to be able to manage the orders that customers place with me."

This might be formalized into an ER model that has three entities:

- Products
- Customers
- Orders

The final physical database design might consist of four tables:

- Product
- Customer
- Order
- Order/Details

with appropriate joins between them, referential integrity established, indexes applied as appropriate and so on.

More about the logical model

ER modeling is essentially a specific way of representing the logical model. What the business analyst and the user need is a common vocabulary for discussing and describing the user model and that's just what ER modeling provides. In order to create the logical model, the user need only understand three new terms and concepts. These are Entities, Attributes and Relationships.

An entity can be thought of as an object in just the same way as described in Chapter 12 where we cover the identification of objects as part of the process of determining what data should go in which table. A customer is an entity, as is an item for sale and an order.

An attribute is a piece of information about an entity. A customer entity will have an address, a phone number and a fax number amongst other things, while an item entity may have attributes such as size, color and country of manufacture.

A relationship is, as you might guess, a connection between entities: customers place orders, orders comprise items and so on.

We said earlier that the problem with building a database is essentially one of communication – as part of the process to overcome this problem the users have to learn to think and talk about their business in terms of entities, attributes and relationships.

So, using this new vocabulary, the BA and the user can discuss the project and then build up a more formal description of how the business works. The user will typically still imagine the database in terms of the user model but translates that into entities, attributes and relationships. For instance, the user might say that a customer can place one or more orders and that orders can be for one or more items. The BA asks questions to further refine the user's understanding (is more than one customer ever associated with an order, for example) and should end up with a clear picture of what the user has in mind. The process has the major benefit of encouraging the user to think more precisely about the business process, about the data to be stored and how the various elements of data are related. Often users have never had the need or the motivation to formalize the picture they hold in their heads and this process can often be quite informative about the business process itself. It is this formal description, couched in terms of entities, attributes and relationships, that makes up the logical model.

The creation of the logical model will almost invariably be an iterative process. Things will be forgotten, exceptions will surface and changes are inevitable – that's a perfectly normal progression. The BA must keep on asking pertinent and searching questions to extract as much information as possible to feed into the model.

When the logical model is as complete as possible, another important benefit is available to both BAs and users. The logical model can, and should, form part of the specification that is signed off by both parties as a step towards a fully documented project. Unless this is done there is no defense on either side against changing minds, fading memories or jumping to conclusions.

To summarize so far, the user model is how the users see the database. The logical model is a more formal description, couched in terms of entities, attributes and relationships. Both users and database designers can understand this model. It also, quite deliberately, lacks a huge amount of detail that would confuse the user. That detail is added in the physical model.

CASE tools

So far, all of this must sound horribly abstract. It must also sound extremely tedious and time consuming. The truth is that, indeed, this used to be the case. Back in the olden days when the ANSI/SPARC committee was rolling out its ideas, all of this would have been done on paper. That really was tedious and the overhead that it added to a project was very high. Nevertheless, it was well worth doing, particularly on a large project, because the risk and cost of failure were also both high.

Since then life has become much simpler. CASE (Computer-Aided Software Engineering) tools have been developed which allow us to perform much of the donkey work on-screen. Interestingly, this not only makes the whole process much faster, it also brings several additional benefits which may not be immediately apparent. The easiest way to see these extra benefits is to step through a typical database design process and see one of these tools in operation.

There is a range of tools from which to choose. Somewhat confusingly, they are sometimes called 'ER modeling tools' which implies that all they can do is help create the logical model. In fact, the better ones can often do much more than this. An example of such a tool is Computer Associates' ERwin (formerly Platinum's ERwin) so we'll use that to demonstrate the process.

As a BA, you start by educating the user to think in terms of entities, attributes and relationships. Then you talk to them, long and hard, helping them to translate the user model they carry in their heads into a logical model. Then you sit at a computer, fire up a copy of ERwin and create a logical model which might look something like this:

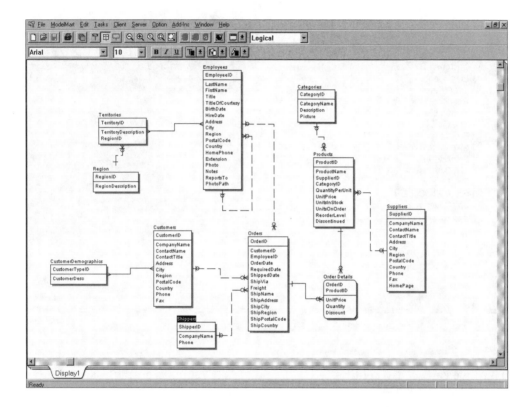

We can zoom in a little to see more detail:

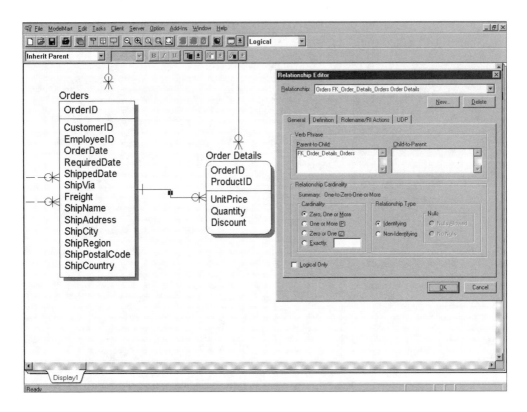

Here we can see two entities – Order and Order Details. Examples of attributes are OrderID, OrderDate etc. The relationship between the entities is shown diagrammatically by the line between them. The additions to this line (the circle, the cross bar and the so-called crow's feet) are there to represent detailed information about the join. In ERwin, double-clicking on the line opens a box where this information can be altered; making alterations will update the representation on screen. As you can see, a fair amount of detail can be contained within this logical model. When you are a BA who is talking to the user it is your job to find out exactly what sort of relationship exists between the entities and represent it accurately in the logical model.

Think about a question like "Do all orders have to have a product attached to them?" If the user says "Yes" we would need to change the 'cardinality' of the relationship to 'One or More' instead of 'Zero, One or More'. Clearly it is essential that you know what all of the symbols mean and it's useful if the user understands what some or all of them mean: this is often part of the education process described above. (We talk more about this in the section on Methodologies below but for now we'll continue with the practical bit.)

So, let's assume that the logical model is complete. How do you get to the physical model to add the detail that the user won't see? In terms of tools like ERwin, it is just a combo box away. Up on the menu bar is a box where you can select Physical Model to see more detail.

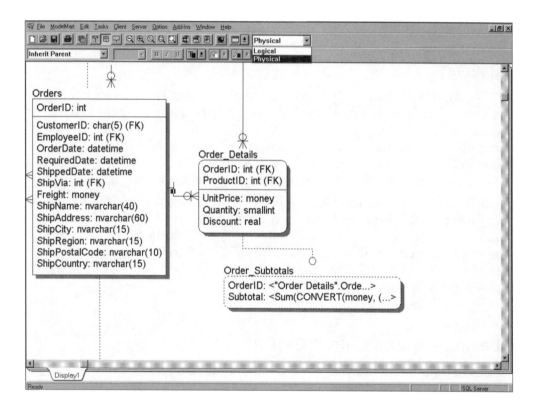

Here you can define the data types, add views such as the one called Order_Subtotals shown here, add indexes – in other words, all of the structural detail. Indeed, you can continue to flip between the two models with the same ease. This enables the user to work with the familiar and fully understood logical model and for the DBD to see the detail of the physical model as necessary. Furthermore, the software ensures that a change made in either model is reflected in the other. In other words, although the logical model comes before the physical, there is no reason why the development of the two cannot proceed to some extent in parallel.

And there is another important advantage of using a tool like this. Suppose a BA and DBD design a database for a client, create it and the database goes live. The one certainty about that database is that the user will, at some point, ask for changes. Given that you have a model like the one we've shown, the BA can discuss the changes with the user while showing them the logical model even though the underlying physical model is stuffed full of detail. And even this isn't the best bit... but we'll come to that in a minute, just after we summarize the story so far.

Summary so far

There is a user model that lives in the head of the user. There's a logical model that formalizes the user model using a vocabulary that's common to the user and the database designer; this model is held in an ER modeling tool. In the same tool is a physical model that describes how the functionality encapsulated in the logical model can be translated into a database structure. There's a great deal more detail in the latter but it can be hidden from sight easily.

And what are the benefits of all this hard work? A formal description of what the finished database is expected to do has been agreed by the user and the BA. As changes occur as they inevitably will, modifications can be made to the physical model that are automatically reflected in the logical model and vice versa. This benefit alone can be of huge significance for both sides involved in a project.

The final big advantage of CASE tools

Once the final version is agreed, the biggest and best feature of CASE tools comes to light which is that they can generate database schemas automatically. And what's a database schema? In its broadest sense it's simply a description of a database; more specifically it means a complete database description expressed in a formal language such as SQL (Structured Query Language: in Chapter 29 we go into details about the querying part of this language but the language also has commands for creating all of the parts of a database such as tables, joins, indexes etc.).

At the press of a button, an ER modeling tool can generate a complete SQL script which, when exported to the database engine, will build the entire database structure for you, tables, fields, data types, keys, joins, indexes and all. This means that as the BA and DBD work away, talking to the users and creating the logical and physical models, they are, at the same time, doing all of the work necessary to create the database itself. When you finally want to create the database, all you have to do is to throw the switch and it will be done for you.

As detailed in Chapter 29, not all implementations of SQL are the same; just as there are dialects in the English language, so there are SQL dialects. In which flavor of SQL will the CASE tool write the database schema? It's simple; you choose. If you plan to run the finished database on Oracle, choose to generate an Oracle SQL schema; if you've gone for DB2, choose an IBM DB2 SQL schema.

"OK, you've convinced me, ER modeling tools are wonderful".

They certainly are, but in order to convince you that I don't have shares in any company that sells them, let me tell you about their down side.

For a start, bear in mind that although they will automatically generate a database for you, that doesn't include the extra elements that lie outside the basic structure and which make up a complete application such as the forms and reports that comprise the user interface.

Secondly, these tools are not yet perfect. The facilities they offer may not be matched by those of your chosen database engine. An ER modeling tool might, for instance, allow the definition of domains but different database engines are likely to interpret this with varying degrees of efficiency and some may not support it at all. The bottom line is that once you've generated the schema from a complex physical model, don't be surprised, when you set it to generate the database for the first time, if it returns a bunch of errors that require hand tweaking to fix.

Despite this, the gain from using an ER modeling tool does, in my experience, far, far outweigh the pain. I use them frequently and would hate to have to work without one. Implementation inconsistencies are inevitable but once you get to know a database engine and a CASE tool well, you'll be able to use the two together in a highly efficient manner. You'll know and avoid the options that are troublesome and any tweaking will be reduced to a minimum.

To end on a more positive note, there is one more advantage to using ER modeling: ease of maintenance. All databases require maintenance and with both the logical and the physical structure of the database documented, maintenance is considerably easier for those involved from the start and for anyone who arrives once it's up and running. Any changes that are necessary should be made in the logical or physical model and the schema and database re-generated. This ensures that the models always match the database and that the documentation is up-to-date.

More about the differences between the Logical and Physical models

While entities, attributes and relationships map readily to tables, fields and joins, there are still occasions where differences occur between the models. A good (and common) example is a many-to-many join. The user knows that, for example, an Employee can work in many Territories and that each Territory can have many Employees working within it. In the logical model, the Employee and Territory entities may be represented simply as having a many-to-many relationship between them.

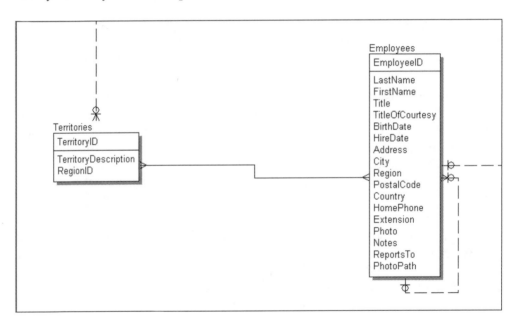

In the physical model, the Employee and Territory entities become tables and a joining table is added so that a many-to-many join can be created between Employee and Territory. In this instance, two tables in the logical model map to three in the physical model.

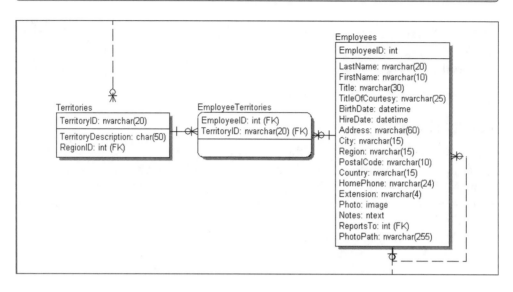

It is not necessary for the user to understand how the join is implemented so its implementation may form part of the physical model and not of the logical model. The meaning of the many-to-many relationship, in terms of database functionality is, however, fully understood by the user and is therefore represented in the logical model. Some ER modeling tools can create such joining tables automatically and in others you have to add the table manually in the physical model.

"Just a minute," you may be thinking, "in your earlier example you showed an entity called 'Order Details' in the logical model. That is doing precisely the same job as the table called EmployeeTerritories which only appears here in the physical model. So do these 'joining tables' appear in the logical model or not?" This is an excellent question and the answer is that it is up to you. In practice, whether you elect to show these 'joining' tables in the logical model will probably depend upon how advanced is the users' knowledge of the whole process.

Another reason for divergence between the logical and physical models is evident when the database structure is tweaked to optimize performance. ER modeling usually produces a normalized structure (one in which certain rules have been applied to ensure that data is stored in the most suitable table – see Chapter 25 for more detail) but there are occasions when you might want to denormalize it for performance gains (see Part 5 for details of performance tuning). If the database in question was for a company operating in America and in the UK, you may decide to split the list of customers into two tables, holding the US-based customer records on a server in the US and the

UK-based ones on a server in the UK. You would also provide a view which shows all the customer records for use whenever the entire customer base is required.

Reality check

I have talked about 'talking' to the users. On large project this may well mean a team of people sending out questionnaires, running workshops attended by groups of users – the process of gleaning information from the users can become quite complex but the principle remains exactly the same. Even though they don't think of it this way, they have a user model in their heads: your first job is to turn that into a logical model.

Normalization can help

There is another way of developing a logical model and that is by acquiring existing data that users may already have collected. For example, suppose they have a spreadsheet in which they've collected data about orders placed by customers but in a totally un-normalized way. If you normalize that data you will end up with a set of tables – for example, customer, order, order details, employee, products etc. These should correspond exactly to the entities that are in the logical model that you created by talking to the user. In practice the two models often do not correspond perfectly which initially appears to be a problem but isn't, it is an opportunity.

Think of it this way. The whole point about building a logical model is to establish as early as possible how the users are actually using their data. If there is a conflict between what they tell you and what they are actually doing, you really do want to find that out at the logical model stage.

What do you do about it? You go back to the user, you talk to them some more, show them the conflict and together you resolve it.

In fact this can all work out very neatly because once you have resolved the conflicts you can build the database. But you also have, because of the work you did with the spreadsheet data, a normalized set of the user's data. This can be squirted directly into the database to provide a set of historical data.

Reverse engineering

At the risk of sounding even more eulogistic than I have already, there's yet another trick up the capacious sleeve of ER modeling tools. Given a copy of ERwin you can reverse engineer the logical and physical models from an existing database. That's how I generated the model of Microsoft's Northwind sample database shown above. It isn't a perfect process but ERwin will report on anything in the database with which it cannot cope so that you can make any necessary tweaks. Not only is it clever, it has the potential to save time and improve the maintainability of existing databases.

Methodologies

Just to make matters fractionally more complex, there are several different ways of representing the same information in a logical model – these different ways are known as methodologies. The two pictures above show the information using a methodology called IE (Information Engineering) but we could elect to use, for example, IDEF1X (Integration DEFinition for Informational Modeling). It's pronounced eye-deaf-one-ex and, yes, I know the acronym doesn't exactly match the words but I didn't design it, I'm just reporting it…

Here is the same information shown in IDEF1X.

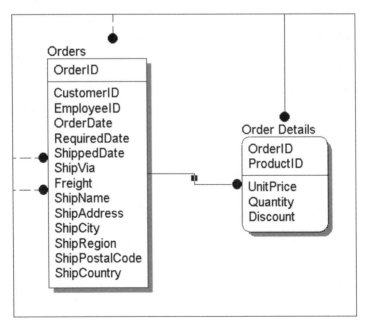

Before you can get involved in database design at this level, you have to take some time to become familiar with at least one of these methodologies. As with virtually everything else in life, as soon as there is choice there is conflict. Database people can become rabidly pro (or anti) a particular methodology. I don't have strong feelings either way but will, if pressed, express a preference for IE. The good news is that tools like ERwin can swap between these two at the flick of an option so you can use whichever you prefer.

We aren't going into the details of any particular methodology because we think that level of detail falls outside the remit of this book. In addition, if you go to work for a company to do design work, it will probably have a standard you have to use and that's the time to learn a particular methodology. What you need to know at this point is that at some time you will probably have to learn one.

Summary of design models

User model – the model that holds the view of what the users want from the database. This is an extremely non-technical view that is simply concerned with functionality and is not expressed in any formal way.

Logical model – A formalization of the user view that captures all the functionality that the users want, but is expressed in a much more formal way (typically as an ER model). It is also true to say that the logical model is a model of the way in which the company processes and manages data (or wishes to do so).

Physical model – The physical model encapsulates the information from the logical and adds the detail necessary to fit it to a particular data model such as the relational model. This will include, for example, deciding on table names, data types, indexing considerations and so on.

Chapter 19

The seven layers of wisdom

"Where did you put that data,

Where did you put that file?"

OK, that covers how we design a database. The next point to consider is how and where you deploy it. In other words we haven't talked about where the components that make up the database – the database engine, the data and the database application etc. – are going to be placed. There's a huge range of possibilities. We don't move the parts around for fun (although the process is intellectually challenging and therefore enjoyable), we do it because each database architecture has a distinctly different set of pros and cons. You may well be called upon to make decisions about which architecture is appropriate for a given database implementation so it is worth understanding the advantages and disadvantages associated with each one. In order to understand these differences, we need to look at the parts into which a database can be dissected, then, in the next chapter, we'll examine where those parts can be located.

The seven layers of wisdom

A database application can be thought of as being constructed from seven layers.

In truth, I would hate to give the impression that this is some form of 'official' layering; someone else might, quite justifiably, describe a database as having eight or perhaps six layers. Exactly how we split up the database doesn't matter too much; what is important is that there are different components and that these can end up in different places.

Layer 1

User interface. This is that part of the application that contains, for example, the forms with which the user interacts. These display information, prompts, provide data and help, allow the entry of information and control the activities undertaken. These are the forms in Access.

Layer 2

Input validation. The checking of the data as it is input to ensure that the data is of the correct form and type (e.g. date format checking, and/or making sure that numbers are put into numeric fields). In Access, this is often performed using the GUI. The important point is that this checking can be performed on the form during data input, as opposed to checking when the row is posted to the table. In addition, this type of validation is often performed on the data in a single field ("Is the value in this field > 500?") as opposed to validation that can be performed between fields (see Layer 4).

Layer 3

Application tasks. These are specific application functions such as calculating the tax payable on an invoice or perhaps the total of that invoice. This is not the same as Input Validation because it isn't applied during data entry; rather, it is applied during data retrieval. An example in Access would be one or more calculated fields in a query which are then used in a report. These manipulations do not permanently affect or alter the data in the database.

Layer 4

Business rules. These check the specific business state and context, e.g. if the total of an order exceeds $1,000 then a 5% discount is applied. Note that this type of validation is often performed on the data in an entire record rather than on a specific field and can often only be performed after some or all of the data has been entered.

Business rules can also make use of data that exists in different tables, for example, an order may be refused if the total exceeds the customer's credit limit.

Typically these checks are performed after the data has been entered into the form, just after the user tries to post the data to the database and before it is actually posted. Again, to put this into Access-speak, it is not unusual for such checks to be bound to the 'Before Update' event of the form.

Layer 5

Data integrity rules. These are the rules that ensure that the integrity of the data as a whole is not compromised. If, at this point you are thinking in terms of:

> Data integrity
>
> Primary keys
>
> Unique indexes
>
> Referential Integrity
>
> Foreign keys

and all that jazz, then you are in the correct ball park (or cricket ground if you prefer). In Access these are applied when the database itself is being built rather than, say, on a form.

Layer 6

Data management. This is the bit that organizes, queries and manages the data; in other words this is the part that actually manipulates data. On the PC this is the Jet engine which sits inside Access. In a multi-user database, this layer also looks after processes like conflict resolution, when two or more users try to modify the same data at the same time.

Layer 7

Data storage. Where the data is actually stored and accessed. In a stand-alone Access application, this is the hard disk of the PC.

OK, those are the seven layers, where options do we have for deployment and what are the consequences?

Incidentally, we are about to discuss where these parts are 'located' and it is worth pointing out that sometimes one needs to distinguish carefully between where the part is actually stored and where it is executed. For example, the code that describes a GUI might be stored on the client or it might equally well be stored on a server somewhere. If we say 'Layer 1 (the user interface) is on the client', we mean that the processor in the client machine is actually reading the instructions (wherever they are located) and drawing the GUI on the screen for the user. The same applies to the data. When we say 'the data is processed on the database server' we mean that when it is queried or edited, the data will pass through the processor in the server, not the one in the client. In turn this means that we can definitely say that Layer 6 is on the database server. The only layer that is solely concerned with where the information is stored is Layer 7.

This may all sound as if we are being very pernickety, but it is worth being pedantic at this stage because otherwise the picture can become obscured.

Chapter 20

Database architecture

Default Architecture in Access

In Access, of course, we often develop an entire database on a PC and use it there. This is an excellent solution for allowing single user access to a set of data. If this is what you need then you certainly shouldn't consider making life any more complex for yourself by starting to move components around; leave it on the PC.

Access – PC front end – data on file server

The most common reason for wanting to move parts of an Access database is to allow multiple users to access the same data. This architecture is much the same as before (that is, as when the entire operation ran on a stand-alone PC). Each user who wants to use the data still runs a copy of Access on their PC. However, the .MDB file itself (which stores all of the data, the forms, the queries, everything) is placed on a file server somewhere on the network so that it can be accessed by all of the PCs.

Now you might argue that since the .MDB file holds everything, we have moved layers 1-7 off the PC – and in one sense we have. However, think about the distinction between processing and storage that was mentioned above. The .MDB file is meaningless without Access… and Access is still running on the PCs, not on the file server. In other words, it is the PCs that are presenting the forms to the users, it is the PCs that are applying the referential integrity rules, it is the PCs that are running the queries against the data. In processing terms all of the work is still being carried out on the PCs so, although the .MDB file has moved, layers 1–6 are still all firmly located on the PCs.

In fact, in terms of architecture, the only real change is that the sole definitive store of data now resides in an area where multiple copies of the RDBMSs can see it, reach it and change it. In other words, layer 7 has moved to the file server:

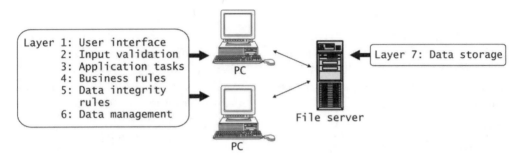

Layer 1: User interface
2: Input validation
3: Application tasks
4: Business rules
5: Data integrity rules
6: Data management

Layer 7: Data storage

File server

Another point is that the very act of sharing data means that the individual copies of Access that are running on the individual PCs suddenly need to communicate with each other. They need to do this in order to resolve the multitude of potential conflicts that suddenly arise when more than one person accesses the same data at the same time. Consider a simple example. You and I both work for the same company and we are trying to update the company's customer records. I open up the record for A. Smith to increase his credit rating from $2,000 to $3,000. While I am doing so, you delete his record. What happens to his record when I finish editing it and send it back to the file server?

The answer is that Access maintains a lock file in the same directory as the .MDB file and this file is used to store information about who is doing what at any particular time. Thus, if I had opened the record to update it before you tried to delete it, you would receive a message saying that the record was in use by "Mark" and that you wouldn't be able to delete the record until I had finished with it. (Other RDBMSs use other mechanisms for dealing with these (and other) potential conflicts – see Chapter 22.)

At first it must seem as if the conflict resolution (layer 6) has surely moved to the server but essentially all that has happened is that some information about who is using the data has moved to the file server. The piece of software that uses this information (the database engine) is still on the PCs.

The important point is that with this database model, only the data has moved off the PC onto the file server. In fact, it is important to note the use of the word file before the word server in that last sentence. The server in question is simply being used as a file store. It is not an 'application server' nor a 'database server' (see below); it doesn't process data, it doesn't even 'know' what the files in question are, it simply stores them and allows applications running on PCs to access them.

The big advantage of this model is that it provides multi-user access to the same data at a relatively low cost. The big disadvantage is that this model is inefficient in two main ways.

First it tends to load the network. Remember that the data is at one end of the wire and the processing is at the other end. Every time you query the data, it has to be moved to the client PC since that is where it is crunched. In a badly designed system this can mean that every query against a 1 Gbyte table requires the entire table to be shipped to the client. Intelligent indexing can reduce this considerably (since the indexes can be shipped to the client for searching and only the relevant records sent out to the client) but it depends upon the RDBMS how effective this process is in practice.

Secondly, the processing is at the client end so each client needs enough resources to cope with the data. If you decide that an increase in the database size warrants an increase in memory of 1 GByte, you will need to add that to all of the clients. Given one hundred clients, that's 100 GBytes and a lot of work upgrading the 100 machines.

These restrictions mean that the number of simultaneous clients and the size of the data are relatively constrained. Think in terms of ten clients and 1 Gbyte of data. Once again, I feel the need to qualify this. I know of one installation that's running such a system with up to 50 simultaneous users but it has been carefully set up, limits what the users can do and is still rather slow.

OK, that is the overview of this architecture completed but a couple of practical details can be added. The first is that it is common for people to split the .MDB file in question into two .MDBs, one of which holds the tables while the other holds the forms, queries, reports etc. The two .MDB files are linked so that the forms etc. in the latter .MDB point to the tables in the former. The 'data' .MDB is then placed on the file server and a copy of the 'interface' .MDB is placed on each of the PCs. This really doesn't affect the model I have described but it is worth mentioning because it can provide a huge improvement in performance. As a further refinement, tables which hold rarely-changing data, often that which is used to populate interface components such as combo boxes, may be stored in the 'interface' .MDB. Again, and for hopefully obvious reasons, this can produce significant performance improvements. As I say, this has almost been a digression into too much detail about actually implementing this particular data model but it seemed worth adding.

The bottom line here is that the entire range of database engines like Access, Paradox, dBASE, FoxPro and Approach were originally designed to run as single-user products. Some of them have been modified over the years to allow a limited level of multi-user access and this is helpful for those times when a database, originally written as a stand-alone application, needs to be shared by a couple of people. However, if you want to allow large numbers of people to access the same data at the same time, these products are the wrong place to start and you need to use an RDBMS such as DB2, SQL Server or Oracle that was written from the ground up with multiple users in mind.

As another aside, Microsoft has made strenuous efforts to make Access better at running with multiple users and to make it easier for you to move an Access application to SQL Server. These include so-called project files that have appeared in the later versions and the ability to use the MSDE (MicroSoft Database Engine) and SQL Server Express 2005. These improvements are to be applauded; however, they still do not make Access a good choice when the number of concurrent users is going to be higher than about 20.

Client-server (or two-tier) architecture

This model is very commonly employed, particularly with database engines like SQL Server and MySQL. The user interface is written as an executable application (written in C++, VB, whatever) and runs on the PC while the data, the processing and the conflict resolution moves to a database server.

Once again, just to try to stop this all sounding too abstract, we'll look at a practical example. Suppose you want to implement a database for 50 concurrent users. You decide to use as the database server, say, a twin processor Intel box running on the most recent version of Windows. The RDBMS engine you elect to use won't be Access but something like SQL Server, Oracle or MySQL.

Let's assume you choose SQL Server. You install it onto the Intel box and then use the tools provided with SQL Server to create the tables. These will sit on the database server, which puts layer 7 firmly on the server.

The applications that provide the GUI might be written in something like Visual Basic. They will run on the PCs so layer 1 sits on the client.

OK, that's the two ends sorted out but what about the five layers in the middle? The client application will present the user with a GUI that enables them to view, edit and add to the data. It is also likely to provide the input validation so layer 2 sits on the client as well. However, the selections made from the GUI by the user will be translated into SQL which will be sent to the database server for processing. The database engine will receive these, execute the queries against the data and return the answer to the client. All of this tells us that layer 6, the data processing layer, is on the server. Database engines are also perfectly capable of enforcing the Data Integrity Rules (referential integrity etc.) so they also look after layer 5.

Layer 4, the Business Rules, can (and typically should) be enforced by the RDBMS engine and, in practice, they usually provide a feature called Triggers (see Chapter 22 for more details on triggers) for this purpose.

That only leaves layer 3, the Application Tasks. RDBMSs typically allow you to set up Views within the database. These are essentially queries that are designed by the database designer and can be run (but not modified) by the users of the database. This means that, for example, the users could be provided with a button on the GUI labeled 'Print end-of-month report'. When they press it, the GUI passes a message to the RDBMS which runs the View and returns the answer to the GUI which prints the report. Since the data is manipulated on the server, layer 3 is running on the server, not on the client.

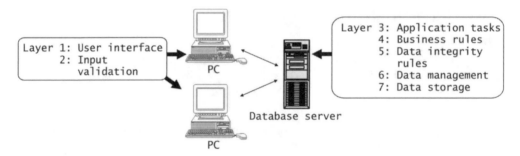

The client-server model is typically not limited by bandwidth. Since the query processing and the data itself are now snuggled together in one place, querying no longer means that masses of data have to move across the network. Instead, when the GUI running on the client is used to construct a question, only an SQL description of that query is shipped across the network to the server. This SQL will typically be a very short ASCII string. The database engine on the server processes the query and simply sends the answer (rather than the entire table) to the client. Conflict resolution is also handled centrally with associated benefits in terms of speed and sophistication. And centralizing the processing means that the whole system is easier and usually cheaper to update. If the database slows down you can throw hardware (in terms of memory and processors) at the server. You don't have to add it to the clients because they are simply handling the user interface.

This type of architecture is also known as two-tier architecture for the relatively obvious reason that there are two tiers, the client and the server.

Three-tier architecture (also known as multi-tier)

After that last sentence, we were bound to be going on to some other number of tiers, and the next is typically three. The classic three-tier architecture inserts a tier in between the client and the server. The job of this middle tier is to... well... do whatever you want it to do.

"This is a rather unsatisfactory explanation, Mark; can't you do any better?" OK, let's get dogmatic for a moment. The middle tier in a three-tier architecture is there to hold all of the user interface information that the clients use; in other words, the code and data that makes up layers 1 and 2 (User Interface and Input Validation).

Why do this? Well, imagine you are managing a two-tier database that has 250 clients. Every time you want to make any change to the user interface, you have to install the application onto 250 machines. If this application can be stored on an application server, you need only change the application in that one single location and all of the machines are updated. Wonderful.

But wait a minute! I've just had an idea. Perhaps we could get the middle tier to queue the requests coming in from the different users to reduce the conflicts generated between them (Chapter 23 talks about these conflicts and ways to resolve them). Yes, we could.

Here is another idea. We might split the database across several different database servers for speed reasons. We could connect the clients to one middle tier machine and we then use that machine to make the split transparent to the user; we'd get the benefit of the increased speed without adding to the users' workload. Yes, we could do that as well.

So which of these is really three-tier? The answer is that all of them are, and there are lots more that may occur to you.

The point I am trying to make here is that two-tier architecture can be excellent, but in practice, some two-tier systems turn out to have problems. These problems are typically to do with speed but they can also be to do with maintenance and/or the ability to upgrade.

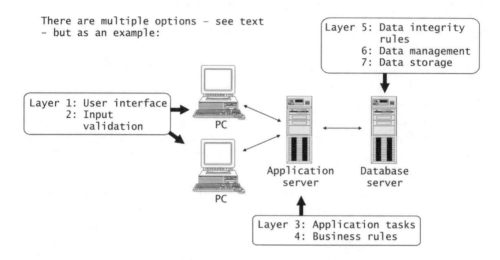

There are multiple options – see text
– but as an example:

Layer 5: Data integrity
         rules
      6: Data management
      7: Data storage

Layer 1: User interface
      2: Input
         validation

PC

PC

Application
server

Database
server

Layer 3: Application tasks
      4: Business rules

In turn many of these problems can be sorted by adding a middle tier. However, it is very important to realize that this middle layer will be of no use whatsoever unless it addresses the specific problem that is affecting the database in question.

If you are ever asked to fix an existing database application that has got into trouble, one of your first questions should be "How many tiers are you using?" and, if the reply is "Three" the next question should be "What is the middle tier doing?" Don't ever assume that you know. (I don't speak from experience here of course; I have never made this mistake myself…)

You don't, of course, have to wait for a database to run into problems before you elect to go three-tier; the decision should be made at the design stage in order to ensure that the problems never arise.

Web-based applications

Ah, the web. We can't possibly discuss databases without including the web, not because it is trendy but because the web model works so well with databases. The 7 layer model also works well with web databases so I'll use it to illustrate one basic way amongst the many in which a web database can be implemented.

Check out the diagram below:

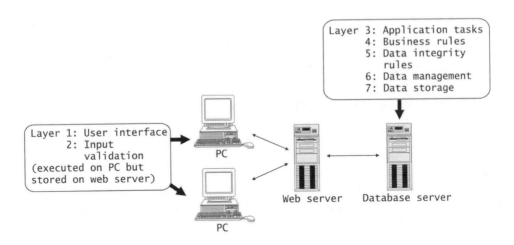

This solution is based upon a database server which holds layers 3–7 just as the client-server architecture does. These layers are the data itself, data management processes, data integrity rules, business rules and application tasks. All the reasons outlined above in the client-server section that tell us that layers 3–7 should be on the server are equally true in this case.

Once a web server is introduced into the architecture, it is that server which talks to the database server. The client runs browser software (the only software on the client that concerns us) and that browser, and therefore the client, will only talk to the web server. The client no longer communicates directly with the database server. Layers 1 and 2, the user interface and the input validation, sit on the web server, possibly in a mixture of HTML (HyperText Mark-up Language) and Java. It is, as discussed above, not where the layers sit physically that's important but where they are executed. Though they're stored on the web server, they are executed on the client.

Why is this model so successful? There are two major factors that give it the edge.

Firstly, the one and only consideration when determining the specification for a client machine is an ability to run a browser. It's known as a thin client (its specification can be pared down to a skinny minimum) and as long as it can run a browser at a reasonable speed, it will do the job of connecting to a database regardless of how complex that database might be.

Secondly, the user interface and data validation elements are stored on the web server so that bug fixes and upgrades can be made in just one place and thereafter all the clients can see the upgraded version.

If this all sounds similar to the description of three-tier architecture, you're right, so is this web database architecture two-tier or three-tier? The honest answer is that I'm not sure. Some people would argue vehemently that it has three tiers and some would insist that it has two. It doesn't really matter all that much: the important point is that you understand the pros and cons of moving the layers around to create an architecture that works. If I had to come down off the fence, I'd say that it is a two-tier solution. My main reason for falling in this direction is that there is nothing to stop you from adding another tier as discussed earlier between the web server and the database server – but I'm not sure I'd like to defend this position too closely. It also serves as a further illustration of why it's so important to find out exactly what people mean when they describe an existing system.

Choosing a database architecture

A database architecture essentially describes the location of all of the pieces that make up the database application.

One of the advantages of getting used to thinking about a database application in terms of the layers that we introduced at the start of this chapter is that it becomes easier to see that these can be distributed between one or more machines. This helps you to understand the common architectures (stand-alone, client-server etc.) and, in addition, it gives you a more flexible view of the whole process so that you can design an architecture that is the most effective solution for a given situation.

The decisions you make will be based upon the interaction of many factors, including:-

- Response time required
- Number of users
- Data size
- Type of data access required (read only, read write)
- Available resources (including hardware, software and money) and so on
- Expertise on site

These factors interact in complex ways. For example, suppose that your system definition makes multi-user access to the data essential: you can instantly rule out a stand-alone PC (unless you want fist fights over the keyboard). However, if the number of users is guaranteed to be small (say, three), then on a given hardware platform, you could allow those users to access a greater volume of data than if there were 50 of them. If the number of users did then increase, the system might still work, but the response time would drop. To make matters worse, the interactions between these factors are often non-linear. For example, doubling the number of users on a given system might have very little impact on response time; doubling it again might bring the same system to its knees.

I bet you can tell where this is leading, and you're right. We are working up the courage to tell you that despite the heading of this section – "Choosing a database architecture" – we can't tell you how to do it. What we have tried to do is to give you some of the basic information you need in order to make the choice between different architectures. In the end there is no real substitute for experience which is what you gain as soon as you start playing with data-bases.

What comes next

Although the joys of Parts 4 and 5 are still beneath your right thumb, this is essentially the end of this book, at least in terms of the 'story' that we have been following. We started with a single-table database and have ended up with a multi-user, multi-gigabyte database.

Part 4 contains chapters which can, essentially, be read in isolation. If you want to know more about SQL, read that chapter now. If normalization fasci-nates you, dip into that chapter over a cup of cocoa this evening.

Part 5 tells you how to make your database run like the wind.

Part 4

Related database topics

Chapter 21

What exactly is a relational database?

Do multiple tables a relational database make?

So far we have skated around the definition of a relational database. It is really tempting to believe that the use of multiple tables marks the transition to a relational database. Indeed, I have read several times that a 'relational' database is so called because it allows you to 'relate' information held in different tables. How can I put this politely? This information is wrong. Anyone who tells you this is incorrect. If they try to sell you anything, say nothing and back carefully away.

So where does the word 'relational' come from? Chris Date says that "The reason that such systems are called 'relational' is that the term 'relation' is essentially just a mathematical term for a table." (*An Introduction to Database Systems*, 6th ed., Addison-Wesley, 1995, p. 22).

He then goes on to define a 'Relational Database' as "a way of looking at data… More precisely, the relational model is concerned with three aspects of data: data structure, data integrity and data manipulation." (ibid., p. 98). All three of these are covered in Parts 1 and 2.

In other words, the term 'relational' comes from the rigorous mathematical background which underpins the model and the relational database model itself is a relatively complex entity of which only a tiny part is concerned with the 'relationships' (more properly called 'joins') between tables.

On names and misnames

For the record, a database is a collection of structured data.

A database application is a broader term that encompasses not only the data, but also the forms, queries etc. that are associated with the data.

In common usage, people often use the term database when they mean database application. For example, when a business person talks about "our new finance database" they usually mean the data, the hardware, the user interface and everything. This common usage isn't a problem – I often use it myself and would only bother distinguishing between 'database' and 'database application' when it was important to do so.

A DBMS (DataBase Management System) is a system which can be used to manage one or more databases. You will also hear it referred to as a database engine.

Again, if we are being pedantic we can actually distinguish between these two. Access, for example, is a DBMS. It has a built-in database engine called Jet which is the specific part concerned with manipulating the tables of data. But again, in common usage, DBMS and database engine are more or less interchangeable.

An RDBMS is simply a DBMS that adheres to the Relational model.

Given the complexity of the relational model, it is possible to argue (as Chris Date has done in the past) that few, if any, of the DBMS currently offered for sale are actually true relational database management systems, since all fail to implement some aspect of the model or other. However, this argument is essentially immaterial. Whatever the rights and wrongs of the situation, almost all of the DBMSs that you will come across today – SQL Server, Access, MySQL, Informix, Sybase, Oracle, DB2 – are, to all intents and purposes, relational and hence can be rightly called RDBMSs.

Chapter 22

Triggers and stored procedures

This chapter covers triggers and stored procedures which are important when you write complex multi-user databases. The Jet engine in Access provides no direct support for triggers although you can provide much the same functionality using VB and, say, the 'Before Insert' property of a form. There is no direct support for Stored Procedures either although again, you can emulate pretty much the same functionality using VB. Of course, Access can also connect to other databases engines which do provide direct support for these features.

Triggers

A trigger can be thought of as a very small program that is set to go off under certain conditions. (Or, less prosaically, think of a trigger as a loyal servant who watches for certain events and, when they occur, carries out your bidding.) The 'program' is typically one or more SQL statements and a trigger is typically activated by one of three types of modification to a row or rows in a table, namely the SQL statements:

DELETE
INSERT
UPDATE

Triggers can be used for many things (limited only by your imagination, really) but they are often used for data integrity checking. Business rules (also part of integrity checking) can also be enforced with triggers. Imagine you had a table of salary data and that you update an employee's salary from grade 1 to grade 2 on a scale. A trigger can ensure adherence to a business rule that states that an employee at grade 1 must have been employed at that grade for x years before being eligible for advancement. More excitingly, triggers can even be used to send out email notifications under certain conditions, like the arrival of a particular value in a table. Perhaps your company has just taken its 1,000th order and a party is called for. A trigger could have been set to detect this event which sends an email ordering champagne. (As a purely personal preference, we see more merit in the latter trigger than the former.)

Trigger terminology

As we said above, a trigger has a triggering operation (i.e. an event that sets it off) which is typically a DELETE, INSERT or UPDATE statement.

A trigger has an activation time (i.e. the time when it's set off) which can be either before or after a DELETE, INSERT or UPDATE statement, giving six possible combinations. Terms such as 'before trigger' or 'after update trigger' are often used to describe the various types that can be built.

Typical usage of Before and After triggers

In general, Before triggers are used to ensure that all is well before a change is made to a row. Think of a typical Before trigger like this: it says 'Before you make this change – check this fact.' If the fact proves to be false, the database is returned to the state it was in before the triggering event occurred. (See Chapter 23 for more details about roll-back.)

In general, you would use an After trigger when you are happy that a particular operation is acceptable and you want some other operation to follow it.

What's needed here is a couple of examples.

Before

Imagine that the CEO of your company decides that no customers can be deleted from the database if they owe your company money (sounds sensible to us). Here you would use a Before trigger – 'Before you delete this row, check that the customer is credit-clean and don't allow the deletion if the customer is in our debt'.

After

Imagine that you want to keep a count of the total number of customers somewhere (not good practice in a fully normalized database, but sometimes useful for performance reasons). In other words, if you add a customer to a table, you want to increment a value in another table. In this case you don't want to prevent the SQL which is performing the Insert, you just want to increment the value when it runs. In this case, you would use an After trigger.

More about triggers

A trigger has a name so it can be identified easily.

A trigger has a body. This is an important bit, the part that determines what a trigger will do when the conditions that fire it are met, and it comprises one or more SQL statements.

A trigger can have conditions that determine whether the trigger body is executed or not. If you only want the trigger to run if, say, the new employee that you are inserting into a table is in a particular department, you add a condition to this effect. Defining a condition for a trigger is typically optional.

Triggers are potentially very secure devices. They can enforce business rules at table level even if you use a range of front-ends. A trigger is attached to the table and will fire regardless of the front-end application which initiates the trigger event. Tables can have multiple triggers attached to them.

So, triggers are great. We could almost, at this point, start to paraphrase A. A. Milne:

> *The wonderful thing about Triggers*
>
> *Is Triggers are wonderful things*

…but we won't, obviously.

As an example, here is a trigger from the Pubs database supplied with SQL Server.

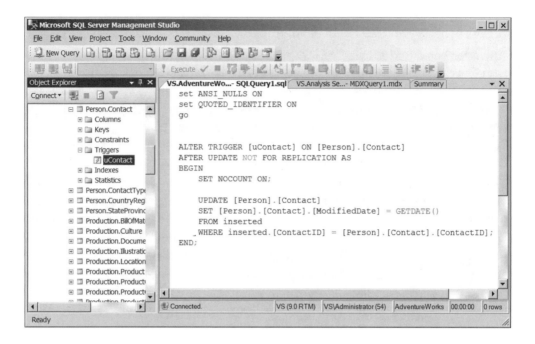

And just to prove the fact that database engines really do differ in the way in which they implement triggers, here is a trigger in IBM's DB2.

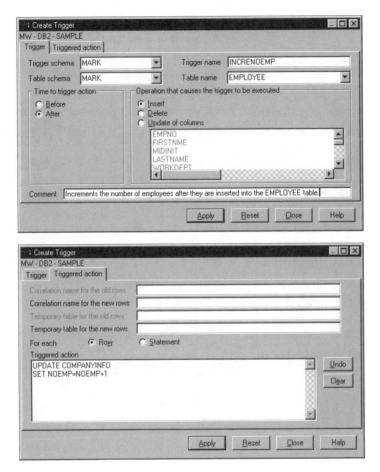

Triggers (and stored procedures) typically use SQL but may well include commands written in an RDBMS-specific language – hence they are typically not highly portable between different databases engines.

Stored procedures

There are times when you want a standard operation to be performed, possibly multiple times, but you don't want it to be tied to any one particular event such as updating a table. You'll have gathered from the heading above that stored procedures have a role to play here.

Imagine you maintain a relatively complex database with tables of sales data, purchases, stock levels, employee costs and so on. Many people in the organization, possibly using several different client applications, are going to want to see the company's net profit. This is a calculation that will involve a number of operations: group by queries against several tables and manipulations of the values thus generated. You could write into each client application a series of SQL statements to do all this whenever you needed to but it is almost invariably neater to use a stored procedure.

As the name implies, a stored procedure is stored not in the client application but in the database itself. It can execute the series of operations necessary to perform the net profit calculation (to stay with the example). The procedure is named (perhaps as NetProfit) and is then available to any client application and when run it will return the net profit. One advantage is that the procedure is written and stored once and is available thereafter as a resource within the database. Another is that individual users don't have to reinvent the wheel whenever they need a calculation performed, and updating or editing the calculation is easy as it only has to be done once. Furthermore, stored procedures run quickly because they are usually 'compiled', that is, turned into a form that can be executed rapidly by the database engine.

Here is a stored procedure from the Pubs sample database in SQL Server.

Summary – triggers and stored procedures

The defining feature of a trigger is that it is attached to a table and cannot be subverted – if an operation that sets off the trigger takes place, there's nothing that the client application can do to stop the trigger from firing. For implementing business rules, triggers are invaluable. If an order has a value of more than $10,000, a 5% discount can be applied automatically and the customer's name can be added, after checking that it isn't present already, to a table of customers who are sent a Christmas card.

Stored procedures can give you the ability to perform useful operations in a standardized way for any client application with the necessary permissions, thus ensuring that when different departments calculate a value, it's always done the same way. Stored procedures are quick to run and, because they're stored once, they're easily maintained.

Knowing about both and acquiring a feel for when each can be used to advantage is a useful skill.

Chapter 23

Transactions, logs, backup, locking and concurrency

Transactions

Tables hold data and that data is constantly being accessed, altered and updated by various operations. It is relatively common in certain applications for two or more of these operations to be logically related.

As an example, suppose Sophie gives Ross a check for amount X, written on her account, in payment for his Dodge Viper (Sophie has excellent taste in cars). Two discrete operations are involved. One is the removal of amount X from Sophie's account, the other is the addition of the same amount to Ross's account. However, it is clear that the two operations are logically related – as demonstrated by the fact that if the first operation succeeds and the second fails both parties are going to be upset (although Ross may be more vociferous).

Logically related operations of this kind are called Transactions.

When we send a transaction to a database three things can happen:

- The entire transaction completes (in which case it is described as committed)
- None of the transaction completes
- Part of the transaction completes

Clearly, committing the transaction is the most desirable conclusion but, of the other two, it is far better if no part of the transaction completes than just some of it.

Typically any one operation within a transaction is a single SQL statement; thus a transaction is usually made up of several SQL statements.

So that's a transaction, but why are they of such fundamental importance?

Transactions are usually generated by client applications that send them to the RDBMS. If an application crashes during a transaction, or the network fails, the transaction may be left half completed; that is, the money has gone from Sophie's account but it hasn't arrived in Ross's. The database itself is fine in the sense that nothing has happened to offend its referential integrity. Both Sophie and Ross's records show a balance in their current accounts; the problem is that the values it shows are inconsistent with reality. So, we need some mechanism for dealing with incomplete transactions.

Rollback

Rollback means undoing the operations of a transaction that have not been committed. In other words, if a transaction fails to complete, rolling it back will leave the database in the same state it was in before the transaction started.

Rollback is amazingly useful because it can be used to deal with much more than simply occasions when just a single application fails and leaves one transaction uncommitted. Imagine a heavily used database running on a server that crashes (perhaps because the power goes down). If there were fifty transactions underway at that moment, the database is likely to be in a highly inconsistent state. However, if the RDBMS can roll back all fifty incomplete transactions, then it will be fine. Some RDBMSs will even do this for you automatically whenever started up after a crash.

Clearly, in order to perform this magic, the RDBMS needs to keep track of incomplete transactions, and it does this with logs.

Logs

Access doesn't support logging. See the end of the chapter for more information. Whenever a transaction starts against a database, the fact is recorded in a log file. Log files store information like:

- when a transaction starts
- what operations are completed
- when the transaction itself is completed (that is to say, committed)

Many RDBMSs use a process known as Circular logging as the default form of logging. Its name reflects the way in which it is implemented.

Circular logging

As anyone who has worked with disk files knows, it is much easier to append information to a file than it is to delete particular pieces of information from within a file. Therefore references to committed transactions are not actually removed from the logs. Instead information is written to a log file until the file reaches a set size. (There will be a default size set for this file and you'll probably be able to configure it should you wish.) Thereafter a second log file is opened and transactions are written into that. The completion of each transaction is still, of course, noted as and when it occurs. When that second file is full, a third is opened. By the time *that* one is full, it is highly likely that every transaction recorded in the first file will have completed. If, and only if, this is the case, the first file will be overwritten. Thus at any time there will typically be three log files in which current transactions are being recorded. Hence the term 'circular' logging because typically three files are used in rotation.

A useful definition at this point is the term 'Active' log file. This describes a log file that contains references to one or more uncommitted transactions. Thus in the paragraph above we could have said "By the time that one is full, it is highly likely that the first file is no longer active. If this is the case, the first file will be overwritten." The opposite of an active file is an inactive file, although the term doesn't seem to be used very much in practice.

Using circular logging, you always have a full and complete record of all currently incomplete transactions, including the operations completed to date within each. If one transaction needs to be rolled back, you have the necessary information in the active logs to do that. If the server on which the RDBMS is running crashes, when it is restarted it can examine the active logs and automatically roll back all of the incomplete transactions.

Secondary log files

You may remember that we said above that many RDBMSs will maintain three log files and that by the time the third one is full, the first is likely to be inactive. You might be wondering what happens if the first file *is* still active. All that happens is that a fourth log file is opened known as a Secondary log file (the default three are Primary log files). "Yes, but what happens if…" then it opens a fifth. Clearly there has to be a limit somewhere and there is. When you first start, your databases are unlikely to need more than the default settings and when they do you will find that you can configure them as you need.

What is stored in a log file?

We said above that the log files store the 'operations' that are carried out during a transaction. This might imply that the actual SQL commands are stored, since each operation is typically an SQL statement. However, this wouldn't work in practice. Consider the SQL statement:

```
UPDATE ORG
SET DIVISION = 'Western'
WHERE DIVISION = 'Eastern';
```

This statement looks for all rows in the ORG table where the value in the column DIVISION is equal to Eastern and sets it to Western.

Imagine that the ORG table has three rows in which DIVISION = 'Eastern' and two where DIVISION = 'Western'. After the SQL statement has run, there are five rows where DIVISION = 'Western'. If all we have in the log file is the SQL statement and we try to roll back, how do we know which of the five to turn back to 'Eastern'? The answer is that we don't. So, in practice, the log file stores a copy of the information that is changed. However, if you imagine the log file as storing a set of 'reversible SQL statements', you have a perfectly functional mental picture of what it contains.

Summary of circular logging

Maintaining circular logs clearly takes up resources, which is another way of saying that doing so must inevitably slow down the database slightly. However, the speed hit is tiny and the pay-off is huge since circular logging enables the database to roll back any or all incomplete transactions. In turn the ability to roll back transactions enables you to protect your database against corruption from:

● network failure

● application or server crash

So circular logs are wonderful, but they don't protect your data against all possible disasters. For example, if the disk on which the database resides crashes, you still lose all of your data. This is, of course, where backup comes in. If you backup your database to disk every night then if the disk crashes you can replace the disk and restore the database.

But suppose that the disk crashes at, say, four o'clock in the afternoon. You can restore the database to the state it was in the previous night, but you have lost all of this morning's transactions.

You can probably see where this is leading. Suppose you perform an off-line backup on Monday evening. On Tuesday morning, as transactions start to run against the database, you perform logging to ensure that you can roll back if necessary. However, instead of using circular logging (which over-writes the inactive log files) you get the database engine to keep all of the log files intact.

Now when the disk crashes at four o'clock, you replace it, restore the database, and then roll forward.

Roll forward

Running complete transactions from a log file against a backup is known as roll forward. (Clearly any uncommitted transactions in the log files are not run during a normal roll forward.)

Of course, as soon as you get the idea of roll forward, you realize that it has great potential. As long as the log files also contain a time/date stamp for each transaction, you can roll the database forward to any chosen point in time. So, if a rogue application (*not to say a rogue employee*) happened to be creating mayhem in your data for some time before the system finally crashed, you can roll forward to a point just before the damage started. Suddenly roll forward is a really powerful tool.

You can also use it as a form of archiving. Imagine you have a backup taken on 1/1/2007 and that you have log files for the next three months. If you wanted to see the state of the database on the 2/2/2007, all you have to do is to restore the database and roll it forward to the date you want.

It ought to go without saying (but I'll say it anyway) that if your database was called, say, ADMIN, you would restore the backup to something called, say, ADMIN2 rather than overwrite your current copy of ADMIN.

This sort of roll forward is also known as point-in-time recovery.

This form of logging, where all of the log files are retained, can no longer be called circular logging and is referred to as Archive logging.

Archive logging

An archived log stores details of all transactions since the last backup and can be used to restore a database to any point between that backup and the failure (as described above).

When all the transactions in an active log are complete, the log is closed and, instead of being recycled as a new active log, it becomes an archived log.

It is worth explicitly stating that Archive logging doesn't prevent you from being able to roll back transactions in exactly the same way as it could with circular logging. Think of archive logging as circular logging plus.

Locations

Log files are kept in a folder on disk and by default this can be on the same disk as the database. For performance reasons, you may well want to move it to another disk. In addition this can have positive data security implications; if the database disk melts down you don't lose the logs as well.

Really paranoid (sorry, really *careful*) DBAs will not only keep the log files on a different disk, they will periodically back up the inactive log files to yet another device (typically tape or a disk on another machine). This leads to yet another form of classification because an archive log is described as 'on-line' when it is stored in the database log path directory and 'off-line' when it has been moved. The 'database log path directory' simply means the place (typically a folder) where the database is currently storing the log files.

You can play games with these classification systems like asking if it is possible to have:

> A. an on-line active log file?
>
> B. an off-line inactive circular log?
>
> C. an off-line active log file?

Answers at the end of the chapter.

Backup strategy

So, there is a whole host of options and possibilities. What we'll do now is to walk through the different options pointing out their pros and cons.

When you create a database and use circular logging, this keeps track of all the transactions that have been started but have yet to complete. Circular logging ensures that any or all uncommitted transactions can be rolled back if necessary. This protects your database against application failure, system crashes and power failure. In fact, this protection is often automated: the RDBMS will automatically roll back uncommitted transactions in the event of a server crash or power failure whenever it is restarted.

However, circular logging does not protect against media failure or, say, the actions of a disgruntled employee. For that you need archive logging.

Archive logging keeps copies of all transactions and allows the RDBMS to roll back uncommitted transactions as before, but also to roll them forward from a backup.

Since this sort of protection is valuable we make the following general recommendations for a production database. (You can be less particular for a test one, but we still recommend backing those up).

Recommendations

As soon as you create a database and before you add data or let users loose on it, make sure that the log files are being saved to a disk other than the one on which the database resides. Make an off-line back up of the database and ensure that your RDBMS is using Archive logging.

You now have a copy of the database on some other medium (presumably tape) and you have told the RDBMS to record every subsequent change to the database. These changes are being recorded away from the database. You are protected from transactions that fail to complete; in addition you should now be protected from a disk crash or an unhappy employee. Finally, we would suggest that you make backup copies of the on-line inactive log files onto another medium such as tape.

We've described what we hope is a safe strategy but clearly only you can decide what is safe for your data. The information above is a broad overview that should help you to determine your own backup policy.

Incidentally, we say that you should put the log files on another disk, but that disk should be located on the same server, not a remote one. The problem with using a remote server is that, should the network glue up (or fail completely) your database will run abysmally slowly or die.

Other points worth considering

Off-line backups

An off-line backup is the most straightforward. Ensure that no one is accessing the database (so that it is in a static state) and make a copy.

On-line backups

It is also possible to make an on-line backup, where users can continue to work with the database. An on-line backup isn't a snapshot of the database at an instant of time. Instead it may be spread over several minutes/hours or even days. Note that an on-line backup is highly likely to contain inconsistent data because some transactions will have started before the backup and will complete during it. Others will start during and complete afterwards. An on-line backup is thus of little value if archive logging isn't in operation. On the other hand, if archive logging *is* running then the backup is perfectly valid – *as long as* you roll the database forward to a point in time that is after the end of the backup.

As general advice, use off-line backups if possible; they generally make your life easier.

Locking

As soon as you have multiple people accessing the same database, the possibility for conflicts of interest is introduced, some of which are illustrated below. In order to overcome these potential problems, database engines typically implement a process called Locking. Locking has two effects, one good, one bad. The good one is that it can resolve conflicts between users. The bad is that, as a by-product, it introduces some problems of its own which also have to be resolved. It all sounds rather like a buck-passing exercise but happily the whole solution usually ends up working satisfactorily.

The entire process does, however, become very complex and reams can be written about it in excruciating detail. We considered writing those reams for you, but decided in the end that you wouldn't thank us because much of what we would write would be specific for a given database engine, since they implement different bits in different ways to end up with their unique solutions. Our purpose here is not to tell you everything you need to know about locking in your chosen database engine but to introduce you to the topic so that when you read or hear about it, or encounter it in a particular database engine, you'll recognize it and have an overview to help you understand that implementation.

Let's start with a simple example. Remember that poor benighted A. Smith from Chapter 20: I open his record with the intention of increasing his credit limit from $2,000 to $3,000 while you open it to delete his entire record. What we have here is a conflict of interests and locking was invented to deal with such conflicts. With locking implemented, if I get to A. Smith's record first and start editing it, when you get there to delete it, you find that the record is 'locked', that is, you can't delete it or do anything else to it until I've finished and posted the record back to the database.

Wow! That's easy! And it is true; expressed like this, locking sounds simple.

Deadlocks

Unfortunately, when you mix locking and transactions, further problems occur which can be referred to as deadlocks. Imagine a banking database with two current accounts, belonging to Eric and Teri, and two transfers of funds that we need to complete. One is to take $50 from Eric's account and put it into Teri's and the other is to take $120 from Teri's account and put it into Eric's. Each transfer is a discrete transaction comprising two operations. So if, for example, we focus on the first transfer, it has two operations. The first opens Eric's account and extracts the money and the second opens Teri's account and pops the money in. The entire transaction must either complete or be rolled back.

So far so good: there is no problem at all unless the two transactions try to occur at exactly the same time. Imagine that the first operation obtains a lock on Eric's record, takes out the money and then tries to obtain a lock on Teri's record. Meanwhile, the second transaction has obtained a lock on Teri's record in order to extract $120 and now tries to obtain a lock on Eric's record. You see the problem: now we have a deadlock. Neither transaction can complete until the lock it requires is released and neither will give up the lock it already has in its grasp. You can make deadlocks as complicated as you like; in fact, they rarely involve as few as two records. Add in a set of concurrent transactions that involve the accounts of Leila, Gus and Claude, and you can create a deadlock that involves five lucky participants.

Transactions are an essential part of databases, as described above, and locking is an essential part of multi-user databases. The bank account tangle is just one illustration of a whole series of new and interesting problems that can arise. So just how do you go about resolving deadlocks?

In the early days of databases, it was left to the database administrator to wait for phone calls from irate users, to hunt down deadlocked transactions and kill off one or more of them so that the others could complete. The situation has improved since then in two main ways: firstly, database engines evolved which were good at spotting deadlocks and dealing with them automatically. Secondly, not all locks on records are equal and a database engine may provide a variety of locks for use in different situations.

As an example of lock usage, imagine a client-server database engine running a database with different client applications all sending complex transactions to the engine. It's perfectly possible for the designers of the applications to actively specify what sort of lock is to be used during the execution of their application. The types of lock available can be important and will vary depending on the engine in use, but support for a good range of locks lets you build applications that generate transactions which are less likely to create deadlocks.

If this begins to make this all sound complex, you will be relieved to hear that you are not obliged to specify the level of locking to be used because defaults will be applied by the database engine, but it is worth knowing that it is possible to change from the defaults. It is also worth knowing that the appalling performance of an application might possibly be due to the locking that's being applied.

It's a natural temptation for developers to use 'strong' locking in their application – so that it grabs all the locks it needs and holds them until it has completed an entire transaction. This can damage the performance of the database as a whole and worse, should that application also let its users go to lunch in mid-transaction, you have the potential to sock the performance of a whole database.

Concurrency

You may hear people using the word 'concurrency' in this kind of context, saying, for example, that a database and its applications have 'good concurrency'. Good concurrency is highly desirable and it's easiest to explain by example. A database with good concurrency allows large numbers of users to access a database without any noticeable impact on performance. This implies that the applications that run against the database have been written to use locking with elegance and sympathy for the needs of others.

Row locking and page locking

Again, we mention these terms because you may hear them in general usage. A row lock will lock a single record in a database and is a very desirable form of locking as it minimizes the impact on other users of the same database. A page lock uses more of a shotgun approach. It locks an entire 'page' of the table, which may embrace several rows (even though the application is only modifying one of them). The number of records locked is determined by the page size implemented in the particular RDBMS you're using. In practice it is best if an engine supports both because either can be optimal under different conditions.

Row and page locking have raised contentious issues in the past, especially during the period when some database engines (SQL Server in particular) were pilloried for not supporting row locking. This is now much less of an issue since any engine worth its salt (SQL Server included) supports both kinds of locking.

Access and the features described in this chapter

As we said earlier, Access doesn't directly support logging. Without logging, individual transactions (supported by the Jet database engine since version 4.0) can still be rolled back but more advanced features, such as roll forward and on-line backup are not possible in the same way.

However, as we said at the beginning of the book, we will tell you about all of the features of relational databases because the book is more about relational databases than about Access. Our slight problem in this case is that, while most client-server database engines support logging, they can do so in quite different ways. It's not a huge problem because the important point here is the underlying principle, not the implementation. So, we have described a relatively common implementation (circular and archival logging) but do make sure, if you connect Access to another engine, that you read up about how that particular engine actually implements logging.

Access does, of course, support off-line backups. It also has a mechanism for locking (and hence provides concurrent access to the data). This is fine for up to 5 concurrent users, perhaps 10, depending on the workload but it is not suitable for larger numbers.

Answers from earlier

A. Yes

B. No

C. No

Chapter 24

Codd's rules

Relational databases are, by now, so widely accepted that many people are unaware that any other form of database can exist. It is also sad (but true) that many people don't know what particular facets of a DBMS make it relational or not. Since the relational model is the brainchild of Dr. Edgar Codd ('the Father of the Relational Database'), the best place to start is with Ted Codd's rules. These rules have been quoted and misquoted so many times that in the interests of accuracy I went back to the original two articles by Codd himself (*Computerworld*, 14th and 21st October 1985). In the first of these he writes:

> *"In this paper I supply a set of rules with which a DBMS should comply if it is claimed to be fully relational."*

In practice these rules have been modified and extended and if you want to know more about Codd's ideas try *The Relational Model for Database Management Version 2* by the man himself.

Economy vs. readability

I have the very greatest respect for Dr. Codd; after all, he was the one who designed the relational database management system. In his writings, Codd expressed his ideas with admirable accuracy and economy. Sadly this combination has left them somewhat unintelligible to the average reader, which is a shame since he was, without doubt, the greatest authority on the subject. What I have tried to do is to make the rules more understandable by expanding them. In the process, inevitably, some of the precision is lost and I apologize in advance for any offence caused. If in doubt, believe Codd's original and not my interpretation.

A little background

Some of the quotes I intend to use from these two papers only make sense if you are aware that by 1985 a great deal had been published about relational databases but few products existed. Several manufacturers were producing systems for mainframes with the word 'relational' on the box (or on the crate in the case of the bigger systems). Most of these products appear to have offended Codd deeply; indeed the articles are, in places, simply a vehicle for his diatribe against them. This can be seen in the introduction to the first paper:

> "...some vendors of nonrelational DBMS have quickly (and recently) added a few relational features – in some cases, very few features – in order to be able to claim their systems are relational, even though they may not meet the simple requirements for being rated 'minimally relational'. We shall refer to this kind of DBMS as 'born again'. It is a safe bet that these Johnny-come-lately vendors have not taken the time or manpower to investigate optimization techniques needed in relational DBMSs to yield good performance."

No-one could ever have accused Codd of pulling his punches.

The rules themselves

There are 13 rules in all. Codd started numbering them at zero rather than one and this has caused confusion ever since because the last one is therefore number 12. It is very common to hear people talk, erroneously, about 'Codd's 12 rules'.

●   **Rule 0:** *For any system that is advertised as, or claimed to be, a relational data base management system, that system must be able to manage data bases entirely through its relational capabilities.*

Note that Codd used a space between the words 'data' and 'base' but this construction has fallen from favor.

Rule 0 is reasonably clear. For a DBMS to qualify as relational it must have *all* of the features of the relational model, not just a subset. At the time Codd formulated these rules, many of the DBMSs which were advertised as relational were actually based on a system other than relational (e.g. hierarchical). The manufacturers had just bolted on a few relational 'features' in the hope that everyone would believe the products were fully relational.

The information rule

● Rule 1: *All information in a relational data base is represented explicitly at the logical level and in exactly one way – by values in tables.*

This rule says that all data should be stored in tables and in no other way. The use of tables to store data has become such a fundamental part of modern database systems that it sounds a little odd to explicitly write it down; it's rather like writing that all cars should have wheels. However, when the rules were written it was less accepted and therefore worth saying.

In case anyone is in any doubt about what a table looks like, this is one called STUDENTS; it has four columns called ID, FirstName, LastName and DOB. It also has five rows.

STUDENTS			
ID	**FirstName**	**LastName**	**DOB**
1	MIKE	WELLINGTON	16 May 1985
2	SALLY	JONES	13 July 1986
3	TZANOVICH	SMITH	12 December 1986
4	GEOFFREY	PHILLIPS	17 April 1976
5	TANIA	NBANGO	12 September 1986

The guaranteed access rule

● Rule 2: *Each and every datum (atomic value) in a relational data base is guaranteed to be logically accessible by resorting to a combination of table name, primary key value and column name.*

First, some terminology; datum is the singular form of data and a datum is a piece of information. The word does not figure much in everyday usage since 'data' is now commonly, if inaccurately, used as both the singular and plural form. An atomic value means the information contained in one field of one record. Codd is using the term 'atomic' in the nuclear sense of an item which cannot be subdivided (at least, not without recourse to a particle accelerator).

Rule 2 says that each entry in a table of data must be locatable with no more information than the name of the table, the field name and the value in the primary key. Thus in the table below, you can find the last name of a given student as long as you know the table is called STUDENTS, that the relevant column name is LastName and that the student's ID number is, say, 4.

STUDENTS			
ID	FirstName	LastName	DOB
1	MIKE	WELLINGTON	16 May 1985
2	SALLY	JONES	13 July 1986
3	TZANOVICH	SMITH	12 December 1986
4	GEOFFREY	*PHILLIPS*	17 April 1976
5	TANIA	NBANGO	12 September 1986

As Codd says when expanding on this rule *'the primary key concept is an essential part,'* so we can take this rule to say also that each table in a relational database must have a primary key and each data value in that key must be a unique identifier.

Systematic treatment of null values

●   **Rule 3:** *Null values (distinct from the empty character string or a string of blank characters and distinct from zero or any other number) are supported in fully relational DBMS for representing missing information and inapplicable information in a systematic way, independent of data type.*

Codd also says in his commentary on the rules that *'it must be possible to specify "Nulls not allowed" for each primary key column.'*

Null values are very important in databases, much more so than their name implies. A null value is supposed to represent an absence of information; it's not the same as a space or a zero, a dash, a hash or any other representation. A null means that we don't know what information should be entered into this field. It certainly does not imply that we don't care about the content of the field. This may seem like a trivial distinction but it isn't. In the context of Rule 3, the important point is that nulls should be handled in a logical and consistent manner. Oddly enough, handling them logically isn't too difficult if the problems that they raise are considered in isolation. Ensuring that an RDBMS is entirely consistent in the way it handles nulls is more difficult. It is interesting to note that Codd simply states that the RDBMS must do it; he doesn't suggest a way in which this ideal can be implemented.

Dynamic on-line catalog based on the relational model

●   **Rule 4:** *The database description is represented at the logical level in the same way as ordinary data, so that authorized users can apply the same relational language to its interrogation as they apply to the regular data.*

An implicit assumption in this rule is that every RDBMS will have a 'database description'; Codd apparently believes this to be so fundamental to the whole concept of an RDBMS that he does not actually state it. A database description is more commonly known as a database dictionary (a term which Codd himself uses in his expansion of Rule 4), a data dictionary, a system catalog and/or the system tables. It is an entity which holds a description of the entire structure of the database – the tables in the database, their internal structure, the joins between the tables, the indexes that have been applied to the columns and so on. (For more details, see Chapter 27, which is about the system tables.) This data is often referred to as the 'metadata'.

The rule says that the structures in which the information in the data dictionary is held should be the same as those for data in the database itself and that there should be no additional complexity for users who need to deal with data in the data dictionary. To put that another way, if you look inside the data dictionary, you should find information about how your database is structured and that information must be held in tables. It all sounds a little incestuous because we end up with tables that define tables (including themselves) but the concept behind this rule is perfectly sound. As you become familiar with a particular RDBMS, you learn how to access the data which is stored in your tables. In learning that process, you also learn how to access the information about the database itself.

Comprehensive data sub-language rule

- Rule 5: *A relational system may support several languages and various modes of terminal use (for example, the fill-in-the-blanks mode). However, there must be at least one language whose statements are expressible, per some well-defined syntax, as character strings and that is comprehensive in supporting all of the following items:*

  - *Data definition*
  - *View definition*
  - *Data manipulation (interactive and by program)*
  - *Integrity constraints*
  - *Authorization*
  - *Transaction boundaries (begin, commit and rollback)*

This rule may appear somewhat anachronistic. After all, we expect to drive most RDBMSs via a GUI nowadays. Do we really care if there is an underlying, unifying language?

The answer is 'Yes' if we expect that database to operate on anything other than a stand-alone PC. Once you expand a database to multi-user operation across a network, the communication between client and database engine is much more efficient if it can be expressed in simple character strings.

Whether Codd had this in mind when he formulated the rule is another matter; he may have simply been trying to ensure that users could always find a consistent way of interacting with their databases. However, the rule is still highly applicable today. The language that has become the de facto standard here is SQL (Structured Query Language). Despite the use of the word 'Query' in the name, SQL is not limited to querying and can be used for all of the above operations.

View updating rule

● **Rule 6:** *All views that are theoretically updatable are also updatable by the system.*

On the face of it, this is a simple rule; it's short, concise and unambiguous. However, reading Codd's further expansion of Rule 6 rapidly disabuses you of that first naïve interpretation. He says '*Note that a view is theoretically updatable if there exists a time-independent algorithm for unambiguously determining a single series of changes to the base relations that will have as their effect precisely the requested changes in the view*'. Oh.

Perhaps some definitions might help to shed light on this obfuscation.

Relation Codd uses the term 'relation' to mean, effectively, a table of data.

Base relation/base table This is a table that exists within a database and is typically stored on disk. It can be distinguished from other types of table, such as an answer table (see below under View). A base table might look like this.

STUDENTS			
ID	**FirstName**	**LastName**	**DOB**
1	MIKE	WELLINGTON	16 May 1985
2	SALLY	JONES	13 July 1986
3	TZANOVICH	SMITH	12 December 1986
4	GEOFFREY	PHILLIPS	17 April 1976
5	TANIA	NBANGO	12 September 1986

View A view is essentially a query that is stored as part of the database and can be run against one or more of the tables. In Access views are not distinguished from queries. In a client-server database (such as SQL Server) the difference is that views are stored on the server as part of the database while queries are generated from the client and sent to the database.

Views are essentially SQL statements, such as:

SELECT STUDENTS.FirstName, STUDENTS.LastName

FROM STUDENTS

WHERE STUDENTS.FirstName="Sally";

However, when the view is accessed it appears as a table of data with rows and columns:

FirstName	LastName
SALLY	JONES

This is an answer table and not a base table.

We can thus rewrite the expansion of Rule 6 as:

Note that a query is theoretically updatable if there exists a time-independent algorithm for unambiguously determining a single series of changes to the underlying tables that will have as their effect precisely the requested changes in the answer table.

So, have my definitions helped to clarify the clarification? Probably not as yet, but we're getting there.

Another way of expressing Rule 6 might be as follows. You should be able not only to look at the data in an answer table, but also to edit and change the data that you see there. However, there are restrictions. You should only be allowed to edit this data if the updating action (be it modifying, inserting or deleting information) makes sense and does not break any of the fundamental rules of the database structure.

As an example of an edit that doesn't make sense, consider this example. Suppose that your base table is like this:

SALES					
SaleNo	*EmployeeNo*	**Customer**	**Item**	**Supplier**	**Amount**
1	*1*	Simpson	Sofa	Harrison	$235.67
2	*1*	Johnson	Chair	Harrison	$453.78
3	*2*	Smith	Stool	Ford	$82.78
4	*2*	Jones	Suite	Harrison	$3,421.00
5	*3*	Smith	Sofa	Harrison	$235.67
6	*1*	Simpson	Sofa	Harrison	$235.67
7	*1*	Jones	Bed	Ford	$453.00

and that the primary key is SaleNo. You then query it to find the average value of a sale:

ANSWER
AvgOfAmount
$731.08

Clearly the RDBMS cannot allow you to edit this value because the figure it shows is derived from a number of different records.

As an example of an edit to an answer table which could cause loss of data integrity, suppose that you create a query which shows the following three fields from the SALES table:

ANSWER		
Customer	**Item**	**Amount**
Simpson	Sofa	$235.67
Johnson	Chair	$453.78
Smith	Stool	$82.78
Jones	Suite	$3,421.00
Smith	Sofa	$235.67
Simpson	Sofa	$235.67
Jones	Bed	$453.00

The act of adding records to this table must be forbidden because it is impossible to include a primary key value to the record that you add. Since all records must have a value for the primary key, allowing the addition of a record will compromise data integrity.

It can now be argued, however, that Rule 6 is of academic interest only because in 1988, a certain H. W. Buff published a paper entitled *Why Codd's Rule No. 6 Must Be Reformulated*. As the title suggests, this paper proves that Rule 6 is fatally flawed. Buff's paper shows that no RDBMS can ever support this rule because 'there does not exist any algorithm which can decide, given any view, whether it is updatable or not.' What's more, he proved it.

In *The Relational Model for Database Management Version 2* published in 1990, Codd acknowledges that Buff's paper is correct and modifies Rule 6 by defining an algorithm which will identify a good percentage of updatable views.

The bottom line is that we have to understand that the system cannot identify all views that can be safely updated. However, it is relatively easy for the system to partition answer tables into two groups:

> — those which are definitely safe to update

> — the others

Clearly an effective RDBMS should allow us to update those which fall into the first category and exclude the update ability from answer tables which fall into the second. Access, for example, does so.

High-level insert, update and delete

- **Rule 7:** *The capability of handling a base relation or a derived relation as a single operand applies not only to the retrieval of data but also to the insertion, update and deletion of data.*

Remembering that Codd uses the term 'relation' to mean a table, we can interpret this rule as follows.

You expect the RDBMS to allow you to retrieve rows with a single command, that is, it should let you query the database in the normal way. Rule 7 says that not only querying but also inserting, updating and deleting multiple rows should be possible with a single command. In other words, if you want to delete all of the invoices which are older than five years, you don't have to locate each one and delete it individually. You should be able to eliminate them all with a single command.

The same applies to inserting and updating, so you should be able to issue one command which, for example, alters the discount rate from 5% to 10% on all items for which the stock level exceeds the weekly usage by a factor of ten.

This rule is important. For a start it significantly reduces the amount of code that you have to write in order to carry out complex processes. It also has important implications as soon as you start to use a system where the database engine is divorced from the front end. Why? Because the ability to perform multi-row changes to a table with a single command dramatically reduces the communication between the front and back ends. When the link is over a network or, indeed, the internet, this can speed up the whole process by an order of magnitude.

Physical data independence

● **Rule 8:** *Application programs and terminal activities remain logically unimpaired whenever any changes are made in either storage representations or access methods.*

Codd expands this rule by saying *'To handle this, the DBMS must support a clear, sharp boundary between the logical and semantic aspects on the one hand, and the physical and performance aspects of the base tables on the other; application programs must deal with the logical aspects only.'*

In practice this means that the logical interaction that the user has with the database ("I want to find all of the orders which are overdue for payment") should be divorced from the physical structure of the tables of data. Suppose that as a database expands, the database manager decides that an index is required on a particular table for performance reasons. This rule says that it should be possible for the index to be added without the users being aware that any change has been made. They (the users are the 'terminal activities' referred to in the rule) and any application programs should be able to work without any alteration after the index is in place. The only difference they should see is a reduced response time.

Logical data independence

● **Rule 9:** *Application programs and terminal activities remain logically unimpaired whenever information-preserving changes of any kind that theoretically permit unimpairment are made to the base tables.*

If this one sounds rather like Rule 8, that's because it is; these rules are often considered as a pair. As an example of what this one means, suppose that you have a table of CUSTOMERS that for performance reasons you want to split into two, CUST_USA and CUST_REST. This allows you to search more rapidly through the customers in the USA, which is good, but what happens to all your existing programs and users which/who are used to interacting with an all-embracing table called CUSTOMERS? This rule says that if a DBMS is to be considered a relational DBMS, it has to allow both applications and users to go on dealing with CUSTOMERS as if it hadn't been split. In practice this can be done by creating a view (or query) which combines the two new tables into a single entity with the original name.

Note that complete conformity with this rule depends on compliance with Rule 6, the view updating rule. That is the one that says that all views which are theoretically updatable are also updatable by the system. If Rule 6 isn't obeyed, then although we can create a view called CUSTOMER from CUST_USA and CUST_REST, the users will be unable to interact with the data it contains in the same way as before.

Rules 8 and 9 are included in the rule set to provide a high degree of flexibility. Codd describes them in order to split the logical interaction with the database away from the physical and base structuring as much as possible. In turn this allows the database manager to make changes to the underlying structure without upsetting the way the user works and without requiring application programs to be rewritten. As Codd says:

'The physical and logical independence rules permit data base designers for relational DBMS to make mistakes in their designs without the heavy penalties levied by nonrelational DBMS. This, in turn, means that it is much easier to get started with a relational DBMS because not nearly as much performance-oriented planning is needed prior to "blast-off".'

Integrity independence rule

- **Rule 10:** *Integrity constraints specific to a particular relational data base must be definable in a relational data sub-language and storable in the catalog, not in the application programs.*

A serious rule this one (of course, all rules are equally serious, some are just more 'equally serious' than others). It contains an important expansion:

> *'In addition to the two integrity rules (entity integrity and referential integrity) that apply to every relational database, there is a clear need to be able to specify additional integrity constraints reflecting either business policies or government policies.'*

After this rather oblique reference to referential and entity integrity as an integral part of relational databases, Codd then goes on to say:

> *'To be more specific, the following two integrity rules apply to every relational database:*
>
> *Entity integrity. No component of a primary key is allowed to have a null value.*
>
> *Referential integrity. For each distinct nonnull foreign key value in a relational database, there must exist a matching primary key value from the same domain.'*

Both referential and entity integrity are really important, not to say essential, parts of a relational database. Why Codd sees fit to introduce them as a mere addition to another rule is not at all clear. However, we have seen before that he has a tendency to include essential information as an expansion of a rule; another example is that no rule explicitly says that an RDBMS needs a data dictionary, though it is implicit in Rule 4.

Rule 10 says that referential and entity integrity rules must be capable of being stored in the system catalog rather than in the application programs. This is clearly essential. If such rules are stored only in the applications, it becomes easier for a user to accidentally (or maliciously) subvert that integrity.

However, this rule says more: it says that, in addition, an RDBMS needs to be able to store other integrity constraints and that we have to be able to store these in the catalog and also to define them in the data sub-language. What might these 'other' constraints be? If you are storing someone's date of birth (DOB) and the date of their entry into school (DOE), it is clearly reasonable to set up a rule stating the DOE must be greater than DOB. In fact, you might decide that DOE has to be greater than DOB + 4 years. In either case, you want this rule to be applied in all cases, without argument. Rule 10 says that you must be able to define such rules in the usual control language that you use and that you must also be able to store the rule in the data dictionary.

One of the reviewers asked "Doesn't this rule preclude the enforcement of constraints by forms?" The answer is "No". Codd is ensuring, by including this rule, that we have the ability to enforce rules at the table level if we so wish. He isn't saying that we have to do so.

Distribution independence

●   **Rule 11:** *A relational DBMS has distribution independence.*

Codd expands the rule as follows:

> *'By distribution independence I mean that the DBMS has a data sub-language that enables application programs and terminal activities to remain logically unimpaired:*
>
> *— when data distribution is first introduced (if the originally installed DBMS manages nondistributed data only);*
>
> *— when data is redistributed (if the DBMS manages distributed data).'*

One of the huge benefits of networking is that it allows multi-user access to a database; that is, the users can be distributed across the network. However, it is also possible to distribute the data across the same network. Thus you can have your EMPLOYEES table stored centrally at company headquarters and the CUSTOMER table held locally at branch level.

This rule says that even if the tables of data are moved around, your users shouldn't be aware of the change in location, neither should any applications that you have developed need to be rewritten. This has several consequences. For a start, you should be able to develop an application on a stand-alone PC and then migrate to a fully networked system employing distributed data without pain. It also means that you should be able to make changes easily to the distribution of the data. So, if the CEO suddenly decides that all data must be held centrally, that should be easy to implement.

Nonsubversion rule

● **Rule 12:** *If a relational system has a low-level (single-record-at-a-time) language, that low level cannot be used to subvert or bypass the integrity rules and constraints expressed in the higher level relational language (multiple-records-at-a-time).*

To put it another way, a user must not be allowed to go directly to a table and add, delete or alter records with the low-level language if such a change would be at odds with the higher level rules (such as referential integrity) which have been applied to the tables and are stored in the data dictionary.

You may remember, way back in Chapter 2, we talked about the distinction between the terms row and record. We said that at times it simply isn't clear which should be used; in which case you are free to use either. Here is a good case. Ted Codd uses the term record where many people might use row. If he can be relaxed about it, so can we.

Summary

So, those are Ted Codd's original rules for defining an RDBMS. As I said at the start, there is a fine line to be drawn between accuracy and verbosity and I have tried to tread it carefully. Nevertheless, it has taken a long time to cover all of the rules, so long that it may be difficult to see the 'take home message'. In addition, the order in which the rules appear is perhaps less than optimal. So, below, I have presented a set of even less exact definitions in what I consider to be a more reasonable order. They may help you to get the general overall flavor.

- Data must be stored only in tables (Rule 1).

- Each table must have a primary key and given the table name, column name and primary key value, it must be possible to identify unequivocally any piece of data in the database (Rule 2).

- The database must have a data dictionary which stores the metadata; that is, the data which describes the database itself. The data in the data dictionary must be stored in the same manner as in the main database, that is, in tables (Rule 4).

- Integrity rules, such as referential integrity, should be storable in the data dictionary (Rule 10).

- There must be a single language which allows the database to be manipulated (Rule 5).

- This language must allow multiple updates, inserts etc. to be performed with single commands (Rule 7).

- However, neither this language, nor any other, must be able to make changes to individual records which subvert the integrity rules stored in the data dictionary (Rule 12).

- Physical, logical and distribution changes to the database structure, such as the addition of an index, the splitting of a table, or the movement of a table onto another disk, should be transparent to the user (Rules 8, 9 and 11).

- Views (answer tables) must be updatable whenever possible (Rule 6).

- Nulls must be treated consistently (Rule 3).

As a final exercise, you might want to ask yourself, as Codd suggested all those years ago "Does my RDBMS really meet all of these rules?". If it doesn't, then it isn't really a Relational DBMS at all (Rule 0).

Chapter 25

Normalization

The tables shown in this chapter are not included on the web site since there is very little that you can do with them. Indeed, some of the tables are demonstrations of how not to construct a table.

A first look at normalization

Part of the attraction of using an RDBMS is that you can manage large complex chunks of data. This can have the advantage of unifying the data handling within your organization. For example, it means that all your customer names and addresses are stored once only and everyone within the company can access up-to-date information. The disadvantage of building complex collections of tables is that you need to be highly organized – you have to be careful to get the right data into the correct tables. If you get it wrong, you are likely to find that some queries are difficult or impossible to build and run. You might, for example, find it impossible to check for a correlation between the hours that your sales people spend on the road and their sales of a particular product. You will also find that you are storing multiple copies of the same information.

As I said in Chapter 12, there is an excellent rule of thumb that we can apply. It is so important I'll repeat it here.

As a general rule, you should identify the real world objects that you are trying to model with your database (Employees, Orders, Customers, Products etc.) and give each one its own table.

Take this table, for instance.

EMPLOYEES			
EmployeeID	**FirstName**	**LastName**	**DOB**
1	Sally	James	01/01/1985
2	Brian	Fish	02/04/1986
3	Fred	Gribbens	02/05/1985

It is clearly storing information about the employees in a company. All of the information in the table refers to the employee and not to any other object. It is a good, well structured table and easily seen as such because it's a very simple table. However, as tables become more complex they can reach a stage where it is more difficult to decide which fields should go into which tables. In other words, the rule of thumb is exactly that – a very useful general rule that works most of the time. It's not a set of precise rules that can be applied to all tables so it is comforting to know that there is also a more formal process to fall back on when you need it. That process is called Normalization and it is defined as a series of levels or 'forms' – First Normal Form (1NF), Second Normal Form (2NF) and so on. The first three normal forms are by far the most important, so we're going to look at these in detail.

One of the problems with normalization is that being a formal process, it has a collection of formal expressions/definitions that are associated with it. These terms provide an excellent short-hand for professional database designers when they are discussing tables in a large production database but, like all formal definitions, they can actually get in the way when you are initially learning the process. We don't want to bog you down in pages and pages of formal definitions while we're explaining normalization because that simply obscures what is, in truth, a relatively simple process. On the other hand, if we don't ultimately give you the formal definitions, we leave you without the necessary framework to talk to (and ultimately to become) a professional database designer. So, we're going to run through the first three normal forms in English. Then we'll go over the formal definitions expanding on the information as we do so ending with a final summary of normal forms 1 to 3 using the formal terminology.

First normal form (first level of normalization): 1NF

First normal form is essentially just a description of a basic table. Remember that a 'Table' (as defined in Chapter 3) has to have a primary key (see Chapter 14), so this requirement is not technically part of the definition of first normal form because it is assumed that any table we are considering for first normal form already has a primary key.

Given a table that has a primary key, we can say it is in first normal form if it doesn't have multiple columns holding the same kind of data. You've already seen tables that break this rule, and the disastrous effect that it has on the ability to retrieve data easily. You may remember that in Chapter 14 we looked at how we could store information about customers who place orders for multiple items. One of the solutions we discussed looked like this:

BAD-ORDERS-TABLE								
OrderNo	*EmployeeNo*	*CustomerNo*	**ItemNo1**	**ItemNo2**	**ItemNo3**	**ItemNo4**	**ItemNo5**
1	1	2	1	4			
2	4	1	3				
3	1	3	4	3	3	3	3
4	2	4	2	1	3		
5	3	2	3	2			
6	2	4	2	4			
7	2	2	1	2			

As you can see, this table uses multiple columns to represent items that we sell. In Chapter 14 we had other associated tables – EMPLOYEE, CUSTOMERS and ITEMS. Looking at ITEMS we can see that item number 3 is a Chair and 4 is a Table, so order number 3 is for a table and four chairs. The correct information is actually stored here but, for all of the reasons already discussed in that chapter, this is a very poor solution to the problem. This table is not in 1NF. How can we fix this? Easy, we split it up into two tables that don't contain multiple columns for item information – like this:

ORDERS		
OrderNo	*EmployeeNo*	*CustomerNo*
1	1	2
2	4	1
3	1	3
4	2	4
5	3	2
6	2	4
7	2	2

ORDER/ITEMS		
OrderNo	*ItemNo*	**NumberOfItems**
1	*1*	1
1	*4*	1
2	*3*	1
3	*3*	4
3	*4*	1
4	*1*	1
4	*2*	1
4	*3*	1
5	*2*	1
5	*3*	1
6	*2*	1
6	*4*	1
7	*1*	1

These two tables are in 1NF and the querying problems disappear. Easy.

Second normal form (second level of normalization): 2NF

To be in 2NF a table must already be in 1NF. That is, it must not have multiple columns containing the same kind of data.

Both second and third normal form are concerned with how the information in one column may depend on that in another column. This dependency is best illustrated by looking first at a well structured table.

CARS				
LicenseNo	**Make**	**Model**	**Year**	**Color**
CER 162 C	Triumph	Spitfire	1965	Green
EF 8972	Bentley	Mk. VI	1946	Black
YSK 114	Bentley	Mk. VI	1949	Red

The license number is a unique number issued by the government so EF 8972 refers to one and only one specific car. That means we can use LicenseNo as the primary key.

We are interested in the dependencies that may exist between the data in the different columns. For a start, do you think that color depends on the make of the vehicle? In other words, are all Bentleys black? Well, in practice, many of them are green but it isn't an obligatory color scheme and, in fact, the two in our sample are different colors. So, quite clearly, Color doesn't depend on Make. In the same way, for example, Year doesn't depend on Model because a particular model of car can be produced for several years.

So are there any dependencies here at all? Yes, all of the columns in the body of the table (in other words, those columns that aren't the primary key) are dependent on the primary key. After all, 'CER 162 C' refers to one and only one car. That car is a Triumph, it is a Spitfire, it was made in 1965 and it's green. This dependency holds true for all of the cars, so we can say that, for example, Color is dependent on LicenseNo, as are Make, Model and Year.

It turns out that this is an excellent way of defining a good table – all of the columns in the body of the table should be dependent on the primary key. In fact, 2NF and 3NF are simply concerned with identifying those tables where this isn't the case and fixing them.

So let's take a look at another table.

ORDER/ITEMS			
OrderNo	*ItemNo*	**NumberOfItems**	**OrderDate**
1	*1*	1	1/1/2006
1	*4*	1	1/1/2006
2	*3*	1	2/1/2006
3	*3*	4	4/1/2006
3	*4*	1	4/1/2006
4	*1*	1	5/1/2006
4	*2*	1	5/1/2006
4	*3*	1	5/1/2006
5	*2*	1	7/1/2006
5	*3*	1	7/1/2006
6	*2*	1	8/1/2006
6	*4*	1	8/1/2006
7	*1*	1	9/1/2006

This is very similar to the table we used above to store information about which items appear on which order. All I have added is a column to hold the date of the order.

OK, forget 2NF for a moment. What does your database instinct tell you about this table? Every time we add another item to the order, we need to repeat the date of the order itself. We can see that there is already repeated data in here and it's only going to get worse. Instinctively we know that the date of the order really belongs in a table that contains information about the order itself (the ORDERS table), so this is a badly designed table.

Now back to 2NF. What does it tell us about table design? It says that each of the columns in the body of the table should be dependent on the entire primary key. That means that they must not, for example, be dependent on just part of the primary key.

In this case the primary key of the table is composed of two columns – OrderNo and ItemNo. OrderDate doesn't depend on both of them together; it simply depends on OrderNo. That's only part of the primary key so this table is not in second normal form.

If this isn't immediately clear, think of a specific example. Take OrderNo 4. Every row in the table that has the value 4 in the OrderNo column must have the same date in the OrderDate column (in this case 5/1/2006). Why? Because OrderDate refers to the data on which the order was placed. If Order 4 had 20 different items in it, there would be 20 rows in this table for that order number and every one would have a date of 5/1/2006.

The point here is that in this simple table, common sense tells us that we need to move the OrderDate column to another table – 2NF tell us exactly the same thing only in a more formal way. As we build more and more complex tables, common sense becomes more difficult to apply but the 2NF rule remains exactly the same and remains easy to apply.

Third normal form (third level of normalization): 3NF

3NF simply carries on the good work started by 2NF. Remember that we are trying to achieve a table in which all of the columns in the body of the table are solely dependent on the entire primary key. 2NF ensures that we deal with any column that is dependent on part (not all) of the primary key. That is one kind of undesirable dependency, but there is another. Take a look at this table.

CARS						
LicenseNo	**Make**	**Country**	**PhoneNo**	**Model**	**Year**	**Color**
CER 162 C	Triumph	UK	01234 5678	Spitfire	1965	Green
EF 8972	Bentley	UK	04321 1234	Mk. VI	1946	Black
YSK 114	Bentley	UK	04321 1234	Mk. VI	1949	Red

The new columns, Country and PhoneNo refer to the location and contact details of the manufacturer of the vehicle. There is clearly a dependency between each of these new columns and Make. No matter how many different cars we enter into the table, every time we enter the word Bentley in the Make column, we will have to enter UK under County and 04321 1234 under PhoneNo.

Once again, what does your intuition tell you? Hopefully it says that we need to pull these columns out and put them into a separate table.

CARS				
LicenseNo	*ManufNo*	**Model**	**CC**	**Color**
CER 162 C	*1*	Spitfire	2500	Green
EF 8972	*2*	Mk. VI	6500	Black
YSK 114	*2*	Mk. VI	4500	Red

MANUFACTURERS			
ManufNo	**Make**	**Country**	**PhoneNo**
1	Triumph	UK	01234 5678
2	Bentley	UK	04321 1234

Correct. And that is exactly what 3NF tells us. It says, in order for a table to be in 3NF it has to first be in 1NF and 2NF and, in addition, there must be no dependencies between columns in the body of the table.

Summary so far

- First Normal Form (1NF)
  - Mainly concerned with basic table structure. Table must have a primary key and there must be no columns that store the same kind of data.
- Second Normal Form (2NF)
  - Table must already be in 1NF.
  - Concerned with the relationship between the columns in the primary key and those in the rest (the body) of the table.

- Each column in the body of the table must be dependent on the entire primary key. As in the example above, given a primary key that is composed of two or more columns, none of the columns in the body of the table must be dependent on part of the primary key.

- Third Normal Form (3NF)
  - Table must already be in 1NF and 2NF.
  - Concerned with the relationships within body of the table.
  - Columns in the body of the table must not be dependent upon each other.

Adding some definitions

As you can see, normalization is a very simple process. What we'll do now is to add some of the formal definitions for the terms below and, at the same time, add some more detail about the process of normalization.

- Atomic data
- Primary key
- Table body
- Keyed and non-keyed attributes
- Functional dependency
- Transitive dependency
- Lossless decomposition
- Requirement definition
- Modification anomalies – insert, update and delete

Atomic data

Atomic data is simply a formal way of saying that tables must not contain repeating information – either within or between columns.

BAD-ORDERS-TABLE			
OrderNo	EmployeeNo	CustomerNo	Items
1	1	2	1 4
2	4	1	3
3	1	3	4 3 3 3 3
4	2	4	2 1 3
5	3	2	3 2
6	2	4	2 4
7	2	2	1 2

In this example, CustomerNo contains atomic values, but Items doesn't; it contains what is called a 'repeating group'.

Of course, an obvious (and bad) way around this would be to use multiple columns to contain the repeating group.

BAD-ORDERS-TABLE							
OrderNo	EmployeeNo	CustomerNo	ItemNo1	ItemNo2	ItemNo3	ItemNo4	ItemNo5
1	1	2	1	4			
2	4	1	3				
3	1	3	4	3	3	3	3
4	2	4	2	1	3		
5	3	2	3	2			
6	2	4	2	4			
7	2	2	1	2			

Good try, but this is still considered non-atomic data.

As you will already have worked out, 1NF simply says that a table must contain only atomic data – there must be no repeating groups.

Primary keys, table body, keyed and non-keyed attributes

It is often useful, particularly in discussions about normalization, to be able to distinguish between the columns of the table that make up the primary key and the rest of the columns in the table. Columns that aren't primary keys form the body of the table.

You might wonder why foreign key columns don't figure in this description. It is because normalization is performed on each table in isolation and we aren't concerned with relationships between tables. Foreign key columns are simply treated as part of the body.

You can also use the rather formal term 'keyed attributes' to refer to the columns that make up the primary key ('attribute' being a formal term for column). The rest of the columns are then, of course, the non-keyed attributes. Or, as a third alternative, you can talk about keyed and non-keyed columns.

Functional dependency

We've already talked about dependency, and the formal term for the kind of dependency we have discussed is 'functional dependency'. In database terms we are concerned with the functional dependencies between columns. Functional dependency is very important because we need to understand it in order to be able to ensure that tables are in 2NF and 3NF. So let's look at another example.

ORDERS					
OrderNo	**ItemNo**	**EmployeeNo**	**CustomerNo**	**ItemName**	**Quantity**
121	*3*	*4*	1024	Nut	3
121	*4*	*4*	1024	Bolt	67
121	*8*	*4*	1024	Washer	3
122	*3*	*9*	176	Nut	9
122	*8*	*9*	176	Washer	9
123	*3*	*4*	234	Nut	345
123	*8*	*4*	234	Washer	345
124	*4*	*9*	321	Bolt	9

Order Number 121 was processed by Employee Number 4. Since each row in this table is recording information about a part of an order, we can have several rows for each order. (This is, incidentally, a badly designed table which my fingers itch to normalize but we are using it for illustrative purposes so I'll leave it alone.) If I tell you that in this particular company, only one employee is ever credited with any given order, you can now be sure that whenever you see the value 121 in the OrderNo column, you will find the value 4 in the EmployeeNo column. There is no doubt, no uncertainty.

Given that information we can say that, in this table:

● EmployeeNo is *functionally dependent* on OrderNo.

● OrderNo *functionally determines* EmployeeNo.

● OrderNo is the *determinant*.

It is important to note that the relationship is one way – we cannot say that OrderNo is functionally dependent on EmployeeNo. Why not? Well, if you look at the table and find the value 4 in EmployeeNo you cannot with certainty predict the value that will be found in OrderNo since in this case it could be 121 or 123.

Which columns are functionally dependent on the primary key (remembering that in this table the primary key is made up of two columns, OrderNo and ItemNo)?

Answer – all of them, since the primary key uniquely identifies each row.

Are any of the columns functionally dependent on *part* of the primary key?

Answer – yes. EmployeeNo and CustomerNo are both functionally dependent on OrderNo. In addition, ItemName is functionally dependent on ItemNo.

In fact, the only column that is solely functionally dependent on the entire primary key is Quantity.

As we have said above, you will find that the process of normalization involves attempting to remove various forms of functional dependency. However, it is worth stressing again that there is nothing wrong with functional dependencies as such. Indeed in a well designed table, every single column in the body of the table is functional dependent on the entire primary key, and not functionally dependent on any other column.

In essence, normalization is all about preserving the functional dependencies that work to our advantage while removing those that don't.

Transitive dependency

A relatively subtle one, this, but still useful. Consider this table.

CARS						
LicenseNo	**Make**	**Country**	**PhoneNo**	**Model**	**Year**	**Color**
CER 162 C	Triumph	UK	01234 5678	Spitfire	1965	Green
EF 8972	Bentley	UK	04321 1234	Mk. VI	1946	Black
YSK 114	Bentley	UK	04321 1234	Mk. VI	1949	Red

If you remember, the values in Country and PhoneNo refer to the company that made the vehicle.

LicenseNo is the primary key. The column Year (for example) is functionally dependent on LicenseNo because the car bearing that LicenseNo was really made in that year. Make is also functionally dependent on LicenseNo because there really is a unique car with that license number and it is a Triumph and only a Triumph. No question.

So far, so clear. In addition, it so happens that the company called Triumph was (and still is) based in the UK. So Country is also functionally dependent on LicenseNo but that dependency is dependent (if you'll pardon the expression) on Make because we have a chain of dependencies here. 'CER 162 C' is a Triumph and Triumph is based in the UK. So we can say that LicenseNo determines Make and Make, in turn, determines Country. In other words, the dependency of Country on LicenseNo is reliant on another dependency.

This type of indirect dependency is called a Transitive Dependency.

Why have we bothered to inflict this rather subtle distinction on you? Because it's useful. We told you earlier that a good table is one in which all of the columns are dependent on the entire primary key. That is true, but it is also a simplification because dependency can be either functional or transitive. And while it is true that Country is dependent on LicenseNo, that dependency is transitive. As soon as we realize that, we know that the Country column is going to have to move to a new table.

So we can now be more precise in our statement about what makes a good table. A good table is one where every column is non-transitively dependent on the primary key.

Incidentally, it is important to note that we aren't springing a whole new level of normalization on you here. When we looked at this table earlier in terms of 3NF we spotted the functional dependency between Make and Country. Since these two columns are in the body of the table, we knew immediately that they were going to be moved into another table in any case.

Also note that the term 'transitive dependency' is useful as shorthand if the two people involved in a conversation understand it. Imagine that you and I are discussing the table above. I say something like "Well, the Country column is fine in this table because it is dependent on the primary key."

You could say "True, it is dependent on LicenseNo. But that dependency is actually a result of the functionally dependency that exists between LicenseNo and Make, and then another between Make and Country. Make and Country are both in the body of the table. That means that there is a functional dependency between two columns which are in the body of the table, so the table fails 3NF. All of which means that you are wrong and the Country column must to be moved to another table."

Or, you could say "True, but that dependency is transitive via Make." Which is a killer argument and ends the discussion – the column will be moved to another table.

Lossless decomposition (and requirement definition)

During the process of normalization we often start with one table and end up with two (or more) because we identify some columns in the first table that shouldn't be there, so we move them into a second table. For example, as a demonstration of 3NF we took this table:

CARS						
LicenseNo	**Make**	**Country**	**PhoneNo**	**Model**	**Year**	**Color**
CER 162 C	Triumph	UK	01234 5678	Spitfire	1965	Green
EF 8972	Bentley	UK	04321 1234	Mk. VI	1946	Black
YSK 114	Bentley	UK	04321 1234	Mk. VI	1949	Red

and turned it into these two.

CARS				
LicenseNo	*ManufNo*	**Model**	**CC**	**Color**
CER 162 C	*1*	Spitfire	2500	Green
EF 8972	*2*	Mk. VI	6500	Black
YSK 114	*2*	Mk. VI	4500	Red

MANUFACTURERS			
ManufNo	**Make**	**Country**	**PhoneNo**
1	Triumph	UK	01234 5678
2	Bentley	UK	04321 1234

The process of breaking one table down into multiple tables is known as 'decomposition' because we are breaking something down into its components. If (as we very often do) we also preserve all of the information that was in the original table, we can also call the process 'lossless decomposition'. Lossless implies that the original table could be perfectly reconstructed (if need be) from the two tables.

Incidentally, some people will use the term 'projection' instead of decomposition. Essentially it means the same, it is just a rather more database specific word. See Chapter 28 for more information.

Consider this table:

STAFF				
EmployeeNo	**LastName**	**FirstName**	**Type**	**Pay**
4	Whitehorn	Mark	Sales Person	25000
5	Jones	Sally	Manager	40000
6	Williams	Henry	Sales Person	25000
7	Johnson	Margaret	Sales Person	25000
9	Smith	Fred	Manager	40000
12	Smith	Sarah	Manager	40000
15	Johnson	Sally	Sales Person	25000
17	Romanus	Eithi	Manager	40000

The data implies that all sales people are paid the same salary and that, while managers are better paid, they also, as a group, are all paid the same. There appears to be a functional dependency between Type and Pay. But is this really a rule or are there exceptions? It matters because if there is a functional dependency this table is not in 3NF; if there isn't, then it is in 3NF.

In other words, the data doesn't tell us the whole story: we need to talk to the company and find out 'what the data means' in this case.

Some databases are well designed from the outset. If this is the case, then all of these questions will have been resolved before the tables were constructed and the information will be contained in some form of 'Requirement Definition' which, as the name suggests, formally describes the requirements that the database has to meet.

Sadly, not every single database that you will meet in your career as a database designer will have a formal requirement definition. Indeed, though it pains me to mention it, you may come across the odd requirement definition that contains one or more tiny flaws.

In these cases, you will have to return to the people for whom the database is being built (or modified) and seek elucidation.

However, the general point is crucial: determining the structure of the data within a database (in other words, deciding which tables you need and which data will go into which tables) is impossible without obtaining information from the people for whom it is being built.

In fact, this brings us to another point. It is sometimes said that, since normalization is a purely mechanical process, surely we could write software to do it for us. Indeed, some people have written such software; for example,

Access has a Table Analyzer Wizard that does essentially this. Such software can be useful, but can never be guaranteed to do a perfect job. The problem is two-fold. For a start, given only a sample of the data, you can never be sure that the functional dependencies have been correctly deduced. For example, in the table above we might, by chance, have 100 rows in which the pay for each job was always identical. The software would then deduce a functional dependency that a conversation with the Human Resources manager would deny. As humans, you and I can have that conversation with the HR manager, the software can't. In addition, suppose that you saw this table:

STAFF				
EmployeeNo	**LastName**	**FirstName**	**Type**	**Pay**
4	Whitehorn	Mark	Sales Pirson	27500
5	Jones	Sally	Manager	40000
6	Williams	Henry	Sales Person	25000
7	Johnson	Margaret	Sales Person	25000
9	Smith	Fred	Manager	40000
12	Smith	Sarah	Manager	40000
15	Johnson	Sally	Sales Person	25000
17	Romanus	Eithi	Manager	40000

The difference is in the first row – a Sales Pirson (sic) is receiving a salary of 27500. The software would see three job types, each example of each job type always receives the same salary, so it would deduce a functional dependency. You and I would see a spelling mistake and an exception that suggested that no functional dependency existed.

Also remember that, as humans, we absorb a great deal of information and meaning without even noticing. Take a look at this table:

X1				
AAA1	**AAA2**	**AAA3**	**AAA4**	**AAA5**
Sdfg	QAA	S	43	V2
Njytty	DFS	A	SD	40000
Gho	SWA	B	42	V
Vhk	DCF	M	42	V
Boghhok	HYU	F	SD	40000
Herrjhlling	FCD	J	SD	40000
Gfhjk	GW	A	42	V
Hghjj	JNM	P	SD	40000

Unless you speak fluent Venusian, it takes considerably more effort to spot the potential functional dependencies in this table than in the one above, despite the fact that they have exactly the same structure in terms of columns, rows and dependencies. You and I would make an assumption that, for example, a column called LastName is not a candidate key because, even if we don't see any duplicates, we expect them to arise eventually. We cannot say the same for a column called AAA3.

Unless the normalizing software has quite extensive semantic capabilities, it can't deduce information about the meaning of the data. So it would see these two tables as essentially equivalent in a way that we never do because we make deductions from the meaning of the information that we see.

The bottom line is that deciding whether functional dependencies really exist requires common sense, an understanding of the business and often quite extensive dialogue with the potential users of the system that you are designing.

Modification anomalies – insert, update and delete

Tables that have not been normalized suffer from a number of problems; that's why we normalize them. The problems from which they suffer can be referred to as 'modification anomalies'. There are three types of modification anomaly that are possible – update, insert and delete. These are easiest to describe as examples, so we'll start with a table that is in dire need of normalization.

CARS						
LicenseNo	**Make**	**Country**	**PhoneNo**	**Model**	**Year**	**Color**
CER 162 C	Triumph	UK	01234 5678	Spitfire	1965	Green
EF 8972	Bentley	UK	04321 1234	Mk. VI	1946	Black
YSK 114	Bentley	UK	04321 1234	Mk. VI	1949	Red

1. Imagine that this table has, let's say, 2,000 rows rather than just three and that 50 of the cars are Bentleys (which would make it a fabulous car collection). If Bentley (the company) suddenly decides to change its telephone number, we will have to update 50 rows instead of just one. We are trying to change one piece of data but we have to alter 50 rows. This is known as an update anomaly.

2. Suppose that we don't have a Ford in our collection. We do, however, have the telephone number for Ford and we want to store it. We now have a prob-

lem because we cannot insert a complete row into this table, we can only insert a partial row. And, if we did that, what would we insert as the primary key value? This is an example of an insertion anomaly.

3. If we only have one Triumph in the collection and we sell it, we have to delete the row for that car. However, this means we will also delete the phone number for Triumph which we may not wish to do. This is an example of a deletion anomaly.

If we normalize these tables:

CARS				
LicenseNo	*ManufNo*	**Model**	**CC**	**Color**
CER 162 C	*1*	Spitfire	2500	Green
EF 8972	*2*	Mk. VI	6500	Black
YSK 114	*2*	Mk. VI	4500	Red

MANUFACTURERS			
ManufNo	**Make**	**Country**	**PhoneNo**
1	Triumph	UK	01234 5678
2	Bentley	UK	04321 1234

all three classes of modification anomaly disappear.

Summary (again)

These more formal definitions are useful and, having covered them, we can now make use of them in redefining the first three normal forms.

- First Normal Form (1NF)
    - Mainly concerned with basic table structure.
    - Table must have a primary key and all of the data must be atomic.
- Second Normal Form (2NF)
    - Table must already be in 1NF.
    - Concerned with the relationship between the keyed and non-keyed columns.
    - Every non-keyed column must be functionally dependent on the entire primary key.

- Third Normal Form (3NF)
  - Table must already be in 1NF and 2NF.
  - Concerned with the relationships between non-keyed columns.
  - There must be no functional dependencies between non-keyed columns.

Chapter 26

More about normalization

The only tables from this chapter that you might find useful are the READINGS tables.
They are included in case you want to play around with the SQL statements.

Higher normal forms

It turns out to also be possible to describe normalization in two different ways.

A – you can assume that you know very little about the tables you are normalizing. For example, you can assume that you don't even know which column(s) will form the primary key. In one sense this is the best way to describe normalization because the description then covers those rare cases where you don't know that information. The down side of describing normalization in this way is that the description becomes much more complex.

B – you can assume that you do, in fact, know the primary key of each table, in which case the descriptions become much simpler.

As you will have guessed by now, we have taken the easy route and assumed that we are talking about real tables that have clearly identifiable primary keys. True, this has made life easier for us (so perhaps we were just being lazy) but it has also made it easier for you because the explanations are much more understandable. In addition, in the real world, we don't really come across tables where we can't identify the primary key, so we think the way we have explained it is genuinely more useful.

However, if you want to know the much more detailed and formal definitions of normalization we would recommend *"An Introduction to Database Systems"* by C.J. Date, published by Addison Wesley ISBN: 0321197844.

Not only does Date cover the subject in great depth, he also covers some of the higher levels of normalization:

- BCNF (Boyce-Codd Normal Form) which is a reinforcement of 3NF

- Fourth normal form (MVD: MultiValued Dependencies)

- Fifth normal form (PJ/NF: Project-Join/Normal Form) also known as (Projection Join/Normal Form)

- DK/NF (Domain Key/Normal Form)

What are these all about? Well, it is possible to construct tables which are in third normal form yet which still have modification anomalies that can be removed by lossless decomposition. Normalization is all about making the database usable so at first sight it seems only reasonable to tell you that you must normalize all databases to DK/NF and to show you how to do it.

However, this is supposed to be a practical book and in practice very few people need to think about normalizing above third normal form. If this sounds unlikely, spend a couple of minutes trying to design a table that is in third normal form and yet still has modification anomalies.

Perhaps you can, but I found it difficult the first time I tried. The point I'm trying to make is that tables which are in third normal form and which still have modification anomalies are very rare. In fact, they are usually counter-intuitive; in other words, people usually never even think of building them. This means that most tables that are in third normal form are also in the four higher levels of normal form mentioned above.

After due consideration I think we'll stop here. If you are trying to get a database built and you are reading this chapter to ensure that you eliminate most of the problems that are realistically going to crop up in your database, you already know enough.

An example

Of course, it is grossly unfair to ask you to try and think of a table that is in third normal form and yet has modification anomalies and then not show you one. If you couldn't come up with one, you now wouldn't be able to sleep at night. So, just for amusement (and to illustrate why such tables are contrived), consider this.

Suppose we need to store information about the items that we manufacture in a factory. Each item can be composed of one or more material, and each has to be subjected to one or more 'treatments' after assembly.

INVENTORY		
ItemNo	**Material**	**Treatment**
25	Steel	Warming
25	Rubber	Warming
27	Steel	Pressure test
27	Paper	Oil pre-soak
27	Steel	Oil pre-soak
27	Paper	Pressure test
35	Brass	Pressure test
35	Brass	Flow test
39	Steel	Heating
40	Steel	Heating

You can run through the definitions and you should find that the table is in third normal form.

It has no repeating columns, so it is in first normal form. Then you'll notice that all three columns are needed to form the primary key. Second normal form is all about functional dependencies from the body of the table to the primary key. This table has no body, so the table has to be in second normal form. Third normal form is about dependencies within the body of the table. Again, since there is no body here, the table must also be in third normal form.

Nevertheless, it has modification anomalies. You will notice that item 27 has four rows in this table. This is because it is made of two materials and has two treatments. We need at least two rows to store this information.

INVENTORY		
ItemNo	**Material**	**Treatment**
27	Paper	Oil pre-soak
27	Steel	Pressure test

However, using only two rows is misleading since it implies that a relationship exists between the material and the treatment. In fact this is not true: item 27 is not being pressure tested because it is made of steel.

Tempting as it might be, it is also false to assume that we are oil pre-soaking the component because it contains paper. We may well have other paper components, such as user manuals, which it would be highly inappropriate to pre-soak in oil. We are pre-soaking this item in oil because it is a filter; in other words, there is no direct relation-

ship between treatment and material.

In order to make it clear that there isn't a relationship between material and treatment, we need to duplicate the rows as shown in the original table. This in turn leaves us with an update anomaly. If we want to add another treatment to, say, Item 27, we will have to add two more rows.

You see what I mean about contrived. I really don't think that many people would have built the initial table in the first place. To resolve the problem (and to create the structure that I think most people would intuitively have used in the first place) we can indulge in a little lossless decomposition to produce:

ITEM-MATERIAL	
ItemNo	**Material**
25	**Steel**
25	**Rubber**
27	**Steel**
27	**Paper**
35	**Brass**
39	**Steel**
40	**Steel**

ITEM-TREATMENT	
ItemNo	**Treatment**
25	**Warming**
27	**Pressure test**
27	**Oil pre-soak**
35	**Pressure test**
35	**Flow test**
39	**Heating**
40	**Heating**

Normalization doesn't automatically remove all redundancy

I said above that one of the aims of normalization was to remove redundant information – and it is. However, it is worth stressing that normalization doesn't *guarantee* to remove all redundancy, it guarantees to remove only that redundancy which can be removed by lossless decomposition. Therefore, it is possible to normalize a table and still have redundancy, and hence update anomalies, lurking in the tables.

To illustrate this, consider a table which stores information about the readings taken from electricity meters. Let's assume that each meter is numbered and the same meter is never read more than once on the same day. A sensible table structure might be:

READINGS		
MeterNo	**Date**	**Reading**
1	18 May 2001	20
1	11 Nov 2001	91
1	12 Apr 2002	175
1	21 May 2002	214
1	01 Jul 2002	230
1	21 Nov 2002	270
1	12 Dec 2002	290
1	01 Apr 2003	324
2	18 May 2001	619
2	17 Sep 2001	712
2	15 Mar 2002	814
2	21 May 2002	913
2	17 Sep 2002	1023
3	19 May 2001	20612
3	11 Nov 2001	21112
3	15 Mar 2002	21143
3	21 May 2002	21223
3	17 Sep 2002	21456
3	21 Mar 2003	22343

with MeterNo and Date combining to form the primary key.

However, this table doesn't show, for example, how much electricity has been used between each reading.

The obvious solution is to run a query to produce an answer table like this:

MeterNo	Date	CurrentReading	PreviousReading	UnitsUsed
1	11 Nov 2001	91	20	71
1	12 Apr 2002	175	91	84
1	21 May 2002	214	175	39
1	01 Jul 2002	230	214	16
1	21 Nov 2002	270	230	40
1	12 Dec 2002	290	270	20
1	01 Apr 2003	324	290	34
2	17 Sep 2001	712	619	93
2	15 Mar 2002	814	712	102
2	21 May 2002	913	814	99
2	17 Sep 2002	1023	913	110
3	11 Nov 2001	21112	20612	500
3	15 Mar 2002	21143	21112	31
3	21 May 2002	21223	21143	80
3	17 Sep 2002	21456	21223	233
3	21 Mar 2003	22343	21456	887

The problem is this query can take a long time to run if there is a reasonable number of rows in the table. For example, given 550 rows, the following SQL statement took 55 seconds to run (on a test machine which is, by today's standards, slow but the figure is still useful for comparative purposes).

SOLUTION1

SELECT READINGS.MeterNo, READINGS.Date, READINGS.Reading AS CurrentReading, Max(READINGS_1.Reading) AS PreviousReading, READINGS.Reading-Max(READINGS_1.Reading) AS UnitsUsed

FROM READINGS, READINGS AS READINGS_1

WHERE (((READINGS.MeterNo)=[READINGS_1].[MeterNo]) AND ((READINGS.Reading)>[READINGS_1].[Reading]))

GROUP BY READINGS.MeterNo, READINGS.Date, READINGS.Reading;

See Chapter 29 for more information about SQL.

The problem is that the query has to find, in effect, the row that corresponds to the *previous* reading for the specific meter. It is this notion of some type of interconnection between the rows which makes the query tortuous.

One tempting solution is to store a reference to the previous reading in the base table like this:

READINGS2				
ReadingNo	**MeterNo**	**Date**	**Reading**	*PreviousReadingNo*
1	1	18 May 2001	20	
2	1	11 Nov 2001	91	*1*
3	1	12 Apr 2002	175	*2*
4	1	21 May 2002	214	*3*
5	1	01 Jul 2002	230	*4*
6	1	21 Nov 2002	270	*5*
7	1	12 Dec 2002	290	*6*
8	1	01 Apr 2003	324	*7*
9	2	18 May 2001	619	
10	2	17 Sep 2001	712	*9*
11	2	15 Mar 2002	814	*10*
12	2	21 May 2002	913	*11*
13	2	17 Sep 2002	1023	*12*
14	3	19 May 2001	20612	
15	3	11 Nov 2001	21112	*14*
16	3	15 Mar 2002	21143	*15*
17	3	21 May 2002	21223	*16*
18	3	17 Sep 2002	21456	*17*
19	3	21 Mar 2003	22343	*18*

Queries which run against this, for example:

```
SOLUTION2

SELECT DISTINCT READINGS2.MeterNo, READINGS2.Date, READINGS2.Reading AS
CurrentReading, READINGS2_1.Reading AS PreviousReading,
[READINGS2].[Reading]-[READINGS2_1].[Reading] AS UnitsUsed

FROM READINGS2 INNER JOIN READINGS2 AS READINGS2_1 ON READ-
INGS2.PreviousReadingNo = READINGS2_1.ReadingNo

WHERE ((([READINGS2].[Reading]-[READINGS2_1].[Reading]) Is Not Null))

ORDER BY READINGS2.MeterNo, READINGS2.Date;
```

produce exactly the same answer table as shown above but are very much faster to run when used with large sets of data (less than two seconds on the same machine).

We could even use a table like this:

READINGS3			
MeterNo	**Date**	**CurrentReading**	**PreviousReading**
1	18 May 2001	20	
1	11 Nov 2001	91	20
1	12 Apr 2002	175	91
1	21 May 2002	214	175
1	01 Jul 2002	230	214
1	21 Nov 2002	270	230
1	12 Dec 2002	290	270
1	01 Apr 2003	324	290
2	18 May 2001	619	
2	17 Sep 2001	712	619
2	15 Mar 2002	814	712
2	21 May 2002	913	814
2	17 Sep 2002	1023	913
3	19 May 2001	20612	
3	11 Nov 2001	21112	20612
3	15 Mar 2002	21143	21112
3	21 May 2002	21223	21143
3	17 Sep 2002	21456	21223
3	21 Mar 2003	22343	21456

whereupon the SQL:

```
SOLUTION3
SELECT DISTINCT READINGS3.MeterNo, READINGS3.Date, READ-
INGS3.CurrentReading,
READINGS3.PreviousReading, CurrentReading-PreviousReading AS UnitsUsed
FROM READINGS3
WHERE (((CurrentReading-PreviousReading) Is Not Null));
```

becomes trivial and very rapid indeed.

However – and this is the crucial point – the second and third base tables shown (READINGS2 and READINGS3) are very odd. Despite being normalized to any and all reasonable levels, both still suffer from update and delete anomalies. In addition READINGS3 contains redundant data.

For example, suppose that we discover that Meter No 1 was also read on 01 Feb 2003 and yielded a reading of 300. We can add a record to READINGS2 like this:

ReadingNo	MeterNo	Date	Reading	PreviousReadingNo
1	1	18 May 2001	20	
2	1	11 Nov 2001	91	1
3	1	12 Apr 2002	175	2
4	1	21 May 2002	214	3
5	1	01 Jul 2002	230	4
6	1	21 Nov 2002	270	5
7	1	12 Dec 2002	290	6
8	1	01 Apr 2003	324	7
9	2	18 May 2001	619	
10	2	17 Sep 2001	712	9
11	2	15 Mar 2002	814	10
12	2	21 May 2002	913	11
13	2	17 Sep 2002	1023	12
14	3	19 May 2001	20612	
15	3	11 Nov 2001	21112	14
16	3	15 Mar 2002	21143	15
17	3	21 May 2002	21223	16
18	3	17 Sep 2002	21456	17
19	3	21 Mar 2003	22343	18
20	1	01 Feb 2003	300	7

The fact that the row is 'out of sequence' (at least, in terms of dates) is of no consequence whatsoever. However, the addition of this latest record has rendered the pointer in the record with ReadingNo = 8 incorrect. The value that it has in PreviousReading now points to the wrong row. Unless we locate the errant record and correct it, the table now has an internal inconsistency. It should be reasonably apparent that deleting records introduces the same sort of problem.

This is a major problem. Simple updates and/or deletions to/of one record can cause anomalies in other records. In order to *ensure* internal data integrity, some or all of the table has to be checked for integrity after every update. This is clearly not impossible to do but it makes extra work for the developer and may well slow the database down, particularly in a multi-user environment.

In addition, even if the developer's work is perfect, later maintenance work on the database may unknowingly circumvent the checks and lead to a loss of integrity.

It is important to realize that normalization doesn't, on its own, remove all update and deletion anomalies or even all redundant data.

I became aware of this problem via the database column that I write for *Personal Computer World*. (In fact, readers of that magazine provided the solutions shown.) I became intrigued by this idea of normalization being an imperfect tool and when I had the privilege of interviewing Chris Date, I showed him the tables and asked him to discuss them. His answer is enlightening, not just about normalization but about the database design process as a whole.

Chris Date: *"Most of database design is still an art not a science; it's very subjective, precisely because it is not, mostly, very scientific. There is some science – normalization is a science – but 90% of it is gut feel.*

[When] we talk about normalization [we can ask ourselves] 'What is the effect of normalization?' Well, basically it's to reduce redundancy but in order to consider that question carefully we have to have a careful definition of what redundancy is, but without getting into such a careful definition (because I don't think I could give you one) I will simply point out that normalization per se does not in general eliminate all redundancy.

What normalization does is – normalization to the ultimate normal form – it gets you to a position that guarantees that you will not have any anomalies, update anomalies, that can be removed by taking projections [that is, by splitting the table up into subtables]. Here it is; it doesn't say it'll get rid of all anomalies, it just says get rid of anomalies that can be removed by taking projections. So yes, you can have redundancy and normalization doesn't help with this question. Normalization is the one tiny piece of science we have but it is not enough – there are all kinds of other questions – is this (here he indicated READINGS2) *a good design, a bad design? I don't know because it is subjective – there is no science there. The only sort of working definition of redundancy you can have is if somehow you can make something smaller, then you have redundancy. My gut feel is that it's a bad design and I can't quantify or qualify that really."*

Summary

Where does all of this leave the process of normalization? Is it really a useful process?

Absolutely. Failure to use normalized tables brings the threat of reduced data integrity. It also may well result in a situation in which certain questions become impossible to ask of a database. Or rather, you are welcome to ask the question but you will not be able to generate a correct answer. So, normalization is very important.

Does this mean that professional database developers spend hours poring over their tables, ferreting out functional dependencies?

No, but once you get used to building databases you should find that you don't either. Most developers, either consciously or unconsciously, apply the general rule of thumb described at the start of this chapter. In addition, as people get used to building tables, redundant data begins to stick out like a sore thumb and they split it out into a separate table as a matter of course. The combined effect is that good developers build tables that do not contain redundant data and do not have modification anomalies. Which is, after all, what normalization is all about.

Is the terminology really useful? Absolutely, as long as you use it as an aid to communication and not, as I have sadly heard it used, to impress non-database people over coffee. "Guess what I found this morning? A table in Simpson's database with a non-key attribute transitively dependent on the primary key! Of course I had to give him a written warning."

Chapter 27

The system tables

You design tables, you give the tables columns, you name the columns, you create joins between tables, you build queries etc. Have you ever stopped to wonder where that information is stored? Where does the database store the information about which tables have which columns, which tables are joined and so on?

In a relational database, this information, according to Codd (see Chapter 24) must be stored in a 'data dictionary'.

A 'data dictionary', also known as a 'system catalog', is a centralized store of information about the database. It contains information about the tables – their number, names, the columns they contain, data types, primary keys, indexes, the joins which have been established between those tables (foreign keys), referential integrity, cascade update, cascade delete etc. This information, stored in the data dictionary, is called the 'metadata'.

The next question is "In what way should the data dictionary store the metadata?". In Codd's view, the answer is quite simple. Tables are where data is stored, so when we need to store data about the actual database itself that data has to be stored in tables. It sounds a little recursive but it works well in practice.

The idea of storing all of this information in tables is to provide consistency. No matter what information you need from, or about, a database, you will find it in the same format, i.e. in tables. Given that these tables store system information, yet another name for them is the 'system tables'.

Microsoft Access conforms to this model, though in normal use the data dictionary tables are hidden because they can be dangerous in inexperienced hands. However, it is interesting (and educational) to play with these tables and it's perfectly safe to do so provided you make a copy of the entire database and put it somewhere safe first. If you don't take heed of this warning, you have only yourself to blame if your database goes up in a puff of pink smoke.

If you do wish to see these tables (in your copy database), click on Tools, Options, View and choose System Objects. The dictionary tables will then appear amongst those you're used to seeing in the normal list of tables. They all start with the letters MSys which makes them easy to spot. There are several of them; for instance, there are separate tables for relationships, queries and objects, and these can be opened and viewed in the normal way. Certain others, MSysACEs, for example, can only be viewed or modified if you change the security permissions to allow you to do so. Now I'm *not* suggesting that you do modify the structure, but…

To change permissions, first have a look at how the permissions are set for one of the tables you can access. Click on Tools, Security, User and Group Permissions and note the settings. Then do the same for a table that you can't access and make the settings identical.

One of the major functions of a true data dictionary is to enforce the constraints placed upon the database by the designer, such as referential integrity and cascade delete. In the early days of the PC, none of the 'relational' DBMSs offered a true data dictionary but for two reasons this wasn't a major concern. Firstly, the early PCs were very slow and incapable of manipulating large, complex, multi-table sets of data. Instead, they tended to be used for fairly simple, single-table work (address lists, for example) so the deficiencies in the DBMS didn't show up as much as they might have done. Secondly, few PCs were running truly mission-critical systems, so if the data became a little 'damaged', who really cared? (Well, of course, the companies involved cared very much but the software world which sold the DBMSs didn't seem overly concerned.)

So, the early PC-based RDBMSs passed responsibility for this level of control to the programmer. This meant that writing a totally secure database was perfectly possible in, say, dBASE. The snag was that you had to be a good programmer; it took a great deal of effort and you had to be very familiar with the relational model. In addition, there was no centralized area where the relationships could be found and examined, so maintenance was difficult. If you suspected a join was being incorrectly supported, you had to hunt through, and understand, all of the relevant code to find the area which was compromising the data.

As PC-based RDBMSs have grown up and come of age, there is now a strong need for a data dictionary. Access does maintain a data dictionary and, as a result, doesn't inflict this extra workload on the developer and, as I said in Chapter 24, most client-server RDBMSs maintain a data dictionary.

Chapter 28

More on queries: data manipulation

Data manipulation is a vital part of the relational model. After all, there is little point in storing data correctly, safely and securely if that is all you ever do with it. Stored data has no value if you cannot question it and extract it in some way for humans to examine. So if you want to know more about databases, you will probably want to know about querying more than any other part.

In turn, you may want to know about SQL which is covered in the next chapter. SQL is based upon the use of 'relational operators' which is what this chapter is all about. You do *not* need to read *this* chapter in order to understand the one on SQL; indeed you can get through the whole of the rest of your life without reading this chapter. The only reason for reading it is that occasionally you will hear people in the database world referring to 'Projection', 'Union' etc. When you want to know what they are talking about, read this chapter. It won't change your life (unlike the one on SQL which is full of genuinely useful information) but it will allow you to understand what other people are talking about.

Relational operators

Most of us are familiar with the standard algebraic operators (+, -, x and /) which signify addition, subtraction, multiplication and division. We use these operators almost without thinking to manipulate numerical values or variables that represent values.

Thus if we know that A=5, B=6 and C=10 and that D=A+(Bx(C/A)) we can calculate that D=5+(6x(10/5))=5+(6x2)=5+12=17.

In a database, we store the data in tables (also known as relations) and the relational model provides a set of operators (known, therefore, as relational operators) with which we can manipulate tables (that is to say, relations). The discerning, sensitive reader will have noticed that I am showing a slight tendency to slip into 'database speak' at this point. In fact, since the very term 'relational operators' includes the word 'relational', the temptation to write this chapter using the more correct terms – relation, tuple, attribute etc. – was strong. I admit I was tempted. On balance I finally resisted, preferring consistency within the book. However, it is worth noting before we start that tables are relations and relations are sets of rows.

Also worth noting is that in general RDBMSs do not expect (or even allow) you to perform relational algebra directly upon tables of data. These operators are simply the building blocks from which operations like queries are built up by the RDBMS.

In order to demonstrate these operators we need a sample table or three:

EMPLOYEES

EmployeeNo	FirstName	LastName	DateOfBirth	DateEmployed
1	Bilda	Groves	12 Apr 1966	01 May 1999
2	John	Greeves	21 Mar 1977	01 Jan 2000
3	Sally	Smith	01 May 1977	01 Apr 2002

SALES

SaleNo	EmployeeNo	Customer	Item	Supplier	Amount
1	1	Simpson	Sofa	Harrison	$235.67
2	1	Johnson	Chair	Harrison	$453.78
3	2	Smith	Stool	Ford	$82.78
4	2	Jones	Suite	Harrison	$3,421.00
5	3	Smith	Sofa	Harrison	$235.67
6	1	Simpson	Sofa	Harrison	$235.67
7	1	Jones	Bed	Ford	$453.00

SALES2

SaleNo	EmployeeNo	Customer	Item	Supplier	Amount
3	2	Smith	Stool	Ford	$82.78
5	3	Smith	Sofa	Harrison	$235.67
213	3	Williams	Suite	Harrison	$3,421.00
216	2	McGreggor	Bed	Ford	$453.00
217	1	Williams	Sofa	Harrison	$235.67
218	3	Aitken	Sofa	Harrison	$235.67
225	2	Aitken	Chair	Harrison	$453.78

In 1972 Ted Codd proposed a set of eight relational operators, as follows:

- Restrict (also known as 'Select', but not the same SELECT as found in SQL)
- Project
- Union
- Difference
- Intersection
- Product
- Join
- Divide

Other operators are possible but these are by far the most commonly used. We'll look at each of them in turn.

Five of these relational operators (Restrict, Project, Product, Union and Difference) are primitive. That means that they are 'formally undefined'. Given these five we can define Intersection, Join and Divide.

Restrict (Select)

Restrict simply extracts rows from a table. Thus if we perform a restriction on the table SALES where Customer = 'Simpson', the result would be:

ANSWER					
SaleNo	**EmployeeNo**	**Customer**	**Item**	**Supplier**	**Amount**
1	1	Simpson	Sofa	Harrison	$ 235.67
6	1	Simpson	Sofa	Harrison	$ 235.67

Project

Projection selects zero or more columns from a table and generates a new table that contains all of the rows and only the selected columns. Thus if we project EMPLOYEES on FirstName and LastName the result is:

ANSWER	
FirstName	**LastName**
Bilda	Groves
John	Greeves
Sally	Smith

This seems straightforward; however, if we project SALES on EmployeeNo and Customer the result is:

SALES	
EmployeeNo	**Customer**
1	Johnson
1	Jones
1	Simpson
2	Jones
2	Smith
3	Smith

Despite the fact that SALES has seven rows, the answer table has only six. This is because one of them:

1	Simpson

would be duplicated in the answer table and tables are not permitted to contain duplicated rows.

If we projected SALES on SaleNo, EmployeeNo and Customer then the answer table will contain seven rows because in the original table the values in SalesNo are unique.

ANSWER		
SaleNo	**EmployeeNo**	**Customer**
1	1	Simpson
2	1	Johnson
3	2	Smith
4	2	Jones
5	3	Smith
6	1	Simpson
7	1	Jones

Union

Union creates a new table by adding the rows in one table to another. Clearly, for this to work well, it is essential that the tables have the same structure. The union of tables SALES and EMPLOYEES is unimaginable because the two tables are very different in structure. In order for tables to be 'union compatible', they must have the same number of columns and each of the column pairs have to draw their values from the same domains (see Chapter 30 on domains for more details). The tables SALES and SALES2 are 'union compatible' and the result would be this:

ANSWER					
SaleNo	**EmployeeNo**	**Customer**	**Item**	**Supplier**	**Amount**
1	1	Simpson	Sofa	Harrison	$235.67
2	1	Johnson	Chair	Harrison	$453.78
3	2	Smith	Stool	Ford	$82.78
4	2	Jones	Suite	Harrison	$3,421.00
5	3	Smith	Sofa	Harrison	$235.67
6	1	Simpson	Sofa	Harrison	$235.67
7	1	Jones	Bed	Ford	$453.00
213	5	Williams	Suite	Harrison	$3,421.00
216	2	McGreggor	Bed	Ford	$453.00
217	1	Williams	Sofa	Harrison	$235.67
218	4	Aitken	Sofa	Harrison	$235.67
225	4	Aitken	Chair	Harrison	$453.78

Note that two rows:

SaleNo	**EmployeeNo**	**Customer**	**Item**	**Supplier**	**Amount**
3	2	Smith	Stool	Ford	$82.78
5	3	Smith	Sofa	Harrison	$235.67

were shared by the two tables but have appeared only once each in the ANSWER table because duplicate rows are eliminated. Note also that the order in which rows appear as the result of a union is unimportant.

Difference

The difference of two tables is a third table which contains the rows which appear in the first but *not* in the second. The tables concerned must be union compatible. Thus the difference of SALES and SALES2 is:

ANSWER					
SaleNo	**EmployeeNo**	**Customer**	**Item**	**Supplier**	**Amount**
1	1	Simpson	Sofa	Harrison	$ 235.67
2	1	Johnson	Chair	Harrison	$ 453.78
4	2	Jones	Suite	Harrison	$3,421.00
6	1	Simpson	Sofa	Harrison	$ 235.67
7	1	Jones	Bed	Ford	$ 453.00

Note that, unlike Union, the order of the tables is vital. Thus the difference of SALES2 and SALES is not the same:

ANSWER					
SaleNo	**EmployeeNo**	**Customer**	**Item**	**Supplier**	**Amount**
213	3	Williams	Suite	Harrison	$3421.00
216	2	McGreggor	Bed	Ford	$ 453.00
217	1	Williams	Sofa	Harrison	$ 235.67
218	3	Aitken	Sofa	Harrison	$ 235.67
225	2	Aitken	Chair	Harrison	$ 453.78

However, the rows that are 'missing' from the two ANSWER tables are the same:

SaleNo	**EmployeeNo**	**Customer**	**Item**	**Supplier**	**Amount**
3	2	Smith	Stool	Ford	$ 82.78
5	3	Smith	Sofa	Harrison	$235.67

That is to say in both cases it is the rows that are common to the two base tables involved in the difference operation which do not appear in the answer table.

Intersect

The intersection of two tables is a third table which contains the rows which are common to both of them. Thus the intersection of SALES and SALES2 is:

ANSWER					
SaleNo	EmployeeNo	Customer	Item	Supplier	Amount
3	2	Smith	Stool	Ford	$ 82.78
5	3	Smith	Sofa	Harrison	$235.67

Unlike the difference operation, the order of the tables is unimportant and, of course, the two tables must be union compatible.

(If at this point you are wondering if Difference and Intersection do essentially the same operation on the data and just keep different bits at the end of it, you get three gold stars because it shows you've been paying attention. I'm impressed.)

Product

The product of two tables is a third table which contains all of the rows in the first one, added to each of the rows in the second. Thus if the first table has three rows, and the second has seven, the product will have 21 rows. The product of EMPLOYEES times SALES is:

ANSWER					
EmployeeNo	**FirstName**	**LastName**	**DateOfBirth**	**DateEmployed**	**SaleNo**
1	Bilda	Groves	12 Apr 1956	01 May 1989	1
1	Bilda	Groves	12 Apr 1956	01 May 1989	2
1	Bilda	Groves	12 Apr 1956	01 May 1989	3
1	Bilda	Groves	12 Apr 1956	01 May 1989	4
1	Bilda	Groves	12 Apr 1956	01 May 1989	5
1	Bilda	Groves	12 Apr 1956	01 May 1989	6
1	Bilda	Groves	12 Apr 1956	01 May 1989	7
2	John	Greeves	21 Mar 1967	01 Jan 1990	1
2	John	Greeves	21 Mar 1967	01 Jan 1990	2
2	John	Greeves	21 Mar 1967	01 Jan 1990	3
2	John	Greeves	21 Mar 1967	01 Jan 1990	4
2	John	Greeves	21 Mar 1967	01 Jan 1990	5
2	John	Greeves	21 Mar 1967	01 Jan 1990	6
2	John	Greeves	21 Mar 1967	01 Jan 1990	7
3	Sally	Smith	01 May 1967	01 Apr 1992	1
3	Sally	Smith	01 May 1967	01 Apr 1992	2
3	Sally	Smith	01 May 1967	01 Apr 1992	3
3	Sally	Smith	01 May 1967	01 Apr 1992	4
3	Sally	Smith	01 May 1967	01 Apr 1992	5
3	Sally	Smith	01 May 1967	01 Apr 1992	6
3	Sally	Smith	01 May 1967	01 Apr 1992	7

EmployeeNo	**Customer**	**Item**	**Supplier**	**Amount**
1	Simpson	Sofa	Harrison	$ 235.67
1	Johnson	Chair	Harrison	$ 453.78
2	Smith	Stool	Ford	$ 82.78
2	Jones	Suite	Harrison	$3,421.00
3	Smith	Sofa	Harrison	$235.67
1	Simpson	Sofa	Harrison	$ 235.67
1	Jones	Bed	Ford	$ 453.00
1	Simpson	Sofa	Harrison	$ 235.67
1	Johnson	Chair	Harrison	$ 453.78
2	Smith	Stool	Ford	$ 82.78
2	Jones	Suite	Harrison	$3,421.00
3	Smith	Sofa	Harrison	$235.67
1	Simpson	Sofa	Harrison	$ 235.67
1	Jones	Bed	Ford	$ 453.00
1	Simpson	Sofa	Harrison	$ 235.67
1	Johnson	Chair	Harrison	$ 453.78
2	Smith	Stool	Ford	$ 82.78
2	Jones	Suite	Harrison	$3,421.00
3	Smith	Sofa	Harrison	$235.67
1	Simpson	Sofa	Harrison	$ 235.67
1	Jones	Bed	Ford	$ 453.00

Note: This is a single table, the SaleNo and EmployeeNo fields are adjacent.)

This product operation has been applied quite correctly. However, the astute reader will note that this table contains seven rows which appear to be 'meaningful' and 14 which do not. This is because we are dealing with a raw operator that takes no account of the values in columns nor of any meaning that those values may imply or indicate.

In practice, the product operation usually needs to be modified by further operations in order to yield the answer we want.

Join

Join is a word that has several different meanings in the database world. In Chapter 29 on SQL you will find the word 'join' used in SQL itself, a use that is derived from this relational operator. In terms of operators, the word has a fairly specific meaning; it is an operator which behaves just like a mixture of the Product and Restrict operators. Suppose that you want to examine the sales that have been made by your employees. In order to do this, you need information from both the EMPLOYEES and SALES tables. (In fact, the table SALES2 contains information about more sales and if we wanted to include this information we would first use the union operator. However, for the sake of brevity, we will assume that we are only interested in the sales recorded in SALES.)

The first job is to perform a product on these tables. Next we need to perform a selection which removes the rows where SALES.EmployeeNo is not equal to EMPLOYEES.EmployeeNo.

The result would be something like this:

ANSWER					
EmployeeNo	FirstName	LastName	DateOfBirth	DateEmployed	SaleNo
1	Bilda	Groves	12 Apr 1956	01 May 1989	1
1	Bilda	Groves	12 Apr 1956	01 May 1989	2
1	Bilda	Groves	12 Apr 1956	01 May 1989	6
1	Bilda	Groves	12 Apr 1956	01 May 1989	7
2	John	Greeves	21 Mar 1967	01 Jan 1990	3
2	John	Greeves	21 Mar 1967	01 Jan 1990	4
3	Sally	Smith	01 May 1967	01 Apr 1992	5

Note: This is a single table, the SaleNo and EmployeeNo fields are adjacent.)

EmployeeNo	Customer	Item	Supplier	Amount
1	Simpson	Sofa	Harrison	$ 235.67
1	Johnson	Chair	Harrison	$ 453.78
1	Simpson	Sofa	Harrison	$ 235.67
1	Jones	Bed	Ford	$ 453.00
2	Smith	Stool	Ford	$ 82.78
2	Jones	Suite	Harrison	$3,421.00
3	Smith	Sofa	Harrison	$235.67

Divide

In order to demonstrate division, it will help if we cut down and alter the SALES table a little, just for this divide operator:

SALES Customer	Item
Simpson	Sofa
Johnson	Bed
Smith	Stool
Jones	Sofa
Smith	Sofa
Simpson	Sofa
Jones	Bed

We will also invent a new table called ITEMS which lists the names of one or more items.

ITEMS Item
Bed

Now, if we divide SALES by this version of ITEMS, we get an answer table like this:

ANSWER Customer
Johnson
Jones

If we divide SALES by this version of ITEMS:

ITEMS Item
Sofa

we get:

Finally, if we divide SALES by this version :

we get:

ANSWER
Customer
Jones

It should be possible to work out from this that the Divide operator is finding rows in the SALES table which have values in its column Item which match the values in the table ITEMS. The more values that are supplied in the ITEMS table, the fewer rows are likely to be returned in the answer table because the match has to be for all of the data in the ITEMS table.

Summary

The following is not rigorous, nor is it detailed but if you have read and understood the previous section it should provide a quick reference to remind you what the operators are and what they do.

Two of the operators (**Restrict** and **Project**) operate on single tables.

- **Restriction** extracts rows.
- **Projection** extracts columns.

Assuming that each operation is performed on a table with 20 rows, the number of rows in the answer table will be:

- Restriction – between 0 and 20
- Projection – between 1 and 20 (because duplicates are removed)

The remaining six operators (Union, Difference, Intersect, Product, Join and Divide) all perform operations on two tables.

- Union adds the rows from two tables.
- Difference subtracts the rows in one table from those in another.
- Intersection locates the rows that are common to two tables.
- Product multiplies the rows in the two tables.
- Join both multiplies and restricts the rows in two tables.
- Divide extracts rows and columns from one table on the basis of data in the second.

Assuming that each of the following operations is performed on a pair of tables with 20 and 10 rows respectively, the number of rows in the answer table will be:

- Union – between 20 and 30
- Difference – between 10 and 20 (assuming that we subtract the table with 10 rows from that with 20)
- Intersection – between 0 and 10
- Product – exactly 200
- Join – between 0 and 200
- Divide – between 0 and 2

This last figure (for Divide) may seem a little odd. However, as the number of rows in the divisor table increases, the number of rows in the answer table drops rapidly. A more realistic case to consider here might be one where we divide a table with 20 rows by a table with two rows. The number of rows in the answer table in this case will be between 0 and 10.

Chapter 29

SQL

SQL stands for Structured Query Language, which is pronounced either as S Q L (as the three letters) or as Sequel. It appears that the former pronunciation is more common in the UK and the latter in the US but as the two are inter-changeable it shouldn't be a cause of anxiety.

SQL is a language that splits neatly into two parts. There is the DDL (Data Definition Language) section and the DML (Data Manipulation Language) sec-tion. The former is the part of the language that is used for creating database objects, such as tables. DDL statements are very rarely written by hand nowa-days, so we'll focus this chapter on the DML part.

The majority of the SQL statements shown in this chapter are in an Access file called CHAP29.MDB. The SQL statements therein are as shown here; in other words, they are in essentially standard SQL. Since Access will understand standard SQL as well as its own dialect, the queries will run quite happily. However, if you view the queries using the Access GUI query builder, it may rewrite the statements in Access SQL dialect.

Please also note that the SQL statements shown are cross-referenced to the queries in CHAP29.MDB file by name. This name is shown at the left-hand side of the page and should not be confused with the SQL statement itself, which appears directly below it.

More and more database querying is carried out with a GUI tool; Access has a great one and I think it's wonderful. Yet here I am, devoting an entire chapter to SQL – a nasty reactionary text-based querying system. Why am I doing this to you?

Delightful as the current crop of querying tools are to use and excellent as they are for relatively simple questions, they do not have the flexibility to permit you to formulate certain more complex types of question and this is where SQL scores. It is endlessly adaptable and knowing something about it is emi-nently worthwhile for those occasions when it's the only way of reaching the answer you desire. If that doesn't tempt you, remember that in certain social circles, zero knowledge of SQL can seriously damage your street cred. On the other hand being able to drop the odd "Why don't you use a GROUP BY here?" can make you appear to be a database freak of the first water.

SQL is often referred to as a standard but when you actually start using it you find that, like most standards, it's not as standard as all that. The examples given here are in a generic form of SQL – you may well find discrepancies if you use another dialect. Having said that, the differences are not great and should not pose serious problems. For instance, although by default Access uses a slightly different dialect, it will usually accept this generic SQL quite happily. The sample queries included with this chapter are written in generic SQL and almost all will run in Access.

The sample tables shown below are the main tables that are used in the examples.

EMPLOYEES

EmployeeNo	FirstName	LastName	DateOfBirth	DateEmployed	CarNo
1	Bilda	Groves	12 Apr 1966	01 May 1999	2
2	John	Greeves	21 Mar 1977	01 Jan 2000	
3	Sally	Smith	01 May 1977	01 Apr 2002	5
4	Fred	Jones	03 Apr 1996	01 May 2004	3

SALES

SaleNo	EmployeeNo	Customer	Item	Supplier	Amount
1	1	Simpson	Sofa	Harrison	$235.67
2	1	Johnson	Chair	Harrison	$453.78
3	2	Smith	Stool	Ford	$82.78
4	2	Jones	Suite	Harrison	$3,421.00
5	3	Smith	Sofa	Harrison	$235.67
6	1	Simpson	Sofa	Harrison	$235.67
7	1	Jones	Bed	Ford	$453.00

CARS		
CarNo	**Make**	**Model**
1	Triumph	Spitfire
2	Bentley	Mk. VI
3	Triumph	Stag
4	Ford	GT 40
5	Shelby	Cobra
6	Ford	Mustang
7	Aston Martin	DB Mk III
8	Jaguar	D Type

In the screen shot below you can see the joins between the tables, including two further tables introduced during the chapter.

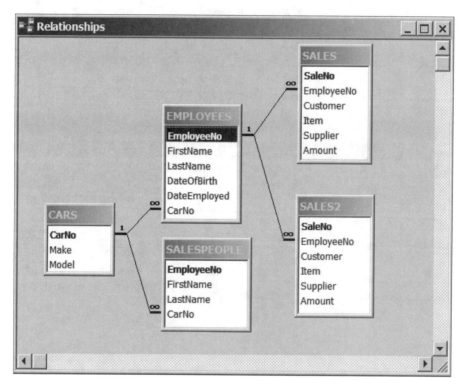

SQL statements are, by convention, written in UPPERCASE. The first ones we'll look at are SELECT, FROM, DISTINCT and WHERE.

SELECT and FROM

The first of these statements is SELECT. It is used to extract a collection of columns from a given table. FROM simply directs attention to the table in question. Thus the statement:

SELECT AND FROM 1

SELECT SaleNo, Item, Amount

FROM SALES;

will yield the following:

SaleNo	Item	Amount
1	Sofa	$235.67
2	Chair	$453.78
3	Stool	$82.78
4	Suite	$3,421.00
5	Sofa	$235.67
6	Sofa	$235.67
7	Bed	$453.00

SQL doesn't eliminate duplicates by default, so:

SELECT AND FROM 2

SELECT Item, Amount

FROM SALES;

will yield:

Item	Amount
Sofa	$235.67
Chair	$453.78
Stool	$82.78
Suite	$3,421.00
Sofa	$235.67
Sofa	$235.67
Bed	$453.00

which has duplicated rows.

DISTINCT

You can force SQL to remove the duplicates by using the statement DISTINCT, which dictates that all rows in the answer table must be unique. The query:

DISTINCT 1
SELECT DISTINCT Item, Amount
FROM SALES;

produces:

Item	Amount
Bed	$453.00
Chair	$453.78
Sofa	$235.67
Stool	$82.78
Suite	$3,421.00

WHERE

SELECT lets you choose the columns with which to work and WHERE lets you choose the rows.

WHERE 1
SELECT Item, Amount
FROM SALES
WHERE Item = 'Sofa';

produces:

Item	Amount
Sofa	$235.67
Sofa	$235.67
Sofa	$235.67

while:

WHERE 2
SELECT Item, Amount
FROM SALES
WHERE Item = 'Sofa' AND Customer = 'Smith';

yields:

Item	Amount
Sofa	$235.67

You will have noticed a general pattern emerging here (I hope) which is that simple SELECT commands follow a basic pattern:

SELECT column name(s)
FROM table name
WHERE condition(s)

All sorts of variations are already possible combining SELECT and WHERE statements; as you can see from the last example, WHERE clauses can contain conditions.

Conditions

We'll digress here to cover the range of conditions that are acceptable within a WHERE clause. Conditions typically consist of logical expressions which can be evaluated for truth; in other words, they are checked to discover whether they are true or false.

Thus if we use the SQL statement:

CONDITIONS 1
SELECT EmployeeNo, FirstName, LastName, DateOfBirth, DateEmployed
FROM EMPLOYEES
WHERE EmployeeNo = 2;

then we can expect the RDBMS to examine every row in the EMPLOYEE table and place in the answer table only those rows for which the condition:

> WHERE EmployeeNo = 2

is true. As you'd hope, this is only true for one row:

EmployeeNo	FirstName	LastName	DateOfBirth	DateEmployed
2	John	Greeves	21 Mar 1977	01 Jan 2000

A condition is constructed from operators such as:

Symbol	Meaning	Example	Notes	Rows returned from Employee table
=	Equal to	EmployeeNo = 2		1
>	Greater than	EmployeeNo > 2		2
<	Less than	EmployeeNo < 2		1
<>	Not equal to	EmployeeNo <> 2		3
>=	Greater than or Equal to	EmployeeNo >= 2		3
<=	Less than or Equal to	EmployeeNo <= 2		2
IN	Equal to a value within a collection of values	EmployeeNo IN (2, 3, 4)		3
LIKE	Similar to	LastName LIKE "Gr*"	Finds Greeves and Groves. Uses wildcards. Wild cards vary between SQL implementations.	2
BETWEEN... AND	Within a range of values, including the two values which define the limits	EmployeeNo BETWEEN 2 AND 4.	Equivalent to: EmployeeNo IN (2, 3, 4)	3
IS NULL	Column does not contain a value	DateEmployed IS NULL		0

The following logical operators have a lower priority than those above and are therefore processed after them, unless parentheses are used to alter precedence.

Symbol	Meaning	Example(s)	Notes	Rows returned from Sales table
AND	Both expressions must be true in order for the entire expression to be judged true	SaleNo > 3 AND Customer = "Smith"	AND is evaluated before OR	1
OR	If either or both expressions are true, the entire expression is judged to be true	SaleNo > 3 OR Customer = "Smith"	AND is evaluated before OR	5
NOT	Inverts Truth	SaleNo NOT IN (2, 3, 4)	(just as well it isn't available for the real world!)	4

The following SQL statement asks for a table of the items and amounts from the SALES table for sale numbers greater than 6:

CONDITIONS 2
SELECT Item, Amount
FROM SALES
WHERE SaleNo > 6;

Item	Amount
Bed	$453.00

while this one only wants to see rows relating to sofas for sale numbers greater than 6:

CONDITIONS 3
SELECT Item, Amount
FROM SALES
WHERE Item = 'Sofa' AND SaleNo > 6;

There are none.

This next statement asks for all rows for sofas, suites and beds, regardless of sale number:

CONDITIONS 4

SELECT Item, Amount
FROM SALES
WHERE Item IN ('Sofa', 'Suite', 'Bed');

Item	Amount
Sofa	$235.67
Suite	$3,421.00
Sofa	$235.67
Sofa	$235.67
Bed	$453.00

and this one adds a condition which specifies rows for the same three pieces of furniture with sale numbers greater than 6:

CONDITIONS 5

SELECT Item, Amount
FROM SALES
WHERE Item IN ('Sofa', 'Suite', 'Bed') AND SaleNo > 6;

Item	Amount
Bed	$453.00

It is worth noting in passing that the use of the operators AND, OR and NOT may seem counter-intuitive at first. For example, if we alter the operator AND to OR in the previous statement:

CONDITIONS 6

SELECT Item, Amount
FROM SALES
WHERE Item IN ('Sofa', 'Suite', 'Bed') OR SaleNo > 6;

would we expect more or fewer rows in the answer table? The answer is more:

Item	Amount
Sofa	$235.67
Suite	$3,421.00
Sofa	$235.67
Sofa	$235.67
Bed	$453.00

Intuition might suggest that AND increases the number of rows while OR restricts them but, in fact, the converse is true. As a general rule, the more ANDs that you add to a condition, the fewer rows appear in the answer table. Of course, this will depend upon the data. What is always true is that adding ORs to a condition must leave the number of rows in the answer table the same or increase it. Adding ANDs must leave it the same or decrease it.

Conditions are nothing if not logical and rendering a series of conditions into plain English is a good way of understanding what it will do in practice.

ORDER BY

I said earlier that a general pattern was emerging. We can expand it a little now by adding another clause called ORDER BY to the statement.

The basic pattern is now:

> *SELECT column name(s)*
> *FROM table name*
> *WHERE condition(s)*
> *ORDER BY column name(s)*

ORDER BY gives you control over the order in which rows appear in the answer table generated by the query. You specify the column by which you want rows ordered, as in the following statement:

ORDER BY 1
SELECT Item, Amount, SaleNo
FROM SALES
WHERE Item = 'Sofa'
ORDER BY SaleNo;

This is the result:

Item	Amount	SaleNo
Sofa	$235.67	1
Sofa	$235.67	5
Sofa	$235.67	6

with the rows ordered by the number of each sale, with the default being ascending order. Note that the column used to ORDER BY doesn't *have* to appear as one of those SELECTed although that is typically the case.

If you feel you want to specify the sort order, the command is ASC, as shown below:

SELECT Item, Amount
FROM SALES
WHERE SaleNo > 2
ORDER BY Item ASC;

Item	Amount
Bed	$453.00
Sofa	$235.67
Sofa	$235.67
Stool	$82.78
Suite	$3,421.00

This is a perfectly acceptable statement but it's tautological, being the equivalent of:

ORDER BY 2
SELECT Item, Amount
FROM SALES
WHERE SaleNo > 2
ORDER BY Item;

since ASC is the default.

The next statement:

ORDER BY 3

SELECT Item, Amount

FROM SALES

WHERE SaleNo > 2

ORDER BY Item DESC;

will produce exactly the same data but it will be sorted differently since DESC, as you'll have gathered, sorts rows in descending order.

Item	Amount
Suite	$3,421.00
Stool	$82.78
Sofa	$235.67
Sofa	$235.67
Bed	$453.00

You can use sorts in both directions, as below:

ORDER BY 4

SELECT Item, Customer, SaleNo, Amount

FROM SALES

WHERE SaleNo > 0

ORDER BY Customer ASC, Amount DESC;

This will sort the customer rows in ascending order, with the amounts each customer has spent shown in descending order.

Item	Customer	SaleNo	Amount
Chair	Johnson	2	$453.78
Suite	Jones	4	$3,421.00
Bed	Jones	7	$453.00
Sofa	Simpson	6	$235.67
Sofa	Simpson	1	$235.67
Sofa	Smith	5	$235.67
Stool	Smith	3	$82.78

If you don't specify an order in the answer table, the rows will be returned in any order that the RDBMS thinks is a good idea at the time. (Bill added 'hopefully chosen for performance or usability reasons!') In fact, you might find when you run the SQL statements in the sample Access database, those which don't contain ORDER BY will show the rows in a different order from that shown in this book. Remember that if the order of the rows in the answer table is important to you, you must use an ORDER BY clause.

Wildcards

Wildcards are used in SQL much as they are used elsewhere for occasions when you want a range of data that fits a certain pattern. The variation below is not uncommon:

WILD CARDS 1
SELECT *
FROM SALES
WHERE SaleNo > 1;

It gives this result:

SaleNo	EmployeeNo	Customer	Item	Supplier	Amount
2	1	Johnson	Chair	Harrison	$453.78
3	2	Smith	Stool	Ford	$82.78
4	2	Jones	Suite	Harrison	$3,421.00
5	3	Smith	Sofa	Harrison	$235.67
6	1	Simpson	Sofa	Harrison	$235.67
7	1	Jones	Bed	Ford	$453.00

In this case, the * symbol is used as a wildcard, meaning 'all columns'. It's a shorthand form of:

WILD CARDS 2
SELECT SaleNo, EmployeeNo, Customer, Item, Supplier, Amount
FROM SALES
WHERE SaleNo > 1;

which yields the same answer table.

Sub-queries

We'll take another diversion, this time into the realm of sub-queries. You already know that the WHERE clause makes use of conditions, such as:

>   WHERE SaleNo > 1

This use of conditions can be expanded into sub-queries to add further refinement to queries. Consider this example:

>   **SUB-QUERIES 1**
>   SELECT Customer
>   FROM SALES
>   WHERE EmployeeNo IN
>   (SELECT EmployeeNo
>   FROM EMPLOYEES
>   WHERE DateEmployed > 5/5/1999);

which produces this table:

Customer
Smith
Jones
Smith

The statement inside parentheses is known as a sub-query and it would work perfectly happily as a query all on its own. Incidentally, this is a good case to illustrate how dialects of SQL differ. Access requires that the date be wrapped up in # symbols, so in Access the last line reads:

>   WHERE DateEmployed > #5/5/1999#;

Any operation performed on a table or tables results in another table, one containing the answer. This is termed 'closure' and it is an invariable rule (see Chapter 15). The sub-query above produces, as you would expect from the foregoing, an answer table which is shown below:

EmployeeNo
2
3
4

By looking at the answer table generated by the sub-query, we can see that the original statement can be simplified to:

SUB-QUERIES 2

SELECT Customer

FROM SALES

WHERE EmployeeNo IN (2,3,4);

and the rows from the SALES table for which this is true are:

SaleNo	EmployeeNo	Customer	Item	Supplier	Amount
3	2	Smith	Stool	Ford	$82.78
4	2	Jones	Suite	Harrison	$3,421.00
5	3	Smith	Sofa	Harrison	$235.67

and so the query actually yields:

Customer
Smith
Jones
Smith

Referring back to the start of the chapter, note that we could eliminate the duplicate rows by adding the word Distinct to the first line of the SQL command.

By now, I hope, it is apparent that this SQL statement translates into English as "Give me the names of all of the customers who have been dealt with by any employee who was employed after 05 May 1999."

Built-in functions

SQL includes several simple statistical functions:

Function	
SUM	Total
COUNT	The number of occurrences
AVG	Average
MIN	Minimum
MAX	Maximum

Thus it is possible (though not normal practice) to write SQL statements such as:

BUILT-IN FUNCTIONS 1
SELECT SUM(Amount)
FROM SALES;

Some systems will actually accept this. Access, for example, generates a 'dummy' field name (Expr1000) and yields the following table:

Expr1000
$5,117.57

However, it is more common to explicitly name the column in which the output should be placed. For example:

SELECT SUM(Amount) "Sum of Amount"
FROM SALES;

or:

BUILT-IN FUNCTIONS 2
SELECT SUM(Amount) AS SumOfAmount
FROM SALES;

or even:

BUILT-IN FUNCTIONS 3
SELECT DISTINCT SUM(SALES.Amount) AS SumOfAmount
FROM SALES;

which is how it appears in the Access dialect of SQL.

All three of the above yield a table like this:

SumOfAmount
$5,117.57

The AS followed by a column name simply tells the SQL statement to put the data into a column of that name in the answer table.

It is permissible to mix two or more functions, for example:

BUILT-IN FUNCTIONS 4
SELECT SUM(Amount) AS SumOfAmount,
COUNT(Amount) AS CountOfAmount,
AVG(Amount) AS AvgOfAmount,
MIN(Amount) AS MinOfAmount,
MAX(Amount) AS MaxOfAmount
FROM SALES;

which yields:

SumOfAmount	CountOfAmount	AvgOfAmount	MinOfAmount	MaxOfAmount
$5,117.57	7	$731.08	$82.78	$3,421.00

One of the reviewers added: "In many SQL dialects one writes either:
COUNT(DISTINCT ColumnName)
or
COUNT(*)
not
COUNT(ColumnName)"

It's also perfectly permissible to mix columns like this:

BUILT-IN FUNCTIONS 5
SELECT COUNT(Customer) AS CountOfCustomer,
AVG(Amount) AS AvgOfAmount
FROM SALES;

giving:

CountOfCustomer	AvgOfAmount
7	$731.08

These functions will even operate correctly on columns which contain no data. If we amend the base table, for the sake of this example only, to be:

SaleNo	EmployeeNo	Customer	Item	Supplier	Amount
1	1	Simpson	Sofa	Harrison	$235.67
2	1	Johnson	Chair	Harrison	$453.78
3	2		Stool	Ford	$82.78
4	2	Jones	Suite	Harrison	
5	3	Smith	Sofa	Harrison	$235.67
6	1		Sofa	Harrison	$235.67
7	1	Jones	Bed	Ford	$453.00

(This table is in the sample .MDB file as ALTEREDSALES)

then the SQL statement:

BUILT-IN FUNCTIONS 6
SELECT COUNT(Customer) AS CountOfCustomer,
AVG(Amount) AS AvgOfAmount
FROM ALTEREDSALES;

(essentially identical to BUILT-IN FUNCTIONS 5) will give:

CountOfCustomer	AvgOfAmount
5	$282.76

The COUNT function finds only five values, AVG sums the values that it finds and divides the result by six (the number of values in that particular column) rather than seven (the number of rows).

However, these functions are designed to yield only a single figure each. Thus a SQL statement like:

BUILT-IN FUNCTIONS 7
SELECT Customer,
AVG(SALES.Amount) AS AvgOfAmount
FROM SALES;

is illegal because:

SELECT Customer

can (and in this case would) have an output consisting of multiple rows, while the second part:

SELECT AVG(SALES.Amount) AS AvgOfAmount

can only have an output of a single row.

Several SQL implementations provide more than the basic functions. For example, Access also provides:

Function	
StDev	Standard Deviation
Var	Variance

It is just this kind of deviation from the standard which demonstrates that SQL is still a fairly 'fluid' language.

GROUP BY – collecting information

GROUP BY seems to be more difficult to understand than some other constructions. Bill agrees; during proofreading he added:

'GROUP BY seems to confuse everyone. It would be nice to describe what it is trying to accomplish. Something like 'Splitting your records into groups and creating one "summary" record in the answer table for each group.'

Which is a good way to think about it.

So far, our generic SELECT statement looks like this:

SELECT column name(s)
FROM table name
WHERE condition(s)
ORDER BY column name(s)

We can expand it with:

SELECT column name(s)
FROM table name
WHERE condition(s)
GROUP BY column name(s)
ORDER BY column name(s)

Above we looked at the command ORDER BY, which provides a way of presenting information in ascending or descending order. Further control over your answer data is given by GROUP BY. The syntax is:

GROUP BY column name(s)

To illustrate its usefulness, we'll consider the simple statement below:

GROUP BY 1

SELECT AVG(Amount) AS AvgOfAmount

FROM SALES;

which gives:

AvgOfAmount
$731.08

This averages the values found in the Amount column for all rows in the SALES table. Suppose you want to examine the records which refer to customer 'Simpson'. You'd use WHERE, as follows:

GROUP BY 2

SELECT AVG(Amount) AS AvgOfAmount

FROM SALES

WHERE Customer = "Simpson";

AvgOfAmount
$235.67

Now suppose you want to do this for each customer. An inelegant brute force solution would be to run the query multiple times, once for each customer. A particularly clever solution is to get the SQL statement to group the records together by the name of the customer and then apply the AVG function to the values in the groups.

We can visualize the process like this. We go from this table:

SaleNo	EmployeeNo	Customer	Item	Supplier	Amount
1	1	Simpson	Sofa	Harrison	$235.67
2	1	Johnson	Chair	Harrison	$453.78
3	2	Smith	Stool	Ford	$82.78
4	2	Jones	Suite	Harrison	$3,421.00
5	3	Smith	Sofa	Harrison	$235.67
6	1	Simpson	Sofa	Harrison	$235.67
7	1	Jones	Bed	Ford	$453.00

to this one:

SaleNo	EmployeeNo	Customer	Item	Supplier	Amount
2	1	Johnson	Chair	Harrison	$453.78
7	1	Jones	Bed	Ford	$453.00
4	2	Jones	Suite	Harrison	$3,421.00
6	1	Simpson	Sofa	Harrison	$235.67
1	1	Simpson	Sofa	Harrison	$235.67
5	3	Smith	Sofa	Harrison	$235.67
3	2	Smith	Stool	Ford	$82.78

and thence to this, which is a full but compact summary of the required information:

Customer	AvgOfAmount
Johnson	$453.78
Jones	$1,937.00
Simpson	$235.67
Smith	$159.23

The SQL statement required to perform this magic is:

GROUP BY 3
SELECT Customer, AVG(Amount) AS AvgOfAmount
FROM SALES
GROUP BY Customer
ORDER BY Customer;

Impressive, isn't it?

The GROUP BY clause can be used more simply than this. For example:

GROUP BY 4
SELECT Customer
FROM SALES
GROUP BY Customer;

produces:

Customer
Johnson
Jones
Simpson
Smith

At first it appears that this is the same as:

GROUP BY 5

SELECT DISTINCT Customer

FROM SALES;

which yields exactly the same answer table but adding another column demonstrates the difference.

Thus:

GROUP BY 6

SELECT DISTINCT Customer, Amount

FROM SALES;

produces:

Customer	Amount
Johnson	$453.78
Jones	$453.00
Jones	$3,421.00
Simpson	$235.67
Smith	$82.78
Smith	$235.67

whereas:

GROUP BY 7

SELECT Customer, Amount

FROM SALES

GROUP BY Customer;

fails to run. Why is this?

Essentially it is for the same reasons that were raised when discussing the conflict that can arise when using functions. The command:

GROUP BY 8

SELECT Customer

FROM SALES

GROUP BY Customer;

says 'Sort the records in the SALES table so that identical values in the Customer field are together. Then 'crush together' the records with identical Customer values so that they *appear* to be one record.'

Thus:

SELECT Customer, Amount

FROM SALES

GROUP BY Customer;

fails because there is a conflict (real in this particular case, potential in other cases) between the number of rows that should be output. (Grouping by Customer, Amount would work, however.)

SELECT Customer

FROM SALES

GROUP BY Customer;

will output four rows:

Customer
Johnson
Jones
Simpson
Smith

while:

GROUP BY 9

SELECT Amount

FROM SALES;

will output seven rows:

Amount
$235.67
$453.78
$82.78
$3,421.00
$235.67
$235.67
$453.00

Combining these two incompatible requests is impossible and SQL engines will refuse the statement.

As you can see from the above, there is no obligation to combine GROUP BY with one or more of the functions. However, it is commonly done because often we only want to group records in order to be able to perform some type of manipulation on selections of records.

It is perfectly possible to GROUP BY more than one column. Thus:

GROUP BY 10

SELECT Customer, Supplier, AVG(Amount) AS AvgOfAmount

FROM SALES

GROUP BY Customer, Supplier;

produces more groups than the SQL statement above which grouped by one column because it is grouping those records which share the same values in Customer and Supplier. The answer table is this:

Customer	Supplier	AvgOfAmount
Johnson	Harrison	$453.78
Jones	Ford	$453.00
Jones	Harrison	$3,421.00
Simpson	Harrison	$235.67
Smith	Ford	$82.78
Smith	Harrison	$235.67

which raises another interesting question. How can you tell how many rows are actually contributing to each group?

One answer (although by no means the only one) is:

GROUP BY 11

SELECT Count(*) AS NumberInGroup,

Customer, Supplier, AVG(Amount) AS AvgOfAmount

FROM SALES

GROUP BY Customer, Supplier;

The only addition is the 'Count(*) AS NumberInGroup' bit which simply says that the number of rows in each group should be counted.

NumberInGroup	Customer	Supplier	AvgOfAmount
1	Johnson	Harrison	$453.78
1	Jones	Ford	$453.00
1	Jones	Harrison	$3,421.00
2	Simpson	Harrison	$235.67
1	Smith	Ford	$82.78
1	Smith	Harrison	$235.67

We could equally well use:

GROUP BY 12

SELECT Count(Customer) AS NumberInGroup, Customer, Supplier, AVG(Amount) AS AvgOfAmount

FROM SALES

GROUP BY Customer, Supplier;

which returns the same answer table.

GROUP BY is an incredibly powerful tool and it can be made even more so with the addition of HAVING.

GROUP BY...HAVING – collecting specific information

Whereas the GROUP BY clause puts rows into logical groupings, the HAVING clause allows you to select the groups that you want to see, based on values which appertain to that group. Consider the example given below:

GB&H 1

SELECT Customer, Supplier, AVG(Amount) AS AvgOfAmount
FROM SALES
GROUP BY Customer, Supplier;

Customer	Supplier	AvgOfAmount
Johnson	Harrison	$453.78
Jones	Ford	$453.00
Jones	Harrison	$3,421.00
Simpson	Harrison	$235.67
Smith	Ford	$82.78
Smith	Harrison	$235.67

Suppose, now the rows are grouped in this way, that we are only interested in the groups where the average amount is $250 or more.

The foolish solution is:

GB&H 2

SELECT Customer, Supplier, AVG(Amount) AS AvgOfAmount
FROM SALES
GROUP BY Customer, Supplier
ORDER BY AVG(Amount);

Customer	Supplier	AvgOfAmount
Smith	Ford	$82.78
Smith	Harrison	$235.67
Simpson	Harrison	$235.67
Jones	Ford	$453.00
Johnson	Harrison	$453.78
Jones	Harrison	$3,421.00

which, although it renders the desired values easy to find, still leaves the job of actually locating them to the user.

Note that I have slipped in an ORDER BY into that last statement. Bill said "Whoa! ORDERing groups seems like a whole new concept! Maybe comment somewhere that 'operations' on groups are similar to those on records." He is, as usual, quite right.

A much better solution is:

283

GB&H 3

SELECT Customer, Supplier, AVG(Amount) AS AvgOfAmount

FROM SALES

GROUP BY Customer, Supplier

HAVING AVG(Amount) >= 250;

Customer	Supplier	AvgOfAmount
Johnson	Harrison	$453.78
Jones	Ford	$453.00
Jones	Harrison	$3,421.00

One reviewer added: "Might be worth saying 'HAVING is simply a WHERE done after GROUPing'."

You can, of course, still order the groups:

GB&H 4

SELECT Customer, Supplier, AVG(Amount) AS AvgOfAmount

FROM SALES

GROUP BY Customer, Supplier

HAVING AVG(Amount) >= 250

ORDER BY AVG(Amount);

Customer	Supplier	AvgOfAmount
Jones	Ford	$453.00
Johnson	Harrison	$453.78
Jones	Harrison	$3,421.00

Working with multiple tables

So far we have looked at using the SELECT statement with a single table. Clearly, since the relational model encourages us to split complex data into separate tables, we will often find it necessary to recover data from two or more tables. In order to do this, we have to use the SELECT statement to draw data from both tables and the WHERE clause to form the joins.

Before we do, let's try querying the tables without using the WHERE clause.

MULTI-TABLE 1
SELECT SALES.Customer, EMPLOYEES.LastName, SALES.EmployeeNo, EM-PLOYEES.EmployeeNo
FROM SALES, EMPLOYEES;

This is the result:

Customer	LastName	SALES.EmployeeNo	EMPLOYEES.EmployeeNo
Simpson	Groves	1	1
Simpson	Greeves	1	2
Simpson	Smith	1	3
Simpson	Jones	1	4
Johnson	Groves	1	1
Johnson	Greeves	1	2
Johnson	Smith	1	3
Johnson	Jones	1	4
Smith	Groves	2	1
Smith	Greeves	2	2
Smith	Smith	2	3
Smith	Jones	2	4
Jones	Groves	2	1
Jones	Greeves	2	2
Jones	Smith	2	3
Jones	Jones	2	4
Smith	Groves	3	1
Smith	Greeves	3	2
Smith	Smith	3	3
Smith	Jones	3	4
Simpson	Groves	1	1
Simpson	Greeves	1	2
Simpson	Smith	1	3
Simpson	Jones	1	4
Jones	Groves	1	1
Jones	Greeves	1	2
Jones	Smith	1	3
Jones	Jones	1	4

It's plain that this table is full of repetitive data that isn't at all helpful: we'll explain why once we've given you a little more detail with which to work.

Note that this SQL statement includes for the first time the table names when columns are being specified. Up to this point our SELECT statements have referred to single tables. Since column names within a single table must be unique, the column name alone allowed us to identify the columns unambiguously. However, column names can (and often are) shared by different tables. For example, both SALES and EMPLOYEES have a column called EmployeeNo. Therefore the only way to identify a particular column uniquely is to use the table name as well. SQL syntax typically has the table name first in uppercase, followed by a dot, followed by the column name in lowercase.

SQL allows you to substitute temporary synonyms for table names:

MULTI-TABLE 2

SELECT S.Customer, S.Amount, E.FirstName, E.LastName, S.EmployeeNo, E.EmployeeNo

FROM SALES S, EMPLOYEES E;

(FROM SALES AS S, EMPLOYEES AS E; is also acceptable).

which can shorten statements considerably but also tends to make them less readable. Note that although the synonyms are not defined until the FROM clause, they can still be used in the SELECT clause, which tells you something about the way in which the SQL statement is read by the RDBMS.

To return to the multiple table query, if we add a WHERE clause like this:

MULTI-TABLE 3

SELECT S.Customer, S.Amount, E.FirstName, E.LastName, S.EmployeeNo, E.EmployeeNo

FROM SALES S, EMPLOYEES E

WHERE S.EmployeeNo = E.EmployeeNo;

we get:

Customer	Amount	FirstName	LastName	S.EmployeeNo	E.EmployeeNo
Simpson	$235.67	Bilda	Groves	1	1
Johnson	$453.78	Bilda	Groves	1	1
Simpson	$235.67	Bilda	Groves	1	1
Jones	$453.00	Bilda	Groves	1	1
Smith	$82.78	John	Greeves	2	2
Jones	$3,421.00	John	Greeves	2	2
Smith	$235.67	Sally	Smith	3	3

Referring to the base tables shows that this is a much more useful answer table than the previous one. Essentially this one is letting us look at the data in the SALES table but instead of seeing the numbers which represent the employees, we can see their names.

Without a WHERE clause (as in Multi-Table 1), the answer table contains every row in the SALES table matched against every row in the EMPLOYEE table, giving 4 x 7 = 28 rows. The WHERE clause ensures that we see in the answer table only those rows in which the EmployeeNo in SALES matches the EmployeeNo in EMPLOYEES. This is reasonable since we are using the value in

SALES.EmployeeNo to indicate which employee made the sale.

In practice, you don't have to have the EmployeeNo columns visible in the answer table and typically they would be excluded, appearing only in the WHERE clause.

MULTI-TABLE 4

SELECT S.Customer, S.Amount, E.FirstName, E.LastName
FROM SALES AS S, EMPLOYEES AS E
WHERE S.EmployeeNo = E.EmployeeNo;

Customer	Amount	FirstName	LastName
Simpson	$235.67	Bilda	Groves
Johnson	$453.78	Bilda	Groves
Simpson	$235.67	Bilda	Groves
Jones	$453.00	Bilda	Groves
Smith	$82.78	John	Greeves
Jones	$3,421.00	John	Greeves
Smith	$235.67	Sally	Smith

It is possible to join more than two tables by adding to the WHERE clause. For example:

MULTI-TABLE 5

SELECT SALES.Customer, EMPLOYEES.FirstName, CARS.Make, CARS.Model
FROM CARS, EMPLOYEES, SALES
WHERE EMPLOYEES.EmployeeNo = SALES.EmployeeNo
AND EMPLOYEES.CarNo = CARS.CarNo;

Customer	FirstName	Make	Model
Simpson	Bilda	Bentley	Mk. VI
Johnson	Bilda	Bentley	Mk. VI
Simpson	Bilda	Bentley	Mk. VI
Jones	Bilda	Bentley	Mk. VI
Smith	Sally	Shelby	Cobra

Note that this query is finding the car driven by the sales person who dealt with a given customer, so it isn't supposed to present particularly meaningful information.

The (SQL-92) SQL standard introduced a new way of expressing joins such that:

MULTI-TABLE 6

```
SELECT SALES.Customer, EMPLOYEES.LastName, SALES.Amount
FROM SALES, EMPLOYEES
WHERE SALES.EmployeeNo = EMPLOYEES.EmployeeNo;
```

which gives:

Customer	LastName	Amount
Simpson	Groves	$235.67
Johnson	Groves	$453.78
Simpson	Groves	$235.67
Jones	Groves	$453.00
Smith	Greeves	$82.78
Jones	Greeves	$3,421.00
Smith	Smith	$235.67

can be replaced by:

MULTI-TABLE 7

```
SELECT SALES.Customer, EMPLOYEES.LastName, SALES.Amount
FROM SALES INNER JOIN EMPLOYEES
ON EMPLOYEES.EmployeeNo = SALES.EmployeeNo;
```

This produces exactly the same answer table and is generally considered to be more readable. However, it does raise another question: "What is this INNER business?"

Inner (Natural) joins

Suppose that your boss says "Give me a list of all the cars and the sales person to whom each is allocated."

You are immediately tempted to use the SQL statement:

INNER JOIN 1

SELECT CARS.Make, CARS.Model, EMPLOYEES.FirstName, EMPLOYEES.LastName

FROM CARS INNER JOIN EMPLOYEES

ON CARS.CarNo = EMPLOYEES.CarNo;

but this will give the answer:

Make	Model	FirstName	LastName
Bentley	Mk. VI	Bilda	Groves
Triumph	Stag	Fred	Jones
Shelby	Cobra	Sally	Smith

which doesn't list all of the cars because, for instance, that delectable D-type Jaguar hasn't been allocated to anyone.

In fact, your boss has phrased the question badly, since her original question assumes that every car *is* allocated to an employee and this is not the case. However, voicing your opinion about her inexact use of English is likely to be a CLM (Career-Limiting Move). It's better to keep quiet and find a query which will list all of the cars and will also show which cars have been allocated to which lucky employees.

But before that, we'll have a look at what's wrong with the query shown above. By default, a join combines the two tables via fields that have identical values; this is known as a 'Natural' or 'Inner' join. However, if one or both of the fields contain exclusive values (I am using the term 'exclusive' to mean that the values are found in one table but not the other) then the join ignores the rows that are associated with these values. Thus the table CARS has a delightful Aston Martin, CarNo = 7, but since there is no corresponding value in EMPLOYEES.CarNo, this fine automobile never appears in the answer table.

So, instead of a natural join, what you need to use here is an unnatural join. OK, I admit it, that was just to see if you were awake. It is really known as an 'outer' join.

Outer joins

There are two distinct flavors of outer join – left and right.

The following SQL statement:

OUTER JOIN 1

SELECT CARS.Make, CARS.Model, EMPLOYEES.FirstName, EMPLOY-
EES.LastName

FROM CARS LEFT JOIN EMPLOYEES

ON CARS.CarNo = EMPLOYEES.CarNo;

yields:

Make	Model	FirstName	LastName
Triumph	Spitfire		
Bentley	Mk. VI	Bilda	Groves
Triumph	Stag	Fred	Jones
Ford	GT 40		
Shelby	Cobra	Sally	Smith
Ford	Mustang		
Aston Martin	DB Mk III		
Jaguar	D Type		

Essentially the substitution of LEFT JOIN for INNER JOIN has made all the difference. It ensures that every row from the first table appears in the answer table.

The other flavor of outer join is RIGHT, which simply ensures that every row
in the table on the right-hand side of the join is included in the answer table,
so:

OUTER JOIN 2

SELECT CARS.Make, CARS.Model, EMPLOYEES.FirstName, EMPLOY-
EES.LastName

FROM CARS RIGHT JOIN EMPLOYEES

ON CARS.CarNo = EMPLOYEES.CarNo;

yields:

Make	Model	FirstName	LastName
		John	Greeves
Bentley	Mk. VI	Bilda	Groves
Triumph	Stag	Fred	Jones
Shelby	Cobra	Sally	Smith

It ought to go without saying (which is another way of saying 'it is important to note') that:

OUTER JOIN 3

SELECT CARS.Make, CARS.Model, EMPLOYEES.FirstName, EMPLOY-EES.LastName

FROM EMPLOYEES LEFT JOIN CARS

ON CARS.CarNo = EMPLOYEES.CarNo;

produces the same answer table. In other words, the LEFT and RIGHT simply refer to the tables as named in the SQL statement. So:

FROM EMPLOYEES LEFT JOIN CARS

and

FROM CARS RIGHT JOIN EMPLOYEES

will include all the employees and some of the cars;

FROM CARS LEFT JOIN EMPLOYEES

and

FROM EMPLOYEES RIGHT JOIN CARS

will include all the cars and some of the employees.

So, you can have all of the cars some of the time and indeed all of the people some of the time. But what you really want to know is, can we have all of the cars and all of the people all of the time? The answer, not surprisingly, is 'Yes'. In order to do so, we can make use of UNION.

UNION

UNION returns all of the rows from two queries and displays them, *minus any duplicates*, in a single table. Thus:

UNION 1

SELECT CARS.Make, CARS.Model, EMPLOYEES.FirstName, EMPLOY-
EES.LastName

FROM CARS RIGHT JOIN EMPLOYEES

ON CARS.CarNo = EMPLOYEES.CarNo

UNION

SELECT CARS.Make, CARS.Model, EMPLOYEES.FirstName, EMPLOY-
EES.LastName

FROM CARS LEFT JOIN EMPLOYEES

ON CARS.CarNo = EMPLOYEES.CarNo;

produces:

Make	Model	FirstName	LastName
		John	Greeves
Aston Martin	DB Mk III		
Bentley	Mk. VI	Bilda	Groves
Ford	GT 40		
Ford	Mustang		
Jaguar	D Type		
Shelby	Cobra	Sally	Smith
Triumph	Spitfire		
Triumph	Stag	Fred	Jones

Clearly the two answer tables that are produced by the separate SELECT statements must be compatible in order for the UNION to combine them sensibly. So:

UNION 2

SELECT CARS.CarNo, CARS.Model, EMPLOYEES.FirstName, EMPLOY-
EES.LastName

FROM CARS RIGHT JOIN EMPLOYEES

ON CARS.CarNo = EMPLOYEES.CarNo

UNION

SELECT CARS.Make, CARS.Model, EMPLOYEES.FirstName, EMPLOY-
EES.LastName

FROM CARS LEFT JOIN EMPLOYEES

ON CARS.CarNo = EMPLOYEES.CarNo;

attempts to put text and numeric data into the same column and should fail. (In practice, some RDBMSs will allow this and convert the resulting column to the lowest common denominator, such as text).

However, the result:

CarNo	Model	FirstName	LastName
		John	Greeves
2	Mk. VI	Bilda	Groves
3	Stag	Fred	Jones
5	Cobra	Sally	Smith
Aston Martin	DB Mk III		
Bentley	Mk. VI	Bilda	Groves
Ford	GT 40		
Ford	Mustang		
Jaguar	D Type		
Shelby	Cobra	Sally	Smith
Triumph	Spitfire		
Triumph	Stag	Fred	Jones

may not be particularly meaningful.

The first example I gave for UNION (combining a LEFT and RIGHT join) serves as an excellent example of the use of UNION but it certainly isn't the only way in which it can be used. Suppose that you have another table of sales people who, for whatever reason, are stored in a separate table from the other employees.

SALESPEOPLE			
EmployeeNo	FirstName	LastName	CarNo
1	Fred	Williams	1
2	Sarah	Watson	4
3	James	Hatlitch	6
4	Simon	Webaston	
5	Sally	Harcourt	
6	Martin	Boxer	
7	Trevor	Wright	7

You want to throw a party for all the employees and to include those sales people with company cars (because they have volunteered to drive the employees home afterwards).

You can use:

UNION 3

SELECT FirstName, LastName

FROM EMPLOYEES

UNION SELECT FirstName, LastName

FROM SALESPEOPLE

WHERE SALESPEOPLE.CarNo Is Not Null;

to yield:

FirstName	LastName
Bilda	Groves
Fred	Jones
Fred	Williams
James	Hatlitch
John	Greeves
Sally	Smith
Sarah	Watson
Trevor	Wright

You can also use UNION to produce a list of all employees and sales people who have company cars:

UNION 4

SELECT SALESPEOPLE.FirstName, SALESPEOPLE.LastName, CARS.Make, CARS.Model

FROM

(CARS INNER JOIN SALESPEOPLE

ON CARS.CarNo = SALESPEOPLE.CarNo)

UNION

SELECT EMPLOYEES.FirstName, EMPLOYEES.LastName, CARS.Make, CARS.Model

FROM

(CARS INNER JOIN EMPLOYEES

ON CARS.CarNo = EMPLOYEES.CarNo);

FirstName	LastName	Make	Model
Bilda	Groves	Bentley	Mk. VI
Fred	Jones	Triumph	Stag
Fred	Williams	Triumph	Spitfire
James	Hatlitch	Ford	Mustang
Sally	Smith	Shelby	Cobra
Sarah	Watson	Ford	GT 40
Trevor	Wright	Aston Martin	DB Mk III

SELECT summary

You are just about to encounter a table which has a column called 'Foo'. 'Foo' is a word used in computing as 'a sample name for absolutely anything'. In other words, in this context it means that the content of this column, and the content of any other columns which might be in this table, don't matter; they could be anything. 'Foo' is one of a collection of these terms (others are 'bar', 'baz', 'qux' and 'fred') which are wonderfully known as the metasyntactic variables. This information is of no use to you whatsoever, except as a long and involved way of saying don't worry about the contents of the column called Foo in the next example table.

We have looked at the SELECT statement and its clauses. What I haven't covered but is worth stressing is that a familiarity with SQL enables you to use it with imagination and that's when it becomes an incredibly powerful tool. For example, suppose you import a table of data like this one:

InvoiceNo	Foo
1	King
2	Baby Blue
3	Royal
2	Crested
5	Humbolt
2	Jackass

into a database and then try to make the column InvoiceNo into a primary key. This should fail because the column contains duplicate values. In this tiny table it is easy to find them but what if it had 50,000 rows? The answer is that with a little imagination, a query will find the errant rows for us.

SELECT SUMMARY 1

SELECT InvoiceNo, Count(InvoiceNo) AS NoOfDuplications
FROM INVOICES
GROUP BY InvoiceNo
HAVING Count(InvoiceNo)>1;

InvoiceNo	NoOfDuplications
2	3

SELECT is undoubtedly the most commonly used SQL statement but we shouldn't forget the other members of the Data Manipulation Language (DML): INSERT, UPDATE and DELETE.

INSERT

A brief note about the sample Access database that we provide. It is tempting to open each query as an SQL view, read it and then look at the answer table by pressing the 'Datasheet View' button. This works for most of the examples provided but not the INSERT, UPDATE and DELETE queries. Press the 'Run' button instead.

It is worth bearing in mind that these queries can change the data in the base tables (one of them deletes the entire contents of a table) so, after running some of them, you may need to start again with a clean copy of the database from the web site. In addition, remember that the tables have primary keys, so if you run the same INSERT query twice without deleting the additional row, the query will fail to run the second time.

INSERT is used to add rows to a table, like this:

    INSERT INTO SALES
    VALUES (8, 1, "Jones", "Sofa", "Harrison", 235.67);

This is not the only allowable construction. Indeed, Access will run this syntactical construction but if you save the query, Access converts it to:

INSERT 1

INSERT INTO SALES
SELECT 8, 1, "Jones", "Sofa", "Harrison", 235.67;

Both constructions will add this record to the SALES table:

SaleNo	EmployeeNo	Customer	Item	Supplier	Amount
8	1	Jones	Sofa	Harrison	$235.67

Simple, isn't it? Note that in these first versions we haven't specified the column names explicitly, so we have to provide a value for each one in the correct order.

A slightly more verbose form is possible:

INSERT 2

INSERT INTO SALES (SaleNo, EmployeeNo, Customer, Item, Supplier, Amount)

SELECT 8, 1, "Jones", "Sofa", "Harrison", 235.67;

which has exactly the same result. We can also add to specific columns:

INSERT 3

INSERT INTO SALES (SaleNo, EmployeeNo, Customer, Amount)

SELECT 9, 1, "Jones", 235.67;

which also adds a single record:

SaleNo	EmployeeNo	Customer	Item	Supplier	Amount
1	1	Simpson	Sofa	Harrison	$235.67
2	1	Johnson	Chair	Harrison	$453.78
3	2	Smith	Stool	Ford	$82.78
4	2	Jones	Suite	Harrison	$3,421.00
5	3	Smith	Sofa	Harrison	$235.67
6	1	Simpson	Sofa	Harrison	$235.67
7	1	Jones	Bed	Ford	$453.00
8	1	Jones	Sofa	Harrison	$235.67
9	1	Jones			$235.67

But don't forget closure. Any operation that we perform on a table (or tables) in a relational database must have, as its result, another table. So, suppose we write an INSERT statement like this:

```
INSERT INTO SALES
VALUES
(SELECT *
        FROM SALES2
        WHERE SaleNo > 200);
```

The table SALES2 looks like this:

SALES2					
SaleNo	**EmployeeNo**	**Customer**	**Item**	**Supplier**	**Amount**
3	2	Smith	Stool	Ford	$82.78
5	3	Smith	Sofa	Harrison	$235.67
213	3	Williams	Suite	Harrison	$3,421.00
216	2	McGreggor	Bed	Ford	$453.00
217	1	Williams	Sofa	Harrison	$235.67
218	3	Aitken	Sofa	Harrison	$235.67
225	2	Aitken	Chair	Harrison	$453.78

and this SQL statement will add the five records for which SaleNo is greater than 200 to the SALES table.

Closure is important here because the statement within the parentheses:

INSERT 4
```
SELECT *
        FROM SALES2
        WHERE SaleNo > 200;
```

generates a table in its own right which is then INSERTed into SALES.

As has been mentioned before, SQL is not always as standard as it should be. As another example, the syntax for this statement in Access is:

INSERT 5
```
INSERT INTO SALES
SELECT *
FROM SALES2
WHERE SaleNo > 200;
```

UPDATE

The UPDATE command is wonderfully powerful and allows you to alter the values in fields.

The general format of the command is:

> *UPDATE tablename*
> *SET ColumnName(s) = value*
> *WHERE ColumnName = value*

although the WHERE condition is optional. Thus:

> **UPDATE 1**
> UPDATE SALES
> SET Customer ="Smith";

will change:

SaleNo	EmployeeNo	Customer	Item	Supplier	Amount
1	1	Simpson	Sofa	Harrison	$235.67
2	1	Johnson	Chair	Harrison	$453.78
3	2	Smith	Stool	Ford	$82.78
4	2	Jones	Suite	Harrison	$3,421.00
5	3	Smith	Sofa	Harrison	$235.67
6	1	Simpson	Sofa	Harrison	$235.67
7	1	Jones	Bed	Ford	$453.00

to:

SaleNo	EmployeeNo	Customer	Item	Supplier	Amount
1	1	Smith	Sofa	Harrison	$235.67
2	1	Smith	Chair	Harrison	$453.78
3	2	Smith	Stool	Ford	$82.78
4	2	Smith	Suite	Harrison	$3,421.00
5	3	Smith	Sofa	Harrison	$235.67
6	1	Smith	Sofa	Harrison	$235.67
7	1	Smith	Bed	Ford	$453.00

As you might imagine, this command can be a little devastating in the wrong hands.

The WHERE command generally limits its scope. So:

UPDATE 2

UPDATE SALES

SET Customer ="Smith"

WHERE Customer = "Simpson";

will act on the same initial table to produce:

SaleNo	EmployeeNo	Customer	Item	Supplier	Amount
1	1	Smith	Sofa	Harrison	$235.67
2	1	Johnson	Chair	Harrison	$453.78
3	2	Smith	Stool	Ford	$82.78
4	2	Jones	Suite	Harrison	$3,421.00
5	3	Smith	Sofa	Harrison	$235.67
6	1	Smith	Sofa	Harrison	$235.67
7	1	Jones	Bed	Ford	$453.00

It is quite possible to use different columns in the SET and WHERE clauses. Thus:

UPDATE 3

UPDATE SALES

SET Customer ="Smith"

WHERE SaleNo < 5;

produces:

SaleNo	EmployeeNo	Customer	Item	Supplier	Amount
1	1	Smith	Sofa	Harrison	$235.67
2	1	Smith	Chair	Harrison	$453.78
3	2	Smith	Stool	Ford	$82.78
4	2	Smith	Suite	Harrison	$3,421.00
5	3	Smith	Sofa	Harrison	$235.67
6	1	Simpson	Sofa	Harrison	$235.67
7	1	Jones	Bed	Ford	$453.00

Other variations are possible and indeed common. For example:

UPDATE 4

UPDATE SALES

SET AMOUNT = AMOUNT * 1.1;

will increase all the values in SALES.Amount by 10%, like this:

SaleNo	EmployeeNo	Customer	Item	Supplier	Amount
1	1	Simpson	Sofa	Harrison	$259.24
2	1	Johnson	Chair	Harrison	$499.16
3	2	Smith	Stool	Ford	$91.06
4	2	Jones	Suite	Harrison	$3,763.10
5	3	Smith	Sofa	Harrison	$259.24
6	1	Simpson	Sofa	Harrison	$259.24
7	1	Jones	Bed	Ford	$498.30

This sort of variant is particularly useful if profits are slumping.

DELETE

The DELETE command allows you to delete specific records from specific tables.

The general format of the command is:

        DELETE ColumnName(s)
        FROM tablename
        WHERE ColumnName = value

The *ColumnName(s)* section of the query can be misleading since it implies that the DELETE command will simply remove individual fields from records. This is not the case, the DELETE command removes any and all *records* which match the WHERE condition. Rather frighteningly, the WHERE condition itself is optional. Thus:

DELETE 1
DELETE *
FROM SALES;

is a particularly powerful (not to say dangerous) statement. The output table looks like this:

SaleNo	EmployeeNo	Customer	Item	Supplier	Amount

To be more specific, this command deletes the entire contents of the SALES table. Please be aware of the consequences of any injudicious use of this command.

More commonly (and less alarmingly) the command is used more like this:

DELETE 2
DELETE *
FROM SALES
WHERE EmployeeNo = 2;

which deletes two records and produces:

SaleNo	EmployeeNo	Customer	Item	Supplier	Amount
1	1	Simpson	Sofa	Harrison	$235.67
2	1	Johnson	Chair	Harrison	$453.78
5	3	Smith	Sofa	Harrison	$235.67
6	1	Simpson	Sofa	Harrison	$235.67
7	1	Jones	Bed	Ford	$453.00

One of the reviewers wrote "What happens if you put field names into the delete statement like:
> *DELETE Customer*
> *FROM SALES*
> *WHERE EmployeeNo = 2;"*

It is a good question, and the answer is that this will have exactly the same effect as:
> *DELETE ***
> *FROM SALES*
> *WHERE EmployeeNo = 2;*

In other words, the DELETE statement works only on entire records; specifying fields has no effect.

A question (and a free SQL diagnostic tool)

The two following SQL statements are perfectly legal and both will run. One of them will find all of the rows where the SaleNo is greater than 200 and order the answer table by EmployeeNo and SaleNo. The other won't and is essentially useless. The burning question is "Which is the useful one?"

Is it:

Q1
SELECT *
FROM SALES2
WHERE SaleNo>200
ORDER BY EmployeeNo, SaleNo;

or

Q2
SELECT *
FROM SALES2
WHERE SaleNo>200
ORDER BY EmployeeNo AND SaleNo;

The only difference, to save you wasting time comparing them, is in the ORDER BY statement.

Answer: Q1 is sensible and returns:

SaleNo	EmployeeNo	Customer	Item	Supplier	Amount
217	1	Williams	Sofa	Harrison	$235.67
216	2	McGreggor	Bed	Ford	$453.00
225	2	Aitken	Chair	Harrison	$453.78
213	3	Williams	Suite	Harrison	$3,421.00
218	3	Aitken	Sofa	Harrison	$235.67

Q2 returns:

SaleNo	EmployeeNo	Customer	Item	Supplier	Amount
225	2	Aitken	Chair	Harrison	$453.78
218	3	Aitken	Sofa	Harrison	$235.67
217	1	Williams	Sofa	Harrison	$235.67
216	2	McGreggor	Bed	Ford	$453.00
213	3	Williams	Suite	Harrison	$3,421.00

because it has a very odd construction:

ORDER BY EmployeeNo AND SaleNo

Despite appearances, this does *not* say, "order the rows by EmployeeNo and then by SaleNo". Instead it says "evaluate the expression 'EmployeeNo AND SaleNo' for truth (the answer will come back as -1 (True) or 0 (False)) and then stack the rows based on this value", You can prove this to yourself by adding the expressions which are being evaluated to the list of information that you want to see.

Thus:

SELECT SaleNo>200 AS 'SaleNo>200',
EmployeeNo AND SaleNo AS 'Emp AND Sale',
EmployeeNo, SaleNo, Customer
FROM SALES2
WHERE SaleNo>200
ORDER BY EmployeeNo AND SaleNo;

produces:

'SaleNo>200'	'Emp AND Sale'	EmployeeNo	SaleNo	Customer
-1	-1	2	225	Aitken
-1	-1	3	218	Aitken
-1	-1	1	217	Williams
-1	-1	2	216	McGreggor
-1	-1	3	213	Williams

In all of the rows the expression 'EmployeeNo AND SaleNo' happens to evaluate to -1, so the sorting has no effect.

I take the trouble to show you this not because I think you are likely to make this particular mistake, but if you are human, you will make some mistakes somewhere along the line. If and when you come across an intractable SQL statement that runs but doesn't give you the answer you expect, then you can use SQL's own ability to show you the results of expressions as a diagnostic tool.

Incidentally, Access will run the last SQL statement exactly as shown but when the query is saved the SQL syntax is converted to:

Q3
SELECT SaleNo>200 AS ['SaleNo>200'],
EmployeeNo AND SaleNo AS ['Emp AND Sale'],
EmployeeNo, SaleNo, Customer
FROM SALES2
WHERE SaleNo>200
ORDER BY EmployeeNo AND SaleNo;

which is therefore how it appears in the sample database.

Summary

SQL is extremely powerful and, if you spend any time at all with databases, it well repays the effort required to learn it. One of the best ways to learn it is to practice using it, which is why the sample database has more than 70 example queries.

Chapter 30

Domains

The concept of a domain is a crucial part of the relational model, which is strange because it is ignored by almost every RDBMS I can call to mind.

A domain is a pool of values from which the values found in a given field in a particular table can be drawn. For example, suppose that we are defining a table to hold information about Employees. We decide that we will store the number of their parents who are living, so we declare a field to have the name ParentNo and we make it of type Integer. We decide to include only those parents who are related by direct involvement (thus eliminating problems with uncertain numbers of step-parents) and decide that there are only three possible values for this field, namely 0, 1 and 2. So, the domain for this field is defined as a subset of integers, namely 0, 1 and 2.

Domains don't have to contain numeric values. Consider a field called City in which are stored, quite reasonably, the names of cities. There is a finite number of cities in the world so the domain for the field contains a finite number of values such as 'London', 'Seattle' or 'Dundee'.

The domain for a field type called Day might well contain the values 'Monday', 'Tuesday', 'Wednesday', 'Thursday', 'Friday', 'Saturday' and 'Sunday'.

Domains come into their own when we start to join tables. The bad news is that very few RDBMSs fully support domains; instead they simply ignore them. In order to understand why they shouldn't ignore such a fundamental (and fundamentally useful) part of relational theory, consider the following example.

EMPLOYEES				
EmployeeNo	**FirstName**	**LastName**	**DateOfBirth**	**DateEmployed**
1	Bilda	Groves	12 Apr 1966	01 May 1999
2	John	Greeves	21 Mar 1977	01 Jan 2000
3	Sally	Smith	01 May 1977	01 Apr 2002

SALES					
SaleNo	**EmployeeNo**	**Customer**	**Item**	**Supplier**	**Amount**
1	1	Simpson	Sofa	Harrison	$235.67
2	1	Johnson	Chair	Harrison	$453.78
3	2	Smith	Stool	Ford	$82.78
4	2	Jones	Suite	Harrison	$3,421.00
5	3	Smith	Sofa	Harrison	$235.67
6	1	Simpson	Sofa	Harrison	$235.67
7	1	Jones	Bed	Ford	$453.00

Let's assume that EMPLOYEES.EmployeeNo, SALES.EmployeeNo and SALES.SaleNo are of type Integer.

If you join the two tables using the two EmployeeNo fields, then all will be well. If, however, you make, say a one-to-many join between EMPLOYEES.EmployeeNo and SALES.SaleNo then the result will be meaningless.

The typical PC-based RDBMSs of today will happily allow you to make joins between two fields as long as those fields are of the same data type; in this case all three fields are of type Integer, so both meaningless and meaningful joins can be made. However, suppose that we declare two domains like this:

Name of domain	Permitted values
Emp	Integer between 1 and 2,000 inclusive
Sales	Integer between 1 and 100,000 inclusive

We then declare both of the EmployeeNo fields to be of type Integer and declare that both will draw their values from the domain called Emp. We further declare SaleNo to be of type Integer and also that it will draw its values from the domain Sales. Thereafter the RDBMS should only allow us to make joins between fields which are of the same data type and which draw their values from the same domain.

Domains are simply another safety mechanism; they prevent later users of the database from unfortunate errors. Since almost all RDBMSs fail to support them, they remain a theoretical consideration, which is a shame.

Chapter 31

What does null mean?

A given field in a given record can contain data, or not. If you don't enter a value into a field in a particular record, you might think that the field was simply empty, but life isn't that simple. Instead the field is said to contain a null value. If, for example, a field is supposed to contain the phone number of a friend but you don't know the phone number, you don't enter any data. The field is then said to contain a null value.

At the most basic level, a null value simply denotes missing information. I was talking to a friend on the phone once about a database problem when our conversation was suddenly replaced by an electronic tone for about three seconds. At least, I had heard a tone which blotted out everything else but I had no idea what my friend had heard. "Did you hear a tone then?", I asked. "No," replied my friend, "I just heard a null." She hadn't received any data during those three seconds – she had received an absence of data.

The odd thing about nulls is that we tend to refer to nulls positively. We don't say "The field is empty"; we say, "The field contains a null", meaning that it contains nothing.

Nulls can cause unending problems in databases at two distinct levels.

Firstly, at a theoretical level, what exactly is meant by a null has been causing problems for years. Date, in *An Introduction to Database Systems*, devotes more than 20 pages to the problems of trying to represent missing information in a database. He comes to the conclusion that despite the fact that vendors provide support for nulls in their products, we should ignore this and not use nulls at all.

Secondly, in the real world most RDBMSs do support nulls and, of course, people make use of nulls in their applications. This causes problems and the problems are all the more difficult to tie down because of the different ways in which vendors support nulls!

To try to give a flavor of the problems that they can cause, consider the following.

Imagine a hospital blood bank that receives un-typed blood from various sources (hopefully human). Each bottle has a unique identifier that is entered in a table called BLOODBANK, along with the physical location of the bottle in the store. There is also a field for the Type that is filled in once the blood in each bottle has been tested in the laboratory. Values such as A+ and O- are entered as appropriate and a null means that the laboratory report on that bottle is has not yet arrived.

BLOODBANK	
Identifier	Type
32WWE	A+
45555	B+
456FF	O-
45FFG	AB+
4FGGG	
55EE4	B-
676FG	A+
FDD5F	AB+
FFFF4	
FGF66	B-
FGGGG	A+
GFGHG	A+

The hospital also receives patients and each has his or her details entered into another table, called PATIENTS, along with a unique patient number. All patients have their blood group determined as soon as possible after admission and this too goes into the table. If the blood group field for a patient shows a null value, it means that, for whatever reason, the information is not yet available from the lab.

PATIENTS			
PatientNo	FirstName	LastName	Type
1	Bilda	Groves	O-
2	John	Greeves	A+
3	Sally	Smith	
4	Fred	Jones	AB-

If patient 2 is in need of a transfusion, you would query the database to find which bottles in the store contained blood of the correct type. John is type A+, so the query finds several matching entries in the BLOODBANK table.

FindBloodForPatientNo2				
FirstName	**LastName**	**PatientNo**	**Type**	**Identifier**
John	Greeves	2	A+	GFGHG
John	Greeves	2	A+	FGGGG
John	Greeves	2	A+	676FG
John	Greeves	2	A+	32WWE

What about patient number 3? She hasn't been typed as yet, so what should happen if we query the database to find blood for her?

The answer should be that no records are returned; that is, no blood is identified as suitable for this patient. Access handles this 'correctly' but not all RDBMSs do so. Some, for example, match the null values in PATIENTS.Type and BLOODBANK.Type, suggesting that Sally Smith could be given the blood in 4FGGG or FFFF4. Would you be prepared to put un-typed blood into a patient? If you were that patient, would you be happy with this arrangement?

Ignoring the arguments about *whether* RDBMS should support nulls, in my view when they do they should never treat null values as equal. I know it is tempting because of the way we use the word 'null'. Expressions like "Oh, there is a null value in that field" implies that the field actually contains something. But remember that a null isn't a type of entry like a one or a zero, it is the absence of an entry.

Take another example. Suppose that we are trying to match not patients to blood but hotel guests to rooms. If a room is occupied, then the guest number is inserted into a field (ROOMS.GuestNo), otherwise it is left as a null value. Surely in this case the use of a null value is OK?

No, nulls are being misused here. A null value means that you don't *know* the state of the real-world object represented by the data in the field. Assuming that the hotel is run correctly, we know which rooms are unoccupied, so a null value, which implies uncertainty, is inappropriate.

Instead of a null, we might insert an agreed value in here (perhaps a zero) to indicate an unoccupied room. However, this causes its own problems.

In my less rigorous moments, I have been known to argue that it doesn't matter too much how a particular RDBMS treats nulls, as long as that treatment is always consistent and as long as you are sure you know the rules by which it operates. However, the bottom line is that I still have a strong preference for ones that don't match on nulls. (*Bill added "That is what the 'is null' operator is for!"*).

The take-home message is that a null doesn't mean 'the default value', nor does it mean 'we don't care what value goes in here'. It means 'We don't *know* what value goes in here'. The difference, particularly in the blood bank example, is vital and could be fatal. But…

…there is a big 'but' lurking here. I have only just begun to scratch the surface of the problems that nulls bring. For each argument that I have raised here, someone, somewhere has a counter-argument. I would not for a moment suggest that in a trite thousand or so words I have done anything except alert you to the fact that there are problems associated with using nulls. Be careful out there.

Chapter 32

Primary keys

In the database column that I write for *Personal Computer World*, I was discussing primary keys a while ago and offered the opinion that for a small car restoration business, the registration number (also known as a license number) of the cars in the workshop would make a good primary key. A reader questioned this opinion and the point is interesting because it illustrates the scope that a primary key must cover.

He wrote:

Car registration numbers are very poor primary keys because they can easily change and therefore do not uniquely identify a vehicle. The chassis or VIN (Vehicle Identification Number) is far more suitable although not as easily obtained. People often argue that the registration number is good enough in the 'real world' but would probably not like to buy a written-off and repaired car just because it had a new reg.

In absolute terms the writer was perfectly correct. However, much as I hate to be contentious, I am also one of those people who thinks registration numbers are (sometimes) good enough for the real world. Which brings us neatly to a point which has a wider relevance than car registration numbers; indeed, it is an important principle about primary keys in general.

The identifier that you choose as your primary key doesn't have to be unique in global terms, it just has to be unique within the context of the database in which it is used. In other words, a database exists to model a subset of the real world; as long as the identifier you choose remains unique within that subset, it is a suitable candidate for a primary key.

For example, if I was building a database which recorded every car in the country, I would without question use the VIN as the unique identifier because it is the one property of a vehicle that cannot (legally) be changed. So, there's no argument in this case.

However, consider a garage which services and repairs cars. Suppose that the owner of the garage uses a database to track the work done on the customers' cars and that the sole function of this database is to ensure that each customer is billed correctly. Within the world of this particular database, the registration number uniquely identifies the car, so it is an excellent primary key. Even if the car happens to be legally re-registered during its time in the garage, the garage proprietor can simply change the registration number in the database because the new number will still be unique.

Now, let's make it more complex. Suppose that the garage tracks the service and repair history of its customers' cars for several years. The chances are that one of the cars will eventually be legally re-registered and this will make the tracking of the car's service history problematical. So, in this case should the garage owner use the VIN or the registration number? My practical experience of garages suggest it would be a disaster to use anything other than the registration number.

Typically, mechanics fill out worksheets which identify the number of hours they have worked on each car and they identify the cars by registration number. Why use the registration number? For the simple reason that it is plastered on the front and back of the car in big letters, so it's convenient. This leaves us with a stark choice.

We can elect to use the registration number:

>**Advantage** – easy to find and use
>
>**Disadvantage** – it may change with time

We can use the VIN number:

>**Advantage** – unlikely to change with time
>
>**Disadvantage** – inaccessible and tortuously long

We (the designers of databases) have to balance two opposing factors. Using the chassis/VIN as the primary key protects against problems as cars are re-registered; using the registration number will cause fewer errors due to finger trouble. Our job is to choose the lesser of two evils; in this case, I would unhesitatingly choose the registration number.

While I have absolutely no experimental evidence to back this up, I have little doubt that insisting that mechanics use the VIN to identify vehicles would introduce more errors into the database than we would reasonably expect to occur from changed registration numbers. In choosing the registration number we also avoid the wrath of the mechanics who will hate using the VIN. Indeed, human nature being what it is, if we force them to use the VIN they might well introduce errors just to spite us.

I also suspect that a garage that welded cars together in a haphazard and illegal manner wouldn't cavil at altering its own database records in the dead of night.

Before we leave the subject, it is worth noting that genuinely global primary keys are very difficult to find. For example, even assuming that every person was honest, chassis/VINs are imperfect. Early in the history of cars, there was little standardization and several manufacturers (such as Bentley) used very simple sequences of numbers; a Bentley with chassis number 3 (and hence in modern parlance, VIN 3) still exists, for example. Other manufacturers will have done the same, so we are likely to have multiple cars with VIN 3. This means that in practice, to get a global primary key we would have to use a key combined from the manufacturer's name and the chassis/VIN. But for certain old and valuable cars that have undergone extensive modification, crash damage and subsequent rebuilding, it has been known for two perfectly complete cars from the same manufacturer to vie for the same chassis/VIN!

Candidate keys

In the example above we were discussing a case where one real-world object (in this case a car) had two possible unique identifiers that could serve as the primary key – license number and VIN.

CARS					
LicenseNo	**Make**	**Model**	**Year**	**VIN**	**Color**
CER 162 C	Triumph	Spitfire	1965	QQ1234567890	Green
EF 8972	Bentley	Mk. VI	1946	AA12345678765	Black
YSK 114	Bentley	Mk. VI	1949	AA12345678764	Red

In the database world, like all specialized worlds, it is often convenient to have a shorthand way of referring to a situation. A useful term here is 'candidate key' – the implication being that both are candidates for the exalted position of primary key.

So the conversation might go:

Mark: Well, LicenseNo would make a good primary key.

You: Yes, but VIN is also a candidate.

Mark: Oh yes, so it is. Hmm, which is going to be better?

Part 5

Speeding up your database

Chapter 33

Hardware considerations

If you are a DBA (DataBase Administrator) you get lots of phone calls every day. I can't tell you what your next call will be but I can tell you what it won't be. You are quite definitely not about to receive one that starts "The database is running far, far too quickly. Can you slow it down a bit?" In other words, no matter how fast the database runs, people always want it to run faster.

With any database (indeed, any application) that isn't performing well, something somewhere will be limiting the performance. This limiting factor is often called a bottleneck. The trick is to identify the bottleneck first before trying to fix the problem. I realize this sounds obvious, but I have seen several databases where money has been poured into more memory and faster CPUs, neither of which made the slightest difference because the speed of the database was being limited by the network speed.

Getting a general feel for where the bottleneck lies doesn't have to be rocket science. When you are asked to investigate a slow database, your first move can be as simple as standing next to the server. If all you can hear is the frenetic thrashing of the disks, it's almost certain that CPU cycles are not the limiting factor. If, on the other hand, all is silence bar the humming of the cooling fans and the occasional chirrup of a disk, then the CPU(s) and the network are worth investigating. I'm not suggesting that this is the be-all and end-all of diagnosing CPU activity, but it's a worthwhile rule of ear.

There are two broad ways in which you can make a database faster: you can either tweak the hardware or the software. In the early days of databases, hardware was very expensive and so software tuning was often preferred but that balance is changing, mainly because the cost of hardware is plummeting.

So, let's take a look at these two broad areas. But first, a warning from your authors.

One problem with writing about tuning databases is that despite what we have just said about rockets and science, it can become a complex business. In even a small database application there are many factors to consider and those factors tend to interact. So the easiest way for us to safely cover the subject of speed tuning is to tell you about the issues but never actually mention any numbers. For example, we can tell you that ensuring you have adequate memory is important (which it is) but not actually give you any idea about how much 'adequate' might be. The beauty of this approach is that we never mislead you; the problem is that it is also likely to be very irritating to read. You can be left wondering whether 128 Mbytes is adequate or should you be thinking about 10 TBytes. The alternative is to try and give you ballpark figures where appropriate and that is what we have tried to do. But, and this is an important 'but', we would never, ever suggest that you base any operational decisions on the figures we provide here. They are simply there to give you a feel for the numbers. Talk to other people, seek advice, find out more about your particular database engine (and even the version you are using) before you ever think about committing your time and money.

Another reason why we are being careful here is that this and the next three chapters are simply an overview, not the definitive work. As a rather terrifying example, in this book we devote about 200 words to the subject of disk I/O (input/output) and speed. The following book devotes 300 *pages* to the subject and just covers one particular database engine.

> *Oracle Disk I/O Tuning: Disk I/O Performance & Optimization for Oracle Databases* by Mike Ault (Author), Donald K. Burleson (Editor) Rampant Techpress (April 2004) ISBN: 0974599344.

So please do treat this as simply an introduction to the subject. Having said that, we have tried to pack as much information as we can into Part 5, so hopefully you'll find it interesting. We'll start now with hardware considerations.

CPUs

A shortage of CPU cycles can cause a bottleneck in a database application and is relatively easy to diagnose and cure. Perform the ear test and then simply measure the CPU activity. If it/they are flat-lining then the answer is simple – add more CPUs to the box, move to a box with faster CPUs, turn the database server into a cluster and/or add more nodes if you're already clustered.

Memory

Database engines love memory. The more you give them (within reason) the faster they will run. Why? Well, they do clever things with it. For example, suppose that you have a large table that is almost always read and rarely updated. It's a base table and so, by default, it's kept on disk. Every query that runs against it requires one or more disk reads. Disks are slow. When compared with RAM, disks are hundreds or thousands of times slower. If you give the database an adequate supply of RAM it can cache the table in memory. Result: the database runs much, much faster.

Then there are queries. Suppose that your users have a very popular view which also happens to be complex and therefore slow. And let's also imagine that they rarely update the base tables that underpin that view. First thing in the morning, a user opens the view. The engine has to run the underlying query and then send out the result to the user, but imagine that it then caches the answer in memory. There is a good chance that another user will run the query again before the underlying tables are updated. In that case, the engine can simply pull the result from memory without even touching the base tables.

And so on and so on but I won't go on with examples because the truth is that I don't know all of the clever tricks that a database engine can do with memory. The designers of such engines usually keep the more elegant techniques secret so that their competitors don't copy the ideas. However, the bottom line is that, if you give a database engine more memory, it will usually run faster. This is particularly apparent with multi-user databases.

How much memory is enough? Now that's the 64 kilo-dollar question. It will depend on a whole variety of factors such as the size of the database (obviously), the number of indexes you create (indexes can be cached in memory), the number of users and so on. In addition, even factors such as the database size and the distribution of the queries may interact. For example, suppose you have a 40 GByte database, but it turns out that 99% of the queries only ever hit 1 GByte of the data. In that case, caching more than 1GBtye of data will never give you more than a tiny increase in speed, so you may not need as much memory as the size of the database suggests.

Nevertheless, as a very, very general rule of thumb, think in terms of matching the size of the database with RAM. Even as I write that, I can bring to mind times when that advice is totally inappropriate (200 TBytes of data that are queried only once a week by a single user) but it gives a kind of ballpark figure.

Disks

As you are probably aware, disks can be put together into stacks, often called RAID (Redundant Array of Independent [or Inexpensive] Disks). Each stack might contain five physical disks but once they have been turned into a RAID stack, they appear to the database server to be a single logical drive.

The basic idea of RAID is very simple. A RAID system uses multiple physical drives to provide both fault tolerance and performance gains. Each piece of data is written to more than one of the disks. This can, in some case, slow down write performance marginally but it does ensure that if one disk fails, all of the data is still accessible. Since the data can be read from more than one disk (and the RAID controller is usually smart enough to know which disk can provide the data first) the read performance of the RAID system is usually enhanced. In practice there are various flavors of RAID (level 0, level 1 and so on) all of which have different characteristics. Choosing the correct level is important. As a very general rule level 5 is often used for a relational database although level 1 is sometimes favored in write-intensive applications.

Since speed and redundancy are both very desirable, you can assume from now on that every time we use the word 'disk' we don't mean a single physical disk, we mean a RAID stack of some kind that appears to the database server to be a single logical drive.

Data volume vs. disk capacity

As a general rule, the larger the capacity of the disk, the faster you can read data from it and the faster you can write data to it. (Reading and writing to and from a disk can be described as input/output or I/O).

Disk manufacturers make disks for the average user to use in an average way. If a disk manufacturers makes a disk of, say, 1 TByte capacity, they give it an I/O capability that is appropriate for the average use to which that disk will be put.

Databases are not 'average' applications, they are very I/O intensive applications. So if, for example, you have a database with a size of 1 TByte and you place it on a 1 TByte drive, it is almost certain that the database will be bottlenecked by the I/O of the disk. However, you can make use of the correlation between capacity and I/O performance and put your 1 TByte database on a 5 TByte disk. True, you waste 4 TByte of disk space, but you get the greater I/O capability that you need in order to ensure that the disk is not limiting the performance of your database.

Don't put all your eggs in one basket

As mentioned above, disk I/O is a slow process, relatively speaking, because it takes place within a physical device.

Disk drives have heads which read data from, and writes it to, the disk itself. It's rather like the arm on a turntable, except that scratching is not recommended practice with disk drives.

Head movement is physical and hence very, very slow. Performance can therefore be improved by minimizing the travel undertaken by the read/write head inside the disk drive. We can do this by keeping different files on different disks – a good rule of thumb is to put the data on one, the indexes on a second and the log files on a third. (There's more about indexes in the next chapter, and log files are covered in Chapter 23).

As an example, imagine what happens if the data and log files are placed together on one disk. When a row is updated in a table, the head of the disk drive has to be physically moved until it is over the correct part of the disk and a write performed. Once the row has been updated, the transaction must be recorded in the log files. So the head has to be moved until it is over the log file and another write performed. After that, it has to be moved back to the data and so on. In other words, the head spends the majority of its time thrashing across the disk between the data and the log files.

If, on the other hand, the data and logs are kept on separate disks, the head of one drive can sit over the data, moving only slightly each time it needs to access another row. The head in the other drive hovers over the log file, appending to it as required.

The benefits of storage on separate disks are even more apparent if you consider indexing. Given a one million row table, using an index to locate a specific row means the database engine has to jump between the data and the index anything up to twenty times. If both the data and the indexes are on the same disk that's twenty head moves which is going to be painfully slower.

One of the joys of Access is that the entire database application is wrapped up inside a single .MDB file. You can, if you wish, split the user interface from the data (as discussed in Chapter 20 – Database architecture) but Access does not let you split the data from the indexes, and Access keeps no log files. The good news is that while all of the foregoing chapter is absolutely true about other database engines, you don't have to worry about it at all as an Access developer.

Chapter 34

Indexing

Indexing is the first topic we'll cover in the area of software optimization of database performance.

Indexing techniques

In almost all databases, the largest single improvement you can make to their performance is by applying indexes and they are very cost-effective to implement. Virtually all gain and no pain; so, what is an index and how does it work?

Incidentally, the plural of index is actually 'indices' but in the computing world people typically use the word 'indexes' so we have followed suit.

One way to describe an index is to tell you, very briefly, how and why we use them. Imagine that you have a 20 million row table which has many columns, one of which is LastName. You query the table looking for "Whitehorn" in the LastName column. It takes 2 hours to return an answer set of one row. You then apply an index to the LastName column and rerun the query. It takes three seconds to return the same one row. In a nutshell, that is why we are all interested in indexes. They can speed up the access to data by several orders of magnitude. The next question is "How do they work?"

Well, humans can manipulate lists efficiently, as long as they are sorted – that's why we are taught the alphabet from an early age. An RDBMS can do the same trick on any set of sorted values and therefore find data much more rapidly. So, in essence, an index is simply a sorted list of values.

Binary chop

How does a database engine search a sorted list? Well, there are several ways, and a very common one is the binary chop.

Here is a tiny sorted list. Imagine that it contains 1 million sorted items rather than the paltry nine that are shown.

LastName
Cooper
Falconer
Lynch
Lynch
McColgan
Robb
Thompson
Wellington
Wellington

Let's assume that somewhere in those 1 million items, one is 'Smith'. The database engine doesn't start at the top of the list; instead it jumps to the middle (item 500,000) and reads the item. This happens to be 'Melville'. Since M comes before S in the alphabet, it is now certain that 'Smith' is somewhere below the middle point of the list – in other words, somewhere within items 500,001 to 1,000,000. By making a single read of the list, the engine has eliminated half of the items from the search process.

Now it takes the remaining set of 500,000 and reads the middle item of that set. That is 'Robertson', so 'Smith' must be located in the first 250,000 of this new set, so the database engine can safely ignore the second half.

You can see the pattern that is emerging. By always reading the middle item in the remaining set, the engine can, with each read, eliminate half the remaining items. So, given 1,000,000 rows, how many reads do we need to get down to one possible row?

Reads	No. of items remaining
0	1,000,000
1	500,000
2	250,000
3	125,000
4	62,500
5	31,250
6	15,625
7	7,813
8	3,907
9	1,954
10	977
11	489
12	245
13	123
14	62
15	31
16	16
17	8
18	4
19	2
20	1

Answer: assuming the worst case, it only takes 20 reads to guarantee finding any item in a list of 1 million values, as long as the list is sorted, and we may well find it in fewer reads. If the column isn't sorted and we are very unlucky, we'll need to read all 1,000,000 items; on average we'll find the item after 500,000 reads.

That's a maximum of 20 reads with an index versus an average of 500,000 without. That, in a nutshell, is why indexes are so much faster.

This reason for the name of this technique – binary chop – is now, hopefully, clear. Each read of the list chops the number of remaining items to be read in half. Binary chops are almost frighteningly efficient and, even more unnervingly, their efficiency actually increases as the number of items in the list increases. We can see this if we consider the number of chops necessary for different numbers of items.

Number of items	Maximum number of reads to find one item
100	7
1,000	10
10,000	14
100,000	17
1,000,000	20
10,000,000	24
100,000,000	27
1,000,000,000	31

Very roughly, increasing the size of the list by an order of magnitude (making it ten times larger) only adds another 3 or 4 chops. Wow.

For reasons that will shortly become clear, there are two different flavors of index – clustered and non-clustered. The database engine can utilize the binary chop technique to search either flavor.

Clustered indexes

A clustered index works by actually moving the rows on disk so that they are physically stored in sorted order. For example, consider a table with five columns. If we apply a clustered index to the LastName column, the rows will all be moved so that they are in the order shown.

CUSTOMERS				
CustomerNo	**Title**	**LastName**	**FirstName**	**Town**
6	Ms.	Cooper	Norah	Seattle
8	Mrs.	Falconer	Grace	London
7	Ms.	Lynch	Helen	Boston
5	Mr.	Lynch	Colin	London
3	Prof.	McColgan	Harry	Seattle
9	Mrs.	Robb	Mary	Dundee
1	Mr.	Thompson	Brian	Boston
4	Dr.	Wellington	Sandra	Boston
2	Miss	Wellington	Helen	Dundee

The LastName column has become the sorted list which means that the database can find any value in this column (e.g. 'Robb') very rapidly and it can use a binary chop to do so.

However, bear in mind that while a clustered index on one column speeds up the access to the data in that column dramatically, it doesn't help for any of the other columns. For example, in order to find all of the people with FirstName = 'Helen', the database engine would have to examine every row.

Of course, if you need the database to find all of the Helens rapidly, you could apply a clustered index to the FirstName column instead, in which case all of the rows would be re-sorted on the disk:

CUSTOMERS				
CustomerNo	**Title**	**LastName**	**FirstName**	**Town**
1	Mr.	Thompson	Brian	Boston
5	Mr.	Lynch	Colin	London
8	Mrs.	Falconer	Grace	London
3	Prof.	McColgan	Harry	Seattle
7	Ms.	Lynch	Helen	Boston
2	Miss	Wellington	Helen	Dundee
9	Mrs.	Robb	Mary	Dundee
6	Ms.	Cooper	Norah	Seattle
4	Dr.	Wellington	Sandra	Boston

This is fine but that sort has now disrupted the original sort by LastName, so if you ask the engine to find the Robbs, it will be slow again because it has to check every single row.

The crucial problem here is that a table can only ever be sorted in one particular way at a time. In turn that means that you can only ever have one clustered index for each table.

Of course, there is no reason why you can't create a single clustered index on more than one column at the same time. For example, the table below has been cluster indexed on both the LastName and FirstName columns.

CUSTOMERS				
CustomerNo	**Title**	**LastName**	**FirstName**	**Town**
6	Ms.	Cooper	Norah	Seattle
8	Mrs.	Falconer	Grace	London
5	Mr.	Lynch	Colin	London
7	Ms.	Lynch	Helen	Boston
3	Prof.	McColgan	Harry	Seattle
9	Mrs.	Robb	Mary	Dundee
1	Mr.	Thompson	Brian	Boston
2	Miss	Wellington	Helen	Dundee
4	Dr.	Wellington	Sandra	Boston

The rows are sorted initially by LastName. Where there are two or more rows with identical values in LastName (Lynch, for example), these rows are ordered by the value in FirstName.

This two-column clustered index makes it easy to find any value in LastName. In addition, it makes it easy to find a specific combination of LastName and FirstName ('Wellington' 'Helen', for example). However, even though the FirstName column is part of an index, this particular index doesn't help the database engine to find all Helens because they are still scattered throughout the table. To find all instances of a first name, a complete table scan is required (which means all rows must be inspected).

So, clustered indexes are very fast and they can be applied to multiple columns, but we can still only ever have one clustered index per table. Nevertheless clustered indexes are great because they are the fastest index around and they are the most important step towards fast query response times. Almost all database engines will automatically (and without consulting you) apply the one clustered index that logic allows for a table to the primary key column(s). That means that all of the rows in a table are sorted on disk according to the values in the primary key.

The description we're giving you is, almost inevitably, a simplification. If what we have described was implemented literally, the result would be horribly flawed. Suppose a table holds primary key values including 1, 3, 4, 5 and so on up to 20 million (the value 2 having been omitted). If a row is ever inserted with the primary key value of 2, the database engine would have to physically move 19,999,999 rows on the disk in order to slot the new row into its place. In practice this isn't necessary because clustered indexes are complex entities and are implemented with great care. Despite this, the basic description that we have given you remains perfectly true: the engine really does physically move the rows around on disk when you apply a clustered index.

Non-clustered indexes

Non-clustered indexes give you essentially the same benefits as clustered ones – they speed up access to the data. They are a little slower than clustered indexes (though not much) but their big advantage is that you can have as many of them as you like on a single table.

Sounds almost too good to be true, but it isn't. They really work and how they work is most easily described using an example. Let's suppose that CustomerNo is the primary key of the table below.

CUSTOMERS

CustomerNo	Title	LastName	FirstName	Town
1	Mr.	Thompson	Brian	Boston
2	Miss	Wellington	Helen	Dundee
3	Prof.	McColgan	Harry	Seattle
4	Dr.	Wellington	Sandra	Boston
5	Mr.	Lynch	Colin	London
6	Ms.	Cooper	Norah	Seattle
7	Ms.	Lynch	Helen	Boston
8	Mrs.	Falconer	Grace	London
9	Mrs.	Robb	Mary	Dundee

Imagine for a moment that we re-sorted this table by the values in the LastName column. We would get this table:

CUSTOMERS

CustomerNo	Title	LastName	FirstName	Town
6	Ms.	Cooper	Norah	Seattle
8	Mrs.	Falconer	Grace	London
5	Mr.	Lynch	Colin	London
7	Ms.	Lynch	Helen	Boston
3	Prof.	McColgan	Harry	Seattle
9	Mrs.	Robb	Mary	Dundee
1	Mr.	Thompson	Brian	Boston
2	Miss	Wellington	Helen	Dundee
4	Dr.	Wellington	Sandra	Boston

Now suppose that we delete all of the columns except the primary key:

CustomerNo
6
8
7
5
3
9
1
4
2

We end up with a list of items, one for each row in the table. What is unusual about this list is that it is a set of primary key values which are not is ascending order. Their order is determined by the alphabetical order in another column, LastName.

Now suppose that we start to use this sorted list together with the original table:

CUSTOMERS				
CustomerNo	Title	LastName	FirstName	Town
1	Mr.	Thompson	Brian	Boston
2	Miss	Wellington	Helen	Dundee
3	Prof.	McColgan	Harry	Seattle
4	Dr.	Wellington	Sandra	Boston
5	Mr.	Lynch	Colin	London
6	Ms.	Cooper	Norah	Seattle
7	Ms.	Lynch	Helen	Boston
8	Mrs.	Falconer	Grace	London
9	Mrs.	Robb	Mary	Dundee

Suppose I want to find the first person in the list alphabetically by last name. I don't even look at the CUSTOMERS table. I look at the sorted list of primary key values and pull out the first one I find – 6. Then I go to the CUSTOMERS table, find primary key value 6 and I have now found the first person in the list alphabetically by last name – Cooper. Easy.

A non-clustered index is essentially a list of the primary key values which have been sorted as a result of information in another column. In the above example, the order was determined by the values in LastName.

This one:

CustomerNo
1
5
8
3
7
2
9
6
4

has been sorted by FirstName.

So, if I have the original table and these two sorted lists, I now have two non-clustered indexes that can both be used to find data in particular columns very rapidly.

Of course, non-clustered indexes can be used for more than finding the top of a list. I can easily perform a binary chop on the non-clustered index. Suppose I want to find FirstName = 'Mary'. I jump to the middle of the second non-clustered index and read the value – 7. I move to the CUSTOMERS table and look up that primary key value. The FirstName value is 'Helen' so I know that 'Mary' is somewhere below the mid-point of the non-clustered index. So I have just eliminated half the number of items that I need to examine, and I know that the primary key value of Mary's record is somewhere in the re-mainder.

CustomerNo
2
9
6
4

And I can continue to chop this list down until I find Mary's record. Note that the binary chop is applied to the index and not the table. This explains why, when we were talking about disks and performance, we suggested that you put the data and the indexes on different disks to minimize the head movement.

Once again we are painfully aware that non-clustered indexes can become more complex than this. To give just an idea of how the idea of a sorted list might be modified for speed, imagine that you had a yes/no column in a 20 million row table and that by far the majority of the values are "Yes". In fact, there were only three rows that contain the value "No". Keeping a non-clustered index of 20 million values would work and it would give much faster access to the data. However, the index itself would be very large and a little thought shows that we can store the information much more efficiently. For example, this tells you all you need to know:

Primary Key Value	Value
2,342,345	No
8,231,237	No
11,453,454	No
All the rest	Yes

Another example: we said that a non-clustered index was a set of primary key values sorted by the values in another column (say, LastName). If we also store the values from the LastName column in the index, then a query that just requests LastName will run much faster because only the index has to be queried. Of course, this makes the index larger and slower to maintain but the speed gain can be dramatic.

Applying indexes – which fields/columns should be indexed?

All RDBMS allow you to mark one or more columns as indexed. This is usually done during table design and once you have decided which columns to index, the RDBMS should construct and maintain the indexes transparently.

To give a feel for the speed difference that indexes can make, I ran some queries on tables both with and without appropriate indexes. One particular query on non-indexed tables was aborted after 18 hours owing to boredom on my part. The same query (with the same RDBMS) was completed in under a minute with indexes.

If indexes are such a good idea (and they are), why not simply index every column in every table in every database? Well, despite their efficiency, indexes do take some processing power to maintain. This maintenance occurs whenever rows are updated or added to the table. Every time a new row is added, or an indexed value in an existing row is edited, some or all of the indexes have to be modified as well. Given a huge table and multiple indexes this can produce a significant delay before the RDBMS will allow the next row to be edited or added.

This means that indexes shouldn't be used indiscriminately but there is nothing to stop you from using them intelligently, as long as you are aware of their pros and cons.

Pros: They speed up querying. This makes a dramatic difference with large tables.

Cons: They slow down data entry and editing. This won't be noticeable with small tables but can be a problem with large ones.

Primary keys

The most obvious columns to index in a table are those that make up the primary key but the RDBMS will typically do that for you. It will usually apply a clustered index.

Heavily used columns

Other obvious columns to index are those that users frequently name in the WHERE part of their queries. For example, the query:

SELECT Item, Amount, SaleNo

FROM SALES

WHERE Item = 'Sofa'

would almost certainly run faster if the Item column was indexed.

Table size is important

Note the slightly cagey nature of that last statement; 'would almost certainly run faster'. There are times when indexes make no difference at all to the speed of a query. For example, suppose a table is tiny – perhaps four rows. You can, if you like, put one or more indexes on this table. However, it would be faster for the database to read the entire table into memory and manipulate it there than it would be for it to use the index. The query optimizer (see below) should be able to work this out for you but a general rule goes something like this. If the table is tiny, don't index it (apart from the primary key which is done automatically for you anyway). If the table is huge then you will see massive gains from indexing and it is worth spending a fair time getting the indexing strategy correct. If the table is mid-sized and you are in doubt, then I would err on the side of indexing it. The query optimizer should be able to decide whether or not to use the indexes (there's more about query optimizers in the next chapter).

What is small, medium and large in this context? Here we really can't help you because it depends on the relative size of the table, the server, the memory and so on. On a PC a 10,000 row table can be large, on a mainframe that same table could be tiny.

Foreign keys

Consider these two tables.

CUSTOMERS

CustomerNo	FirstName	LastName
1	Brian	Thompson
2	Sally	Henderson
3	Harry	McColgan
4	Sandra	Wellington

ORDERS

OrderNo	CustomerNo	Supplier	Price	Item
1	2	Harrison	£235.00	Desk
2	1	Ford	£234.00	Chair
3	3	Harrison	£415.00	Table
4	4	Ford	£350.00	Lamp
5	2	Ford	£234.00	Chair
6	4	Ford	£350.00	Lamp
7	2	Harrison	£235.00	Desk

ORDERS.OrderNo is a primary key and ORDERS.CustomerNo is a foreign key to CUSTOMERS.CustomerNo which is a primary key.

Clearly, many of the queries we would expect to run against these two tables will involve finding the orders that correspond to particular customers. Every such query means that the RDBMS has to perform a search on ORDERS.CustomerNo, that is, on the foreign key. In that case, putting an index on the foreign key is likely to be a good idea.

However, there are some instances where indexing a foreign key will not improve performance at all. For example, suppose the users of the database never run that kind of query in practice. Instead they always run queries that, for example, find all the orders for items from the Supplier 'Ford' and list the customers who place them. In that case an index on the foreign key ORDERS.CustomerNo will have no effect at all because that column is never searched.

So, indexing foreign key columns is not always an advantage, which is presumably why databases don't automatically index them in the same way as primary keys. It is very often the case, however, that indexing foreign keys has a profound effect on performance and so we thoroughly recommend that you look carefully at the foreign keys as candidates for indexing.

If you want a more specific guideline then think about it this way. Foreign keys are typically found at the many end of a one-to-many join. In this case, one customer can place many orders and, sure enough, the foreign key under consideration is at the orders end of the join.

If the query restricts on the data in the table at the one end (CUSTOMERS) and then pulls all the associated rows from the many end (ORDERS) then indexing the foreign key should make a significant difference.

```
SELECT CUSTOMERS.FirstName, ORDERS.Item
FROM CUSTOMERS INNER JOIN ORDERS
ON CUSTOMERS.CustomerNo = ORDERS.CustomerNo
WHERE CUSTOMERS.FirstName="Sally";
```

On the other hand, if a query restricts the data in the table at the many end (ORDERS) and then pulls all associated rows from the one end (CUSTOMERS) then indexing the foreign key will make no difference. For example:

```
SELECT CUSTOMERS.FirstName, ORDERS.Supplier
FROM CUSTOMERS INNER JOIN ORDERS ON CUSTOMERS.CustomerNo =
ORDERS.CustomerNo
WHERE ORDERS.Supplier="Ford";
```

However, if you are unsure of the type of queries that your users will be running, then put foreign keys high on your list of probable columns to index.

Intelligent use of indexes

Suppose that you look after a massive database of orders. It just so happens that this table is updated with all the previous month's orders on the first day of every month. For the whole of the rest of the month, the table is frequently queried but never updated. What would you do? Well, I'd index all of the foreign keys and any of the columns which were ever queried, without worrying about how many indexes I was applying.

For the whole of the month, all users of the database would be able to query it and get answers back as rapidly as possible. On the morning of the first day of the month, I would remove all of the indexes. As the new orders were added, the users wouldn't see any speed penalty because the RDBMS wouldn't be constantly rebuilding the indexes after every edit.

You will be way ahead of me by this point. Once all of the new orders were added, I would reapply the indexes, the RDBMS would build them all once and for the rest of the month the queries would run like greased lightning.

Chapter 35

More on optimization

Query optimization

SQL is the language used to query a database and, in some respects, it's a strange language. It's declarative rather than procedural, which means that when you write a query you declare to the database engine what you want it to do, but you don't tell it how to achieve that end result (that would be a procedural approach). For instance, if you want to query for matching values in two joined tables, the query contains nothing to indicate which table should be examined first.

For example, consider this query:

> SELECT CUSTOMERS.FirstName, ORDERS.Supplier
>
> FROM CUSTOMERS INNER JOIN ORDERS ON CUSTOMERS.CustomerNo = ORDERS.CustomerNo
>
> WHERE CUSTOMERS.FirstName="Sally" AND ORDERS.Supplier="Ford";

It says, give me the customer's first name and the supplier's name for all orders where the customer was Sally and the supplier was Ford.

Nowhere in this SQL is the database engine told which table to look at first. Suppose that both tables were huge and there was an index on CUSTOMERS.FirstName but not on ORDERS.Supplier. In that case, as an intelligent human, we'd search the indexed column first because, if we can't find any matches to 'Sally' in that column we know that the answer table is going to contain zero rows so we never even have to look at the unindexed column in ORDERS.

Or suppose that CUSTOMERS.FirstName is still indexed, but ORDERS has only three rows. In that case we'd take a quick look at ORDERS and, if there were no Suppliers called Ford we'd have finished the query.

The point here is that SQL doesn't contain any information about how the query should be performed, it simply asks for a specific set of data. Hence we call it a declarative language.

So who or what does make those very important decisions? Well, it's a very subtle and elegant part of the database engine called the query optimizer. In both of our examples above the optimizer should be easily capable of working out the optimal way of solving the problem.

How does a query optimizer work? When you run a query, it's sent to the engine as a SQL string; that code is broken down into a set of so-called primitive operations which are then carried out against the database by the database engine. It is the optimizer that breaks the query into primitives, making all sorts of decisions which will speed up the query. The end result is called an execution plan which is essentially a strategy for solving the problem.

Clearly there is a tension here: the optimizer has to find the optimal execution plan but, very like a game of chess, there are numerous possible solutions to a complex query (quite literally there can be billions). Imagine that the slowest possible solution takes 20 seconds to complete while the fastest possible (if we can find it) would take ten seconds. Now suppose that the optimizer does finally work out the fastest possible solution, but it takes eight minutes to find it. Well, there's the tension right there. Like a good chess player, the trick is to find the optimal solution – the best one you can find in a reasonable period of time. The fastest solution is no help if it takes too long to find. Query optimization software is indeed subtle.

Query optimizers are very, very clever but they can end up working in the dark if we fail to give them the help they need. This brings us to our next topic, updating statistics.

Update statistics

In Chapter 27 we described how information about a database is stored as metadata in system tables. In general, this information describes the structure of a database (table names, column names, which columns have been indexed and so on) but typically there is no metadata in there that describes the data itself. For example, there is no record of the number of rows in each table nor of how data is distributed within a table.

Data is rarely distributed evenly. For instance, in British English last names, certain initial letters are much more common than others. In my (very) local phone book there are three pages of last names beginning with A, twelve and a half pages of Bs and a mere eighth of a page of Qs. The proportions are likely to differ in different languages and in different parts of the same country: Scotland has a preponderance of names beginning with Mc and Mac, so there's a large chunk of M pages in Scottish directories.

We described a binary chop earlier in the chapter and it is a wonderfully effective technique. But if I asked you to find the phone number of John Abercrombie, you wouldn't open the phone book halfway through but near the beginning. In the same way, if the query optimizer has information about the distribution of the data in a column it can use the indexes even more effectively.

All of this information about the data in a database is known as the database statistics. Unlike system tables which are typically maintained automatically by the database engine, the generation of up-to-date statistics is typically left under the DBA's control. And unless the DBA does actively take control, information about the data in tables is not available to the database engine. In turn that means that the query optimizer will not know which tables are large or small and will be unable to create a good, well optimized execution plan.

Even as I write these words, this is changing and the more advanced engines are now beginning to take over some of the control of updating statistics. However, it is still an area where human intervention will be important for the next few years.

Most database engines allow you to instigate an 'update statistics' operation which will count rows and inspect the distribution of indexed data amongst other things, and store them for use by the query optimizer.

This section boils down into a simple speed tip: run an 'update statistics' operation on your database at regular intervals. Your query optimizer will reward you with even faster queries.

Query analysis

Many database engines give you a tool called a query analyzer. As you might guess from the name, it lets you take a closer look at your queries and how they are being solved. A query analyzer can be a useful investigative tool when, say, a user has alerted you to the fact that a query is running very slowly.

Once you've run a query, you can ask the analyzer to show you the execution plan that the query optimizer has chosen for solving it. Being able to see how the query is broken down into primitive operations gives you the opportunity to spot something you could tweak to improve performance, like adding an index.

Query optimizers and analyzers make a great team: the optimizer does the donkey work but you can review its decisions using the analyzer and get the chance to bring your own understanding into play.

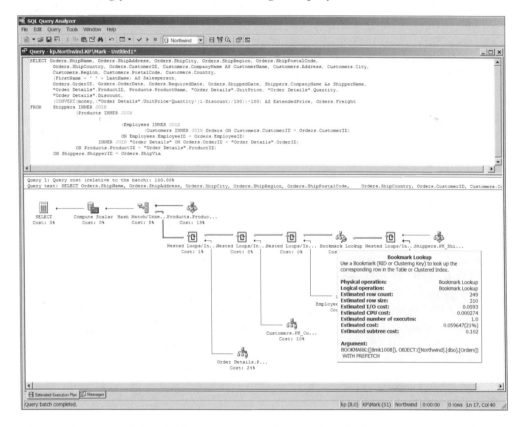

Access has a highly efficient query optimizer but it has no query analyzer. However, it's worth knowing what tools are likely to be available to you if you decide to trade up in terms of RDBMS. The screen shot above also gives you some idea of what such a tool might look like.

Also, in Access you can't manually update statistics. As an alternative, you have the option to compact a database and it's good practice to do this from time to time. It has much the same effect as updating statistics and can speed up querying. This option is found on the Tools menu (Tools, Database Utilities, Compact and Repair Database…)

Writing good SQL code

I wrote above that SQL is a declarative language rather than a procedural one. Using SQL you tell the database engine in broad terms what you want it to do without telling it how.

SQL is a versatile language and it's perfectly possible to express the same request for data in a variety of different ways, using different commands and constructions. A perfect query optimizer would take a query written in any way in SQL, render it into a perfect execution plan and execute it, always performing at top speed. In practice, it turns out to be very, very difficult to build a perfect query optimizer.

The upshot of this is that despite what we said earlier, certain aspects of the way we write our SQL code can still have a dramatic effect on the speed with which the code runs. Unfortunately the optimal way to write SQL depends on the query optimizer for which it's being written: optimizers differ significantly between database engines and can differ significantly between versions of the same database engine.

The message here is that if it comes to your attention that a query or view is not performing well, then inspecting the SQL and re-writing it can increase speed.

This all sounds a little vague, so an example may help. You have a table called Workforce with an indexed column called Profession. The table contains 10 million rows but only four different professions are represented in the Profession column. These are manager, lumberjack, politician and DBA. Furthermore, there are only three rows out of 10 million with 'DBA' in the Profession column. In order to find the three DBA records, you write some SQL. You could write:

```
SELECT Profession
FROM WORKFORCE
WHERE Profession = "DBA";
```

or alternatively you could write:

```
SELECT Profession
FROM WORKFORCE
WHERE Profession NOT IN ("Manager", "Lumberjack", "Politician");
```

These queries will give exactly the same result but the crucial point here is that we only know they're logically identical because we have some specific knowledge about the data and its distribution. We happen to know there are only four different values in 10 million rows. For a human being, it's a simple intuitive leap that these two are equivalent but for a query optimizer that's a very difficult conclusion.

It may know from the database statistics that there are only four different values in this column – manager, lumberjack, politician and DBA. It may be able to see in the query that we have listed three of those – ("Manager", "Lumberjack", "Politician"). But to put those two pieces of information together and to realize that, for this particular set of data:

> WHERE Profession = "DBA";

is the same as:

> WHERE Profession NOT IN ("Manager", "Lumberjack", "Politician");

is a very advanced conceptual leap. We have to remember that query optimizers are not intelligent, they are only programs. Not only that, they have to run within very tight time constraints. The average query optimizer would find this particular equivalence difficult to resolve.

What will happen in practice? Given the first statement, most query optimizers will use the index to identify the three rows with DBA records and return them in an answer table with a sub-second response time. Given the second statement, most optimizers will have to perform a complete table scan and compare every value found in the Profession column with the list supplied in the SQL. Almost all of the rows are of no interest once inspected but much time will be consumed checking and then ignoring them. Eventually all rows have been inspected and the same three-row answer table will ultimately be presented.

This particular class of difference can be expressed straightforwardly. When we write the WHERE clause like this:

> WHERE Profession = "DBA"

we are providing the query optimizer with what's called a searchable argument. We're telling it what to look for. When we write:

> WHERE Profession NOT IN ("Manager", "Lumberjack", "Politician");

we're providing what is known as a non-searchable argument. We're asking for exceptions: things that aren't in the list we provide.

The bottom line is that you can design and build the best database in the world and its performance can still be impacted by how DBAs write views and how application developers write queries. Learning about the SQL language will stand you in good stead: our primer in Chapter 29 will get you started.

Chapter 36

Denormalization

Denormalization is the process of turning a normalized database into one where some or all of the tables are not in 3NF. Denormalization is not only perfectly acceptable, there are times when to build a fully normalized database would be absolutely the wrong decision.

Yes, I know. I know that I spent the whole of Chapters 25 and 26 strongly emphasizing the benefits of a normalized structure. Yes, I know that I made it clear that not using a fully normalized database would render you a social pariah at the Database Designers' Ball. I know all of that. But there is the little matter of speed.

When we create a fully normalized database we take all of the data and split it up into small, discrete packages called tables. We do this so that each piece of data is stored only once. This makes it much easier for us to maintain the integrity of the data, it keeps the data volume low and it ensures that whatever questions we ask of the data we will get the correct answer. These are all the benefits of a fully normalized database and they are all real and all very important.

The problem is that any and all design decisions have their pros and their cons. One of the disadvantages of a fully normalized database is that it can be slow when we run queries against it. Why? Well, precisely because we have taken all of the data and split it up into small, discrete packages called tables. We use pointers between the tables (the primary and foreign keys) so we can always put the data back together, but tracking all of those pointers takes time. The net result is that fully normalized databases can be slow. For that reason it has been relatively common to denormalize parts of the database for performance gains.

But, inevitably, denormalization brings its own problems. As soon as you denormalize a relational structure you re-introduce some modification anomalies. All of these can be kept in check and controlled using some form of data integrity code (often one or more triggers) but those in turn will slow down data entry and update.

Managing denormalized tables is not an insurmountable problem and it's perfectly possible to build a robust system that has been partially denormalized. It will, however, take time and money to hand-code the integrity constraints necessary to keep data in good shape, and further time and money to maintain and document them, and to train new DBAs in their use. It is, as ever, a balancing act between performance and costs.

As we said at the beginning of this section, as hardware costs plummet and database maintenance cost rise, the balance is shifting and fewer people are denormalizing systems now than they were 10 years ago. It's now cheaper to throw hardware at the problem.

Having added all of those warnings, it is true that I would expect all well-qualified database designers to have a good understanding of the pros and cons of denormalization because it is still a perfectly valid technique in the right hands.

Yes, this is a coded way of saying that denormalization is often abused by the wrong hands.

So let's have a look at the types of denormalization that you might want to consider.

Mirroring tables

In this context, mirroring simply means making a copy of a table. It's a slightly curious term because it's not, of course, actually a mirror image but a straightforward copy. So under what circumstances would you want to make even a straightforward copy of a table?

Imagine that you have a huge table that is heavily used by multiple users. The usage is so heavy that the response times are slow all the time, when adding and updating rows, and when querying. The table has becomes a bottleneck to the performance of the entire database. One obvious solution is to create a copy of the table and the direct half of the queries to run against the original table and the other half to run against the copy. Simple. Simple and effective.

A couple of things should, however, be borne in mind here. One is that bottlenecks like this are typically physical – by which I mean that when many people hit one table the speed decrease occurs because of the physical limitations of the disk on which the table is sitting. If you make a copy of the table and place it on the same disk you are unlikely to see any major speed increase. In fact, you are likely to see speed degradation because the disk now has to read from two separate tables.

Secondly, as soon as you mirror a table in this way (whether on one disk or two) you introduce a complete set of modification anomalies. If you delete a row in one table, you have to delete it in the other: if you don't, you are left with an inconsistency between the two copies of the table. So you have to add a substantial set of hand-crafted data integrity constraints to the database (typically implemented as triggers – see Chapter 22) which maintain the integrity. These will, inevitably, slow down the process of updating the data. Mirroring tables is likely to work best on tables that are read heavily and much less frequently updated because reading is a quicker operation than writing and doesn't change the data.

This is our first example of denormalization but it sets the tone for every other example we examine and underlines the fundamental point we made above. Denormalization is only ever implemented to improve performance, but it almost always introduces data integrity issues.

Splitting tables

Another form of denormalization (more accurately a form of over-normalization) is the splitting of large tables into two or more smaller tables. The number of tables into which a large table is split, and whether the splitting is performed vertically or horizontally, depends on the particular circumstances in your database.

Imagine a table with a hundred columns and many rows: it's half a terabyte of solid data. Investigation reveals that 99% of the queries run against this table require data from just the first five columns. You'd split this table vertically, putting the five frequently-queried columns into a separate table, which now occupies a mere 0.01 of a Tbyte and can be queried very much more rapidly. The remaining 95 columns inhabit a table of their own. The 5% of queries that need to access the whole table can do so via a view which pulls the data together so it has the look and feel of a single table. Where a table has been split vertically, both new tables can be stored on the same disk: most of the head activity will be over the small table with rare sorties over the larger one.

If, on the other hand, you imagine a table of customers, roughly half of whom are based in Canada and half in Europe. Your Canadian users almost exclusively query for Canadian customers and European users for European customers. This is a case where you'd consider splitting the table horizontally, sorting the rows into Canada-based and Europe-based customers and putting each category into a separate table. This gives you two tables, both enjoy a reduction in querying load and both are smaller so queries run faster against them. Again, a view can be used to see the complete set of data whenever necessary. Whether these tables were stored on the same or different disks depends on circumstances: if you found that most hits on the Canadian table occurred when your European users were asleep, you could store the two tables on the same disk. If both tables were being heavily hit over the same period, you'd move them to separate disks.

Splitting tables is a common technique for improving query performance where the data is invariably queried by time and/or date. For example, you have a huge table of orders placed with your company. Mostly users want to see current orders, or those in the last week or month or year, and splitting the table into several smaller tables based on time (ORDERS2004, ORDERS2005, ORDERS2006 etc.) can bring impressive performance gains.

Once again there are data integrity issues here. Returning to the Canadians and Europeans example, customers, wherever they're based geographically, are all objects of the customer class and you may still want to inspect and query them as a single class of object. In order for a view to pull the data from two tables together so that it can be queried as if it was a single table, the primary key values must be consistent. If you allow new customer records to be entered to the two separate tables, you must ensure that the same primary key is not allocated twice to two different customers in the two different tables.

EUROPECUSTOMERS		
CustomerNo	**Country**	**LastName**
1	UK	Smith
2	Germany	Schneider
4	UK	Anderson

CANADACUSTOMERS		
CustomerNo	**Country**	**LastName**
3	Canada	McKeith
5	Canada	LeBlanc

If you add a new French customer (Monsieur Soulard) to EUROPECUSTOMERS and issue him with a customer number of 6 you must ensure that Mr. Brown in Canada is not issued with the same primary key value. It fits the familiar pattern: denormalization offers speed but with additional burdens.

OK, we'll stop going on about this; you've got the message.

Redundant data

Redundant data is ruthlessly pursued and expunged during the process of normalization but in the search for speed it can be an excellent tool.

Here are two perfectly unsurprising tables containing order and company data, none of it redundant:

COMPANY	
CompanyID	**CompanyName**
1	ABC Inc
2	Smithsons
3	K & J Ltd
4	LeFranc
5	Penduline

ORDER			
OrderID	*CompanyID*	**Item**	**Quantity**
1	2	300	1
2	2	400	2
3	4	750	1
4	3	350	1
5	1	800	6

Imagine, however, that the COMPANY table has many more columns to the right and that both tables have a vast number of rows. Further imagine that the ORDER table is constantly queried and almost every query requests order details which include the company name. This means each query has to match the value in ORDER.CompanyID with the value in COMPANY.CompanyID and pull the entry in COMPANY.CompanyName into the answer table. Even with indexing, this is slow; too slow.

One solution is to create a column of redundant data in the ORDER table, which simply states the company name in full, as it's wanted by the users, like this:

ORDER				
OrderID	*CompanyID*	**CompanyName**	**Item**	**Quantity**
1	*2*	Smithsons	300	1
2	*2*	Smithsons	400	2
3	*4*	LeFranc	750	1
4	*3*	K & J Ltd	350	1
5	*1*	ABC Inc	800	6

Now each query will run much faster because it can avoid the whole process of using keys to find matching data in a separate table.

There's still an overhead to be considered, however. Every time a new order is entered, the company name must be fetched from the COMPANY table and written into the ORDER table, and if a company record is ever changed, all the instances in ORDER.CompanyName must be updated.

Repeating groups (breaking 1NF)

Can we really mean it? Break first normal form? Well, if you've decided that denormalisation is for you, why not start with the big one? It's not sacrosanct, after all. Let's look at a situation where breaking 1NF could help. 1NF says, simply put, that you must not have repeating groups of data within a table.

You have a table of parts containing information about their progress through your factory. Each part has a code and is checked twice by an inspector. You employ a phalanx of inspectors, and it's not necessarily the same inspector who makes both checks. The inspectors have a table of their own, and there's also a table of check events. The tables, in shiny 3NF, look like this:

PARTS		
PartID	**Type**	**Material**
B3	Milled	Steel
C47	Cast	Iron
D129	Cast	Bronze

INSPECTORS

InspectorID	FirstName
1	Joe
2	Sam
3	Bill

CHECKS

CheckID	PartID	InspectorID
1	D129	2
2	C47	1
3	D129	3
4	C47	1
5	B3	2

It transpires that the database is heavily queried and most queries want to know the name of the inspector who performed a check on a particular part. This means every query must match the value in PARTS.PartID with equivalent values in CHECKS.PartID and then match values in CHECKS.InspectorID to those in INSPECTORS.InspectorID before reaching the requested information. This means following a trail between three tables, a slow process, and inevitably the result is poor performance.

If we know that there are only ever two checks made on a part, and that all parts always have to have both checks, we could re-design the PARTS table to look like this:

PARTS2

PartID	Type	Material	InspectorIDCheck1	InspectorIDCheck2
D129	Cast	Bronze	2	3
C47	Cast	Iron	1	1
B3	Milled	Steel	2	

The INSPECTORS table remains unchanged and the CHECKS table becomes redundant.

Data integrity issues? Not too great in this instance because it so happens that all parts have exactly two inspections.

Derived columns

Derived data is another of those conveniences that we learn to live without in a normalized database. When we want to use derivable data, we derive it using techniques like calculations and concatenations. If we store the cost of an item and we have an order for two of them, it's a simple calculation to multiply the cost by the quantity to give us the total monetary value of the order. Calculations are slow to perform, relatively speaking, and where queries constantly ask for information that has to be calculated, poor performance can result. So, yes, derivable data is up for grabs when you're denormalizing.

Let's look at a couple of tables containing orders and items to illustrate this point.

ORDERS		
OrderID	*ItemID*	**Quantity**
1	*1*	1
2	*2*	8
3	*4*	1
4	*1*	2

ITEMS		
ItemID	**Item**	**Price**
1	Lobster	$12.00
2	Langoustine	$1.50
3	King crab	$10.00
4	Spider crab	$8.00

If every query that runs against the ORDERS table wants the total value for an order, it has to match the value in ORDERS.ItemID to ITEMS.ItemID, find the corresponding price in ITEMS.Price and multiply it by the number in ORDERS.Quantity. Too slow.

This is a situation where deriving some data and storing it can improve query speed. You calculate the value for each order and store it in the ORDERS table, like this:

ORDERS			
OrderID	*ItemID*	**Quantity**	**Price**
1	*1*	1	$12.00
2	*2*	8	$12.00
3	*4*	1	$8.00
4	*1*	2	$24.00

Now queries just have one table to inspect and no calculations to perform.

Summary

This part of the book, although quite chunky, simply gives you an overview of the various techniques at your disposal. However, acquiring just the overview is vital to later optimization success. For instance, a DBA might absorb the ideas of denormalization and mirroring and implement them, but the same DBA may never have seen, read or discussed the point that mirrored tables should be stored on separate disks. (I've seen just this scenario in the wild). If you mirror a table to the same disk, the head spends much time jumping between the two copies and performance gains won't be apparent.

Implementing optimization techniques in isolation doesn't always lead to a good solution. To develop a successful optimization strategy, a solid overview is an excellent place to start.

Appendix 1

GUIs, macros and control languages

Building a user interface and controlling data entry at the form level are typically accomplished in one of three ways:

- using the GUI
- using a macro language
- using a programming language

We'll have a look at all three and examine their pros and cons.

Typically, GUIs are seen as the easiest to use and the least powerful, while programming languages are perceived as the most powerful but the most difficult to learn. Macros sit, like elevator music, slap in the middle of the road (and therefore, in my opinion, deserve most richly to be run over, but more of that later). However, there is often a measure of overlap between these three, so we'll choose a task that can be accomplished by all three to illustrate how they work and how they differ.

It says clearly at the start of this book that it is not about 'How to use Access' but the next few pages are going to read pretty much like a bit out of a 'How to' book. This is not because we have forgotten the original idea, it is because we want to discuss which of these three ways of building a user interface is the 'best'. In order to compare and contrast them, we have to give some idea of how they are used.

Creating a very simple user interface

Suppose you have a database like the one we created in preceding chapters. Customer details are stored in a table called CUSTOMERS and order details in an

ORDERS table. You have also created two forms, as in Chapter 15, one showing the customer details and the other, based on a query, which shows the order information for specific orders from particular customers. So far, so good.

But now you want to weld these two forms together to create a tiny part of a cohesive user interface. You want to be able to move directly from the Customers form to the Orders form. This will enable you (or the other users of your database) to enter the details of a new customer and then move directly to the Orders form to enter that customer's first order.

What is required is a button embedded in the Customers form which will open up the Orders form. In addition, we want the Orders form, when opened up in this way, to show us only the orders which relate to the current customer we are looking at with the Customers form. In other words, if we are looking at Sally Henderson's record in the Customers form, when we press the button we want to see only her orders in the Orders form.

Using the GUI

In Access 1.x the GUI could not provide a solution to this problem. Access versions 2.x and later, on the other hand, allow you to do this using a Control Wizard.

Switch to design mode in the Customers form, pop down the 'View' menu and choose Toolbox. This will cause a modeless (meaning it stays visible on screen until you close it) window to appear – the Toolbox. It has a tool called Control Wizards (the second button at the top of the toolbox in Access 2003). Turn it on and then use the Command Button tool to place a button on the form. The wizard will come into operation and ask you a series of questions.

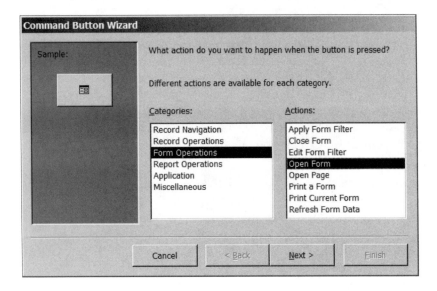

You need to select Form Operations, Open Form, ORDERS, "Open the form and find specific data to display", then match the relevant fields, type in some text for the button (perhaps 'Open Orders', although I have used 'GUI Button') and finally give it a name (which could also be 'Open Orders').

This works beautifully. When you press the button, the Orders form opens up. When you close the Orders form the Customers form should still be visible, since it was never closed.

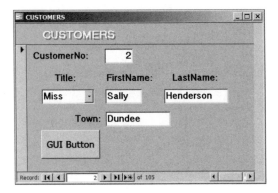

Using a macro

Go back to the database window, click on the Macro tab and then on the New button. A window opens up which is divided into two sections, Action and

Comment. If you click in the first row of the action column, a list pops down. Scrolling down this list is fascinating because it shows all the actions that a macro can perform. We want this macro to open the ORDERS form, so choose the option OpenForm; in fact typing 'o' will save some scrolling time because it jumps to the options that start with that letter. A second dialog area appears at the bottom of the macro window (under 'Action Arguments') and it is here that you can enter details such as the name of the form you want to open. Opposite Form Name you can again click to produce a pop-down list from which you can select the form 'Orders'.

One option listed under Action Arguments for Open Form is 'Where Condition'. This essentially means 'Open the form where the following is true'. In this case we want to see only those orders in which the Customer ID field has the same value as that currently showing in the CustomerNo field in the form called Customers. To put that another way, we use the Customers form to flip through the customer records until we find the customer we want. At that point, the relevant name will be showing in the form, as will the CustomerNo number (say, 2). When we switch to looking at the orders, we want to see only those which have a Customer ID number of 2.

Thus we want to see the records in the Orders form where:

> the CustomerNo field is equal to the CustomerNo field in the form called Customers.

We can express this more formally as:

> Open the form Orders where
> [CustomerNo]=[Forms]![Customers]![CustomerNo]

The expression:

> [CustomerNo]=[Forms]![Customers]![CustomerNo]

is the statement required in the Where Condition section. In Access 2003 you can use the expression builder to help you to construct this.

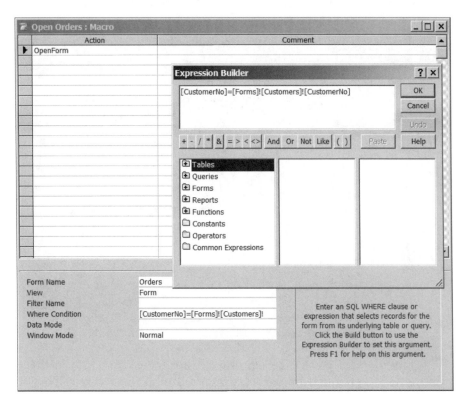

Close the macro window and give the macro a sensible name like 'Open Orders'.

That's the macro written; all you need to do now is add a button to the form and tell it which macro it should run. Open the form in design mode, pop down the 'View' menu and choose Properties. Another modeless window appears – the Properties Sheet. Turn off the Control Wizards, then choose the Command Button tool from the toolbox, click the mouse on the form and a button will appear. Now turn your attention to the Properties Sheet. Find the property called 'On Click' (it is in the list of All Properties and also in the list of Event Properties). Click in the On Click box and you will be able to select your macro from a list (if this is your first macro, you will, of course, get a list of one):

That's it; when you press the button, the macro should operate in the same way as the GUI-generated one. You can give the button a name like 'Macro Button'.

Using the programming language

Modern Windows RDBMSs still allow you write very efficient bits of code but you no longer write them in one huge block. Instead it is normal to use the GUI to create most of the major objects you need (forms, reports etc.) and indeed to populate them with control objects (buttons, combo boxes etc.). The programming language is then used to give these objects a mission in life. For example, you can use the GUI interface to place a button on a form and then to attach a small section of code to it so that it does something when it is clicked by the user. More technically, you supply code which is linked to an event associated with that object.

Every object in the interface has a series of events which are linked to it. For example, a form is an object and has events like 'On Open' tied to it. The events are specified by the designers of Access and reflect the likely uses to which objects will be put. Form objects, for example, do not have events like 'On change color' since, although the color of a form *can* be changed, you are unlikely to want to have a section of code which detects that particularly obscure event and runs when it occurs. On the other hand, forms are continually being opened so we have an event called 'On Open' which will run code every time the form is opened. And buttons have events like 'On Click' which are clearly likely to be useful. In fact, to no one's great surprise, that's the event we are going to use for code in this case.

Open the Customers form in design mode and use the toolbox to place a button upon it. Then use the property sheet to rename the button as 'Press me for Orders' and give it the same caption. Next list the 'Event Properties' and locate the one called 'On Click'. If you click to the right of that event you will find a button with three dots appears. Press it and a dialog box appears which asks whether you want the Expression Builder, Macro Builder or Code Builder: select the third option.

A code window opens up in which you will be able to type the required code.

The code you are going to use is based on the statement:

```
DoCmd.OpenForm
```

The DoCmd bit is a commonly used statement in Visual Basic which allows you to execute most of the Access 'Actions'. It's short for 'do command'. Actions (like the 'actions' described earlier for macros) carry out tasks like opening forms, closing them, opening tables etc. If you search the help system for 'actions reference' you can find a list of them all.

Opening the form is no problem; we just need to write:

```
DoCmd.OpenForm 'ORDERS'
```

The next question is "How do we get the form to open up showing only the orders which refer to the current customer?" In our case, the CustomerNo field in the CUSTOMERS table stores a unique identifier for each customer. Each order for that customer also stores that number. Thus Sally Henderson's number is 2 and all her orders are identified by this number. We can make use of this by looking up her number on the Customers form and asking to see only the orders which appertain to that number.

Most actions can be modified by a series of arguments. The OpenForm action can have a long string of arguments:

```
DoCmd.OpenForm formname [, view] [, filtername] [, wherecondition]
[, datamode] [, windowmode] [, openargs]
```

Frightening, aren't they? In fact, you can ignore them until you need them. In this case, all we need is the wherecondition argument. We can express what we want in English as:

Open the form called Orders where the contents of CustomerNo field in Orders is equal to the contents of the CustomerNo field in the current form Customers.

This actually translates, in Access 2003/Visual Basic 6.3, into :

```
DoCmd.OpenForm "Orders", , , "[CustomerNo] =
Forms![Customers]![CustomerNo]"
```

(Note that in Access 2.0 this reads slightly differently as:

```
DoCmd OpenForm "Orders", , , "[CustomerNo] =
Forms![Customers]![CustomerNo]"
```

The difference is in the lack of a dot between DoCmd and OpenForm)

Note also that there have to be three commas before the where condition, which itself must be wrapped up in double quotation marks. Access is pernickety on these points of syntax. If you enter this DoCmd statement,

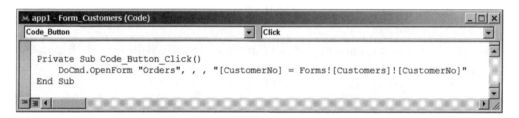

save it and return to the form, it should work.

So which is best?

So what do these three solutions to the same problem tell us about the relative merits of GUIs, macros and programming languages?

As GUIs get better they give us more functionality (as shown by the increased functionality offered by the later versions of Access) but they can never provide all of the versatility that macros and hand-crafted programming can offer. I am all in favor of using the GUI as much as possible; it's faster and easier to use than either of the other two. However, if you develop a moderately complex database application with a reasonable user interface and data integrity checks, you will have to use tools which work at a deeper level.

Macros offer the next level down, extending the functionality of the GUI. Macros are still limited, however, and do not provide anything like the enormous flexibility of a programming language. Both the macro and the programming languages take some effort to learn and, surprisingly, often require relatively different skills; in other words, a good working knowledge of macros may not make it much easier to convert to using the programming language. Perhaps even more surprisingly, I do not believe that programming is *fundamentally* more difficult to learn. Macros *are* easier to use but not by orders of magnitude.

And there is an often overlooked problem here. People who are new to databases tend to assume that their needs are simple. They say things like "Oh, I just need to generate some realistic sample data so that I can see how the system works" or "I just need to change the name 'Smith' to 'Smyth' in all of these records". Both sound simple to the uninitiated but in fact the former is often very complex while the latter is very simple. The only sensible solution for the former requires code; the latter can be accomplished with an update query created with the GUI.

If you are new to RDBMSs, I suggest (with as much deference as possible) that you may well not be in a position to judge whether you need macros or programming. In that case, my advice is clear. Unless you are sure that your needs really are simple, don't bother learning to use macros. Once you find that you need more than the GUI offers, go straight to the programming language. In this way you avoid the pain of climbing one learning curve only to discover that the view from the top is unsatisfactory and another climb awaits you.

If you need further evidence to convince you, consider the GUI solution that I outlined earlier. When you placed the button on the form, a wizard ran and asked questions about which form you wanted to be opened and under what conditions. Once it had collected all of the answers, the wizard wrote a piece of code for you automatically and attached it to the OnClick event for the button:

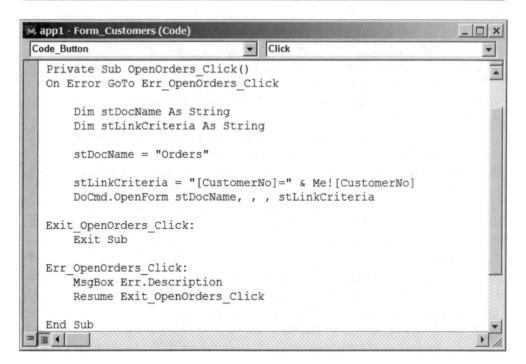

```
app1 - Form_Customers (Code)                          _ □ ×
Code_Button                    ▼   Click                    ▼
   Private Sub OpenOrders_Click()
   On Error GoTo Err_OpenOrders_Click

       Dim stDocName As String
       Dim stLinkCriteria As String

       stDocName = "Orders"

       stLinkCriteria = "[CustomerNo]=" & Me![CustomerNo]
       DoCmd.OpenForm stDocName, , , stLinkCriteria

   Exit_OpenOrders_Click:
       Exit Sub

   Err_OpenOrders_Click:
       MsgBox Err.Description
       Resume Exit_OpenOrders_Click

   End Sub
```

This code appears more complicated than the code I produced but that is simply because it has some rather elegant built-in error-checking. If you decide to expend the extra effort in learning the programming language, you will then be able to do precisely what I and many other developers do. We use the GUI and its wizards as much as possible and then simply edit and modify the code they produce to achieve the ends we need.

Other languages – SQL

Incidentally, you may well have come across SQL (Structured Query Language) in discussions about RDBMSs. You may be wondering, with all of this talk about control languages, how they relate to SQL. Is SQL an example of the sort of control language which has been discussed here? The simple answer is "No, it isn't."

SQL is a standard language which allows a database to be queried (hence the name). It can also be used for other operations such as creating tables but it is never used for interface control as described in this chapter. It is often used to pass queries between a front-end RDBMS running on a PC to a database server sitting somewhere on a network. In other words, SQL becomes quite important when the database you are building expands from a single-user database running on a PC to a multi-user database running on a network. (This expansion is discussed in more detail in Chapter 20.)

SQL is also used internally in Access to describe the queries that you typically create using the graphical query builder. If you build a query and then select View SQL, Access will show you the SQL statement which describes that query. Chapter 29 covers SQL in some detail.

Index